Re-Designing Teacher Education for Culturally and Linguistically Diverse Students

Through a critical-ecological lens, this book examines how to prepare pre-service teachers to be resourceful and responsive practitioners in addressing the intellectual needs of children often labeled as "culturally and linguistically diverse." It explores a comprehensive redesign of a teacher education program grounded in research on the complex factors that affect the teaching and learning of linguistically and culturally diverse children. *Re-Designing Teacher Education for Culturally and Linguistically Diverse Students* challenges hegemonic cultural and linguistic norms, quantitative and static views of "resources," the impact of U.S. education policy, and the limited attention to the agency, identities, and strategic actions of diverse students and their families.

Ana Christina daSilva Iddings is professor of language, literacy, and culture—early childhood at the University of Arizona, USA.

Routledge Research in Teacher Education

For a full list of titles in this series, please visit www.routledge.com

The Routledge Research in Teacher Education series presents the latest research on Teacher Education and also provides a forum to discuss the latest practices and challenges in the field.

Books in the series include:

Re-Designing Teacher Education for Culturally and Linguistically Diverse Children

A Critical-Ecological Approach

Edited by
Ana Christina daSilva Iddings

Routledge
Taylor & Francis Group

LONDON AND NEW YORK

First published 2017
by Routledge

2 Park Square, Milton Park, Abingdon, Oxfordshire OX14 4RN

52 Vanderbilt Avenue, New York, NY 10017

Routledge is an imprint of the Taylor & Francis Group, an informa business

First issued in paperback 2018

Copyright © 2017 Taylor & Francis

The right of Ana Christina daSilva Iddings to be identified as editor of this work has been asserted by her in accordance with sections 77 and 78 of the Copyright, Designs and Patents Act 1988.

All rights reserved. No part of this book may be reprinted or reproduced or utilised in any form or by any electronic, mechanical, or other means, now known or hereafter invented, including photocopying and recording, or in any information storage or retrieval system, without permission in writing from the publishers.

Notice:
Product or corporate names may be trademarks or registered trademarks, and are used only for identification and explanation without intent to infringe.

Library of Congress Cataloguing in Publication Data
Names: DaSilva Iddings, Ana Christina.
Title: Re-designing teacher education for culturally and linguistically diverse children : a critical-ecological approach / [edited] by Ana Christina da Silva Iddings.
Description: New York : Routledge, 2017. | Series: Routledge research in teacher education ; 12
Identifiers: LCCN 2016037770 | ISBN 9781138217447 (hardback)
Subjects: LCSH: Teachers—Training of. | Critical pedagogy. | Linguistic minorities—Education. | Social ecology.
Classification: LCC LB1707 .D375 2017 | DDC 370.71/1—dc23
LC record available at https://lccn.loc.gov/2016037770

ISBN: 978-1-138-21744-7 (hbk)
ISBN: 978-0-367-19435-2 (pbk)

Typeset in Sabon
by Apex CoVantage, LLC

Contents

Re-Designing Teacher Education for Culturally and Linguistically Diverse Children

A Critical-Ecological Approach

Edited by
Ana Christina daSilva Iddings

Routledge
Taylor & Francis Group

LONDON AND NEW YORK

First published 2017
by Routledge

2 Park Square, Milton Park, Abingdon, Oxfordshire OX14 4RN

52 Vanderbilt Avenue, New York, NY 10017

Routledge is an imprint of the Taylor & Francis Group, an informa business

First issued in paperback 2018

Copyright © 2017 Taylor & Francis

The right of Ana Christina daSilva Iddings to be identified as editor of this work has been asserted by her in accordance with sections 77 and 78 of the Copyright, Designs and Patents Act 1988.

All rights reserved. No part of this book may be reprinted or reproduced or utilised in any form or by any electronic, mechanical, or other means, now known or hereafter invented, including photocopying and recording, or in any information storage or retrieval system, without permission in writing from the publishers.

Notice:
Product or corporate names may be trademarks or registered trademarks, and are used only for identification and explanation without intent to infringe.

Library of Congress Cataloguing in Publication Data
Names: DaSilva Iddings, Ana Christina.
Title: Re-designing teacher education for culturally and linguistically
   diverse children : a critical-ecological approach / [edited] by Ana
   Christina da Silva Iddings.
Description: New York : Routledge, 2017. | Series: Routledge
   research in teacher education ; 12
Identifiers: LCCN 2016037770 | ISBN 9781138217447 (hardback)
Subjects: LCSH: Teachers—Training of. | Critical pedagogy. |
   Linguistic minorities—Education. | Social ecology.
Classification: LCC LB1707 .D375 2017 | DDC 370.71/1—dc23
LC record available at https://lccn.loc.gov/2016037770

ISBN: 978-1-138-21744-7 (hbk)
ISBN: 978-0-367-19435-2 (pbk)

Typeset in Sabon
by Apex CoVantage, LLC

Contents

Foreword

This book addresses a central issue in the field of education: how to prepare "preservice" teachers to be resourceful and responsive practitioners in addressing the intellectual needs of children often labeled as "culturally and linguistically diverse." These children, especially Latino and African American students, are now the numerical majority in all urban school districts in the country (Sable, Plotts, & Mitchell, 2010), and a growing presence in the suburbs as well. In sharp contrast, the demographics of teachers have remained fairly stable over the years; about 80 percent of teachers are female and white, whether in urban or rural districts (Snyder & Dillow, 2015). The main challenge of this discrepancy, however, is not only related to race or ethnicity but to social class. Teachers are mostly middle class, befitting their educational attainment; their students are mostly from the working class. In my view, this is a condition that engenders multiple stereotypes about the children and their families, mostly imagined limitations that they are apathetic about education and their lives intellectually barren. These stereotypes are demonstrably false and extremely damaging.

Project CREATE was conceptualized on two encompassing premises. The first one is that preservice teachers, regardless of their characteristics, must be honored; after all, these are the young people who represent the next generation of teachers of our children. As such, they are extremely important colleagues, and one must convey clearly that perception to them. The second premise is that the educator must also be educated. And central to this education is how to develop the professional wherewithal to challenge uninformed perceptions about students and families and facilitate access to knowledge and experiences that can become, in the hands of able teachers, valuable pedagogical resources. This book tells the story, throughout its collection of chapters, of how such an additive education philosophy becomes concrete practice, the formation of a "mediating" structure to support this practice, all in the various conditions for teaching and learning that represent the broader ecology of this novel project.

Luis C. Moll
University of Arizona

Bibliography

Sable, J., Plotts, C., & Mitchell, L. (2010). *Characteristics of the 100 largest public elementary and secondary school districts in the United States: 2008–09* (NCES 2011-301). U.S. Department of Education, National Center for Education Statistics. Washington, DC: U.S. Government Printing Office.

Snyder, T.D., & Dillow, S.A. (2015). Digest of Education Statistics 2013 (NCES 2015-011). National Center for Education Statistics, Institute of Education Sciences, U.S. Department of Education. Washington, DC.

Preface

The first section of the present volume, "Perspectives," sheds light on the theoretical grounding, concepts, and ideas that have provided a direction for the redesign of our early childhood teacher education program and that have guided the research projects in which we engaged. In addition to the present volume introduction, Souto-Manning's chapter, "Why Are Critical Perspectives and Ecological Approaches Needed in Early Childhood Teacher Education?" sketches a strong rationale for why a critical-ecological perspective in early childhood teacher education is necessary in order to challenge the dominant narratives that continuously undermine those who may have different types of knowledge, forms of expression, or ways of knowing.

The second section, "Designing for Change," describes with detail the use of design-based research methodology for the comprehensive reconceptualization and reform of an early childhood teacher education program. This section also addresses the challenges associated with institutional change at the university and district levels as well as changes in the teacher education curricular status quo, including with new requirements, such as home engagements and community events. The chapter entitled, "Using a Design-based Research Approach: Educating Early Childhood Teachers to Understand, Engage, and Teach the Culturally and Linguistically Diverse Child," co-authored by Jurich, daSilva Iddings, and Clift, describes the ways by which, through a series of prospective and reflective cycles of research, we designed and redesigned opportunities for preservice teachers to experience children's learning across contexts. Our findings suggest that the preservice teachers developed a deeper understanding about linguistically and culturally diverse children through their participation in a system of intricately intertwined curricular relations and experiences, as opposed to moving through a set of courses and events that work in isolation.

In the final chapter of the second section, "Engaging Teacher Educators' Commitment to the Principles of CREATE Over Time," Clift, Robbins, and Reinhard report on teacher educators' perceptions of the development of an early childhood teacher education program for over three years. They focus in particular on how the preservice teachers' understanding of the program's principles evolved and how their ability to enact the principles did (and did not) improve over time. Based on the analysis of a series of interviews with participants in five different role groups (Co-Principal Investigators, Instructors, Graduate Teaching Assistants, Graduate Research Assistants, and Coordinators), the authors discuss the challenges posed by curricular change and the responses to those challenges.

The third section, "Learning across Contexts: Toward Community Engagement and Action," presents a series of studies that address the ways by which the preservice teachers were able to develop (or not) an understanding of the families' language and literacy practices and then were able to apply these into their instruction. In "Teacher Candidates Interactions with Families: Understanding Home Context," Gonzalez and Zapien discuss the redesign of field experiences to include home engagements. They foreground the concept of funds of knowledge as a guiding principle for the teacher candidates and its application in a series of engagements with the purpose of providing opportunities for our preservice teachers to deeply envision communities as resources for their own learning and development. Since the majority of prospective teachers in this program were young, mostly middle class, and white, just as they are in most teacher education programs, teacher educators must find ways for meaningful interactions between communities and teachers-in-formation. The authors argue that a funds of knowledge perspective involves transcending classroom walls and engaging with community members, events, practices, and local knowledge bases. Yet, this process is neither transparent nor unproblematic for future teachers to traverse. This chapter describes how scaffolding the emergent understandings of prospective teachers about the communities they are attempting to understand can be enriched through principled activities and an understanding of cultural and linguistic resources. An ethnographic approach to households that is profoundly respectful of practices and processes of 'sense-making' is at the core of the development of teacher candidates as producers of their own knowledge about communities, pedagogy, and families.

Next, in "Teacher Candidates Connecting to Community Resources and Children's Literacies," Reyes, Acosta, Fierro, Fu, and Zapien share findings from a community literacy project where teacher candidates reflected on their experiences of getting to know the local community during their field placements. First, they took a literacy walk together with a case study child to observe and document the print environment—everything from street signs, to product labels, bumper stickers to murals—found around a neighborhood and school community. Second, the teacher candidates documented the community resources found within the neighborhood to examine the existing literacy resources available within the children's community. In addition, the preservice teachers identified and mapped the local community resources to connect to their students' learning experiences. This research aimed to broaden the current notion of literacy and potential resources available to support the learning of emergent bilinguals in their everyday contexts

In the fourth section, "Funds of Knowledge through Story and Play" the chapters describe the formats and procedures that provided an examination of family/preservice teacher interactions around stories. First, in "Thinking with Teacher Candidates: The Transformative Power of Story in Teacher Education," Acevedo, Kleker, Pangle, and Short report on interviews with approximately 35 preservice teachers over a two-year period. These interviews were designed to provide a close understanding about the effectiveness of engagements with context-specific curricular materials, including the *Family Story Backpacks* (to encourage oral stories as a means for families to share their funds of knowledge) and the *Cultural Community Story Boxes* (to encourage young children to explore global cultures through story and play). Their analysis pays close attention to the ways the engagements were valued and practiced by preservice teachers and also by the teachers with whom they cotaught. In addition, they report on the ways institutional obstacles and missteps impeded the effectiveness of such engagements.

In "Understanding Children's Funds of Knowledge through Observations of Play," Yoon describes how preservice teachers learned to create a portrait that included the social and cultural aspects of children's funds of knowledge, connecting cultural knowledge with school experiences. Children's intellectual work around episodes of play reiterates the critical role of play in children's language development. With this in mind, Yoon claims that teachers need the dispositions and tools to listen and learn from children through deep, cultural analysis of classroom events. Such analysis allows teachers to become curriculum makers instead of technicians of scripted curricula. Although this project took place in play-based early childhood centers, Yoon advocates for its relevance to elementary schools, especially in kindergarten classrooms that have replaced play with more "academic rigor."

Following, Butler, Feller, and daSilva Iddings' chapter, "Stories that Travel: Preservice Teachers Using Photography to Understand Children's Funds of Knowledge in Literacy Learning," investigates how preservice teachers make use of coursework-related literacy engagements (such as the *Photobook*) as a tool to promote and bridge children's home language and literacy development. Findings show that through the families' sharing of their own stories (often told in Spanish or in their native language), preservice teachers begin to know, understand, and value the children's family histories, heritage, and language. Thus, they also become more apt to implement some of this understanding in their classroom. Further, the Photobook stories served as a vehicle for the preservice teachers to explore and interrogate their assumptions about cultural and linguistic diversity and to challenge the hegemony of English-only policies and alphabetic monomodal ideologies.

The final section of the volume, "Directions for Research and Practice," poses challenging questions and invites reflections regarding the need to disrupt institutional practices that function to conceal and to maintain repressive relations of power and domination. In addition, this section offers insight into new programmatic and research possibilities for early childhood teacher education.

In "Making Race and Racism Visible and Addressing Issues of Whiteness: Educating Teachers to Work with Students of Color," Gray and Combs explore the experiences of a bilingual, black, female teacher educator in educating a predominately white, female, middle class, monolingual early childhood. Using critical race theory and social justice teacher education to frame her experience, the authors critically analyze the need to recruit and retain both teacher educators and students of color. In addition, they highlight the challenges such a goal presents when working in predominately white teacher preparation programs. This chapter also examines the historical, social, and cultural role educators of color have played in the academic success of diverse students as a way to affirm the need for recruiting more teacher educators and students of color into teacher preparation programs. The authors also discuss the sociocultural benefits for white students learning from and with instructors of color since these instructors' discourse styles and "truth telling"—although oftentimes resisted by white preservice teachers—serve nonetheless as a socialization tool for young white women.

The volume ends with a chapter by Deborah Rowe, "Learning to Teach for Equity, Access, and Inclusion: Directions for Program Design and Research in Early Childhood Teacher Education," in which she offers new directions for research in early childhood teacher education. Rowe argues that the goal of teacher education is not to teach a static set of best practices. Instead, teacher candidates need to be supported in developing ways of *designing* instruction that are nimble in adapting to the needs of students with culturally and linguistically diverse backgrounds. Drawing on themes presented in the chapters of this volume, she argues that future research needs to explore ways of supporting teacher thinking characterized by the following dimensions.

1 Flexibility: allowing for, in the moment, assembly of resources;
2 Personalization: instructional activities and materials link to the experiences of the children with whom we are currently working;
3 Shared sponsorship of instructional content: teachers partner with families and community members to provide culturally and linguistically relevant content for instruction;
4 Two-way sharing of funds of knowledge and linguistic resources between schools and families, and teachers considering "what travels" between home and school, with special attention to designing for community-to-school sharing.

All told, this volume compiles analyses of data collected in different areas of inquiry, and provides a comprehensive redefinition of early childhood teacher education, with specific concern given to the education of the culturally and linguistically diverse child. This volume also offers a window into new pedagogy, one that invokes thoughtful considerations about the child in his or her multiple contexts, and ultimately makes the case for the importance for a critical-ecological approach and praxis in education. We hope that the volume will provoke thought, encourage new teaching practices, and inspire others in the direction of improving and creating new possibilities for the educational circumstances of culturally and linguistically diverse children.

1 Introduction

Ana Christina daSilva Iddings

The issues addressed in this volume are of concern for all of those who would like to see the educational conditions of culturally and linguistically diverse children improved. These children make up the fastest-growing student population in the U.S. (Snyder & Dillow, 2015), yet, in the U.S. public schools, their education has tended to shortchange their academic potential, to be overly restrictive and compensatory, and to be largely driven by policies instead of sound educational theory and research.

At least two decades of research examining key reasons for the inferior-quality education culturally and linguistically diverse children receive (e.g., Gutierrez, Bequadano-Lopes, & Tejeda, 1999, Manyak, 2000; Rueda & de Neve, 1999; Souto-Manning, 2013) have pointed to two major factors: First, schools consistently fail to provide these children with expansive and enriching curricular activities that build on the ample resources available in their broader social environment. Second, teachers are not adequately prepared to work with these populations of students. Indeed, most colleges and universities have not succeeded in providing preservice teachers, as well as teachers pursuing advanced degree work, effective preparation in teaching linguistically diverse learners in their future classrooms (Amatea, Cholewa, & Mixon, 2012; American Federation of Teachers, 2014;Sleeter, 2001, Voltz, Collins, Patterson, & Sims, 2008).

Still, critical issues related educational quality and opportunity begin well before formal K-12 schooling. From much of the research on literacy development, we know that the foundation for success in elementary school begins at birth. According to the United Nation's Children's Fund, "investing in children form birth to age 3 is the only way to ensure that every child has the opportunity to reach his or her future potential" (Bellamy, 2001). How do we best support literacy development beginning with birth? The National Assessment of Educational Progress shows that the literacy achievement gap between Latino and white populations begins in infancy. How do we address the unique challenges posed by families whose first language is not English? In Arizona, which has one-sixth of the nation's Latino immigrants, these challenges are a critical and pressing issue. However, we know from other studies that the gap narrows when certified early childhood teachers work with preschool populations over an extended period of time.

Using and understanding written words is a complex task that involves social, cultural, and language practices that are specific to individual communities. When school-based instruction does not build on the literacy knowledge within the home and community, it is less effective because it underestimates the knowledge children bring to the school setting and thus, their potential achievement. Early literacy practices need to aggressively incorporate strategies that bridge the differences spanning home, school, and community. Teacher education must prepare teachers who know such strategies and who are able to implement them because they have had extensive practice working with these strategies in school and community settings.

To address these overarching issues, there is a pressing need to develop a more encompassing and dynamic way to attend to the learning needs of these children and to prepare teachers to work with this population. This includes opportunities for preservice teachers to develop a closer understanding of the specific sociocultural and linguistic assets of these children, as well as the array of in-school and out-of-school activities, family practices, and communities that mediate learning.

One way of framing the discussion of the sociocultural and linguistic assets, resources, and capital of distinct communities is through the well-developed concept of *funds of knowledge* (Gonzalez, Moll & Amanti, 2005; Moll, 2014; Moll, Amanti, Neff, & Gonzalez, 1992; Moll & Gonzalez, 1994). This volume presents research that serves to generate new knowledge about the *funds of knowledge* of culturally and linguistically diverse students. As such, we employ an ecological educational approach as applied to practice, placing multiple layers of community in the forefront of our educational commitments and pedagogical concern. Within this perspective, and using a design-based research methodology, our research team (Clift, daSilva Iddings, Jurich, Reyes, & Short, Co-Principal Investigators, 2011–2015), funded by the Helios Education Foundation, set out to systematically reform an early childhood teacher preparation program—The Community as Resources in Early Childhood Teacher Education, or CRE-ATE (www.createarizona.org). This program provided a new infrastructure of coursework and innovation in field experiences as well as novel spaces for action and interaction among multiple stakeholders to promote new understandings that would inform curriculum, pedagogy, and educational policy. Through this ecological lens and through the designed experiences of our curriculum, preservice teachers have engaged in intellectual inquiries from different perspectives and angles to form rich learning portraits of culturally and linguistically diverse young children.

Why an Ecological Approach?

Although the term *ecology* has referred mostly to a scientific discipline that considers the relationships of an organism with all other organisms, an expanded notion of ecology in social sciences research (Bronfenbrenner, 1979; Cole, 2006; Gutierrez & Rogoff, 2003) seeks to understand the dynamic relations of learners and the world, whether it is at a macro-level (e.g., culture, history, or socioeconomic status) or at a micro-level (e.g., interactions, physical objects, or dialogs). More specifically, an ecological approach focuses on "*relations* between people and the world, and on learning as *ways of relating* more effectively to people and the world" (van Lier, 2004, p. 4, emphasis added). In this way, studies informed by an ecological perspective include an investigation of dynamic and mutual influences between learners and surrounding contexts through semiotic and material resources.

An ecological approach is neither a theory nor a method with which to do research. Instead, it can be conveyed as a way of thinking (and acting), allowing for broad understandings of cultural, historical, social, institutional, and linguistic phenomena in the classroom. Although not a theory per se, an ecological approach draws from various theoretical positions, including sociocultural theory. For example, at the core of sociocultural theory is the concept of *mediation*, which emphasizes the dynamic interactions and negotiations between learners and material/symbolic artifacts or cultural tools (Vygotsky, 1987; 1977; 2004). In this way, both the ecological approach and sociocultural theory recognize the significance of the context and its mediating role for human minds and actions, and furthermore consider development as inseparable from the contexts of activities.

Two central tenets of ecological approaches to language learning are the concepts of *emergence* and *affordance*. These are intimately related to the notion of mediation. That is, this approach proposes that learning *emerges* as a mediated and situated activity from interactions between a learner and his or her surrounding context. From this perspective, then, learning cannot be understood without considering the physical, social, and symbolic *context* in which learners are engaged. In this way, the ecological approach considers the context of human activity through the idea of *affordance*, which refers to "what is available to the person to do something with" (van Lier, 2004, p. 91). Herein, learning arises from, and is mediated through, various types of affordances, or a myriad of opportunities for meaningful action and interaction offered to an engaged participant.

From an ecological perspective, it is assumed that sociocultural practices *per se* become a mediational process in shaping particular relationships between learner and context, and that a learner's actions are understood in relation to the constraints and affordances of a particular instructional context and its inherent social practices. Using this approach, then, we are able to ask certain questions: "What is it in this environment that makes things happen the way they do?" and/or, "How does learning come about within this particular context of activity?" (van Lier, 2004, p. 13).

An ecological approach was particularly relevant to our CREATE research team as we began to formulate a comprehensive reform of early childhood teacher education. Of primary concern to the CREATE team was the goal to expand, through theory and practice, a *funds of knowledge* perspective. In other words, by applying an ecological approach, we aimed to illuminate the ways by which all stakeholders involved in this process (e.g., preservice teachers, university faculty, participating families) engaged in praxis, defined here as the dialectic unity of consciousness and actions in the world (Lantolf & Pohener, 2011). In addition, within this focus, we aimed to track the critical and self-reflexive discourses and practices that these social agents used to intervene at the level of social action. Following Thibald (2004) praxis leads to "exposing, challenging, and changing those social meaning-making practices that function to conceal and to maintain illegitimate and repressive relations of power and domination in the social order" (p. 8). Thus, this concept was also immanently suited for understanding community development, especially for traditionally disenfranchised populations who may or may not speak the institutionally dominant language—in this case English. An ecological lens with a focus on praxis helped us to understand how critical awareness, or *conscientização* (Freire, 1970), developed for the participants, as they began to overcome monologic institutional views and create new possibilities for addressing the needs of the linguistically and culturally diverse children and their families (cf. daSilva Iddings, McCafferty, & Teixeira, 2011).

A Design-based Approach to Research in Early Childhood Teacher Education: Building a Base of Useable Knowledge

Aligned with our focus on the *ecology* of learning, for the overall purpose of the early childhood teacher education reform, we applied a design-based research approach, which considers the learning process as an intricate system of relations as opposed to a mere set of practices that work in isolation. A design-based methodology generally consists of five main characteristics. First, this paradigm aims to derive theories relating to the process of learning as well as the means by which this process is supported. Second, a design-based research methodology relies upon intervention by bringing about new forms of learning. Third, design-based research has two complementary faces: prospective and reflective. Prospectively, hypotheses are created about a specific form of learning and the means of supporting it. Reflectively, these conjectures are implemented, exposed to scrutiny, accepted, or refuted. Researchers may need to refine their initial hypotheses in light of newly collected data. Fourth, the methodology requires that researchers engage in repeated cycles of hypothesis creation and analysis. Last, as design-based research is heavily reliant on theory, the work done within this paradigm tends to focus on the direct application of seemingly abstract theoretical concepts onto a specific context. In other words, the theories employed within the experiment are useful to impel not only thinking but also practice. Through detailed description and analysis of these interventions, researchers, in collaboration with other stakeholders in the field (e.g., pre- and in-service teachers, families, community members, university faculty) can expand the base of *useable knowledge*—that is, knowledge that could be directly applicable to the contexts of the university classes and our community and school partners and the circumstances of our students and, ultimately, the educational circumstances of the children we want to affect.

Funds of Knowledge as a Foundational Principle for Teacher Preparation

The research on "funds of knowledge," brought forth over 20 years ago, was mainly concerned with the literacy education of Latino, mostly Mexican American, children in the U.S. Southwest (Moll, 1990). In this work, teachers as co-researchers collaborated using ethnographic-like household observations and interviews with household members. Importantly, this research advanced a "sociocultural" orientation in education, seeking to build strategically on the experiences, resources, and knowledge of families and children, especially those from low-income neighborhoods (e.g., Hogg, 2011).

From this perspective, families, especially those in the working class, have been characterized by the practices they have developed and the knowledge they have produced and acquired in the everyday living of their lives. The social history of families, and their productive or labor activities in both the primary and secondary sector of the economy, are particularly relevant to educational contexts and teachers because they reveal experiences (e.g., in farming, construction, gardening, household maintenance, or secretarial work) that generate much of the knowledge household members may possess, display, elaborate, or share with others. This knowledge may develop through their participation in social networks, often with kin, through which such funds of knowledge may be exchanged in addressing some of life's necessities. As Moll, Soto-Santiago, and Schwartz (2013) further explained:

> One might help a neighbor fix a car, because one has the required knowledge and experience as an auto mechanic, and the neighbor incurs an obligation to reciprocate and help paint one's house, a task that is within his or her areas of expertise.
>
> (p. 23)

The authors note that these forms of reciprocal exchange are not of cash for labor as in commercial transactions; instead, it is an exchange in another currency, that of funds of knowledge. One could argue, then, that funds of knowledge in a particular household or in a network of households may form part of a broader (nonmonetary) household economy (Moll, 2014).

Thus this type of research, especially if conducted in collaboration with teachers, provides one with an opportunity to (a) initiate relations of trust— or *confianza*—with families to enable discussion of their practices and funds of knowledge; (b) document families' lived experiences and knowledge that may prove useful in defining households' intellectual resources or assets that may be valuable for instruction; and (c) establish discursive settings with teachers to prepare them theoretically, methodologically, and analytically to do the research, and to assess the utility of the findings for classroom practice(González, Moll, & Amanti, 2005, p. 213). In other words, the studies cited here show that the knowledge base one can accrue through one's approach to households can be treated pedagogically as cultural resources for teaching and learning in schools. A close understanding about families' funds of knowledge represents an opportunity for teachers to identify and establish the "educational capital" of families often assumed to be lacking any such resources, and to leverage this capital in the classroom (daSilva Iddings, Combs, & Moll, 2013).

Many subsequent studies in different parts of the world have pointed to the usefulness of the funds of knowledge concept, especially when working with students and families of diverse backgrounds. Kenner's (2004; 2005) work with immigrant children growing up in London, for example, serves as a clarion call for the use of home language/culture as resources for schooling situations and for reconsiderations of monolingual and Anglocentric practices in schools that continuously undermine the learning capabilities of immigrant students. Drury's (2007) study confirms the findings of an ever-growing corpus of empirical data, making evident the importance of reconciling the complex realities of children's home and school experiences, and of harnessing resources from home contexts in order to foster children's literacy learning. Also along those lines, scholars advocate for educational approaches that help us identify and situate English learners' literacy practices within their specific households, schools, and communities and that focus on the dynamic and mutual relationships between learners and surrounding contexts (daSilva Iddings, Combs, & Moll, 2012; Ovando & Combs, 2012; Reyes & Guitart, 2013). With a basis on the close understanding of these interrelationships, pedagogical and social action toward more equitable education for culturally and linguistically diverse students is possible.

A Critical Perspective

Extending the ecological approach, the contributing authors for this volume also engage a critical perspective to more directly address issues of power, identity, and agency, which are central to our concerns (see also Lewis, Moje, & Enciso, 2007, p. xi). Specifically in relation to literacy practices, Dworin (2012) adds that in addition to understanding them as constituted within specific contexts, such as homes, schools, worksites, and communities, educators must also consider the *conditions* in which literacy practices occur, including the broader social and ideological issues. A critical perspective allows us to capture in our analysis various historical and institutional patterns of exclusion and oppression of minoritized populations and calls for (a) an increased understanding and respect for the values, needs, and aspirations of immigrant families; (b) a greater understanding about immigrant households as places that contain valuable knowledge and experience (as opposed to common misconceptions about immigrant homes as places from which children need to be rescued); and (c) a growing awareness that literacy is fundamentally related to cultural identity, and shaped by ethnicity, primary language, and social class (see daSilva Iddings, 2009 for a review of this literature).

By coupling an ecological approach with critical perspectives on early childhood teacher education, we aim to delineate a much-needed more equitable approach to education and in particular to the education of culturally and linguistically diverse students. Since learning is constituted within the specific practices of a variety of social learning contexts (e.g., homes, schools, and communities) that are ever-changing, we propose that fully considering the relationships among these contexts is necessary in order to envision new possibilities for praxis. Further, we assert that equitable approaches to teacher education need to be advanced in tandem with critical examinations of ideological issues surrounding deficit-oriented language policies and the prevalent educational programs and school reforms that continue to disadvantage the culturally and linguistically diverse student.

The Present Volume

While other studies and research collections have developed and extended funds of knowledge perspectives (Campano, 2007; Compton-Lilly, 2007; daSilva Iddings, 2009; daSilva Iddings et al., 2013; Gillanders & Jimenez, 2004; Hammerberg, 2004; Perez, 2004; Perry, Kay, & Brown, 2008; Reyes & Azuara, 2008; Rodriguez, 2006), this collection is distinctive in that it centers on the actual application of a critical-ecological approach through designed intervention, made visible by a set of research and development studies developed to critically evaluate the design and extend theory. Toward these ends, we present a variety of studies using design-based, ethnographic, and other qualitative research methodologies to account for, theorize, and engage the complex interplay of factors that considerably affect the teaching and learning of linguistically and culturally diverse children. Across the multiple perspectives of our studies, our analyses challenge narrow conceptions of language literacy and stories, bounded or contained learning contexts (e.g., home, community, schools), hegemonic cultural and linguistic norms, quantitative and static views of 'resources,' and limited attention to the agency, identities, and strategic actions of diverse students and their families as they traverse different contexts.

The overarching question we set out to investigate through the associated research projects and vision of CREATE was roughly the following: "What would it take to promote a paradigmatic shift in early childhood teacher education toward an asset-based orientation regarding young culturally and linguistically diverse students?"

We have approached this question through studying the development of four cohorts of preservice teachers in early childhood education, of about 25 participants each, as they participated in courses and engaged in sustained relationships with families, teachers, and other community members across different learning contexts. The series of field experiences and course engagements we refer to in this volume were carefully crafted through the articulation, application, and iterations of four key principles: a) *funds of knowledge within diverse cultural communities*; b) *story as a meaning-making process to understand self and world, c) family literacies for literacy learning*, and d) *professional learning opportunities for educators across community, school, and university settings.*

In their expanded version, these principles were originally elaborated in the following ways:

Valuing the funds of knowledge within diverse cultural communities

This principle, as it pertains to CREATE, involves fostering possibilities for our teacher candidates to learn about their students' home-based contexts and to get to know the child as a whole person who is actively involved in multiple spheres of knowledge and relationships (Gonzalez et al., 2005). From this point of departure, our goal is to develop innovations in teaching that leverage the knowledge and skills found in local households.

Encouraging story as a meaning-making process to understand self and world

The principle of story was centered on the belief that literature offers the potential to transform children's lives as they find themselves reflected in stories and make emotional and reasonable connections that transform their understandings. Transformation occurs as children carry their experiences and inquiries through literature back into their worlds and lives. To enact this principle, in CREATE we used a large international collection of literature (www.wow.lit.org) and provided support through professional development for preservice teachers and family members on ways of interacting with children around written story—reading aloud, talking about story—as well as ways of encouraging family members and children to tell oral stories (Short, 2009; 2012).

Celebrating the significance of family literacies in literacy learning

The third principle that guided CREATE is an expansion of the idea that prospective early childhood teachers and teacher educators who are able to work in and with community-based education centers have powerful opportunities to learn *with and from* children, their family members, and their caregivers. When family members are involved and invited to participate in their children's learning, student motivation increases, and positive relationships between family members and teachers foster optimal development in children (daSilva Iddings, 2009; Reyes, 2006). When family members participate with other family members and early childhood educators in group discussions, similar to *tertulias* (social gatherings with literary or artistic foci that are common throughout Ibero-America), they become engaged in their children's learning and become knowledgeable about how to help their children in school-related activities (e.g., homework).

Providing professional learning opportunities for educators across community, school, and university settings

Through the fourth principle, we aim to convey a coherent message about teaching practices that covers coursework and field experiences (see also Clift & Brady, 2005; Levine, 2006). This necessitates relocating teacher education programs from university classrooms to early childhood centers, and coordinating content of instruction among teachers, families, university educators and administrators, community members, and community literacy organizations. In this way, the curriculum is fluid and the programmatic content does not rely solely on discrete, segmented coursework in theory and pedagogy.

Across all of these principles, we note that the contributing authors for this book have in common the belief that education is always political and fundamentally ethical and as such, we must combat our own biases and fight for inequities at every turn, from the ways we build our schools and arrange our classrooms, to the ways we distribute resources, to the ways we talk to our students and refer to their families and communities, to the stories we choose to tell about them and hear from them. As educators, we strive toward the ideal of a just society as we prepare teachers to build true partnerships between family-community-school that support the language and literacy learning of linguistically diverse learners and that promote educational equity.

Bibliography

Amatea, E. S., Cholewa, B., & Mixon, K. A. (2012). Influencing preservice teachers' attitudes about working with low-income and/or ethnic minority families. *Urban Education*, 47(4), 801–834.

American Federation of Teachers. (2004, March). *Closing the achievement gap: Focus on Latino students* (Policy Brief 17). Retrieved March 28, 2014, from http://www.aft.org/teachers/pusbs-reports/index.htm#english

Bellamy, C. (2001). *The state of the world's children 2001*. Retrieved from http://www.unicef.org/sowc01/pdf/index.html

Bronfenbrenner, U. (1979). *The ecology of human development: Experiments by nature and design*. Cambridge, MA: Harvard University Press.

Campano, G. (2007). *Immigrant students and literacy: Reading, writing, and remembering.* New York: Teachers College Press.

Clift, R. T., & Brady, P. (2005). Research on methods courses and field experiences. In M. Cochran-Smith & K. M. Zeichner (Eds.), *Studying teacher education: The report of the AERA panel on research and teacher education* (pp. 309–424). Mahwah, NJ: Lawrence Erlbaum.

Cole, M. (1996). *Cultural psychology: A once and future discipline.* Cambridge, MA: Harvard University Press.

Compton-Lilly, C. (2007). *Re-reading families: The literate live of urban children, four years later.* New York: Teacher College Press.

daSilva Iddings, A. C. (2009). Bridging home and school literacy practices and empowering families of recent immigrant children. *Theory into Practice*, 48(4), 304–312.

daSilva Iddings, A. C., Combs, M. C., & Moll, L. C. (2012). In the arid zone: Drying out resources for English Language Learners through policy and practice. Urban Education, 47(2), 495–514.

daSilva Iddings, A. C., & Katz, L. (2007). Integrating home and school identities of recent-immigrant Hispanic English language learners through classroom practices. *Journal of Language, Identity, and Education*, 6(4), 1–16.

daSilva Iddings, A. C., McCafferty, S. G., & Teixeira, M. L. (2011). *Conscientização* through Graffiti literacies in the streets of São Paulo neighborhood: An ecosocial semiotic perspective. *Reading Research Quarterly*, 41(6), 5–21.

Dantas, M., & Coleman, M. (2010). Home visits: Learning from students and families. In M. Dantas & P. Manyak (Eds.), *Home-school connections in a multicultural society: Learning from and with culturally and linguistically diverse families* (pp. 156–176). New York: Routledge.

Drury, R. (2007). *Young bilingual learners at home and school: Researching multilingual voices.* Stoke-on-Trent: Trenthan.

Dworin, J. (2012). Insights into biliteracy development: Toward a bidirectional theory of bilingual pedagogy. *Journal of Hispanic Higher Education*, 2(2), 171–186. DOI: http://dx.doi.org/10.1177/1538192702250621

Freire, P. (1970). *Pedagogy of the oppressed.* New York: Herder and Herder.

Gibson, J. J. (1979). *The ecological approach to visual perception.* Hillsdale, NJ, and London: Lawrence Erlbaum.

Gillanders, C., & Jimenez, R. T. (2004). Reaching for success: A close-up of Mexican immigrant parents in the USA who foster literacy success for their kindergarten children. *Journal of Early Childhood Literacy*, 4(3), 243–269.

González, N., Moll, L. C., & Amanti, C. (2005). *Funds of knowledge: Theorizing practices in households, communities, and classrooms.* Mahwah, NJ: Lawrence Erlbaum Associates.

Gutierrez, K., Baquedano-Lopez, P., & Trejeda, C. (1999). Rethinking diversity: Hybridity and hybrid language practices in the third space. *Mind, Culture, and Activity*, 6(4), 286–303.

Gutiérrez, K. D., & Rogoff, B. (2003). Cultural ways of learning: Individual traits or repertoires of practice. *Educational Researcher*, 32(5), 19–25.

Hammerberg, D. D. (2004). Comprehension instruction for socioculturally diverse classrooms: A review of what we know. *The Reading Teacher*, 57(7), 648–658.

Hogg, L. (2011). Funds of knowledge: An investigation of coherence within the literature. *Teaching and Teacher Education*, 27(3), 666–677.

Kenner, C. (2004). *Becoming biliterate: Young children learning different writing systems*. Stoke-on-Trent: Trentham Books.

Kenner, C. (2005). Bilingual families as literacy eco-systems. *Early Years: An International Journal of Research and Development*, 25(3), 283–298.

Lantolf, J. P., & Pohener, M. (2011). *Sociocultural theory and the teaching of second languages*. Oakville, CT: Equinox Press.

Lewis, C., Enciso, P., & Moje, E. (2007). *Reframing sociocultural research on literacy: Identity, agency, and power*. New York: Routledge.

Levine, A. (2006). *Educating teachers*. Education School Project. Retrieved from http://files.eric.ed.gov/fulltext/ED504144.pdf

Manyak, P. (March, 2000). *Participation, hybridity, and carnival: A situated analysis of a literacy practice in a primary-grade English immersion class*. Paper presented at the American Association of Applied Linguistics, Vancouver, BC, Canada.

Moll, L. C. (Ed.) (1990). *Vygotsky and education: Instructional implications and applications of sociocultural psychology*. New York: Cambridge University Press.

Moll, L. C. (2014). *L. S. Vygotsky and education*. London: Routledge.

Moll, L. C., Amanti, C., Neff, D., & Gonzalez, N. (1992). Funds of knowledge for teaching: Using a qualitative approach to connect home and classrooms. *Theory into Practice*, 31(2), 132–141.

Moll, L. C., & Gonzalez, N. (1994). Lessons from research with language-minority children. *Journal of Reading Behavior*, 26(4), 439–456.

Moll, L. C., Soto-Santiago, S., and Schwartz, L. (2013). Funds of knowledge in changing communities. In K. Hall, T. Cremin,, B. Comber, & L. C. Moll, (Eds.), *Wiley Blackwell international handbook of research on children's literacy, learning and culture*. London: Blackwell.

Nierstheimer, S., Hopkins, C., Dillon, D., & Schmitt, M. C. (2000). Preservice teachers' shifting beliefs about struggling literacy learners. *Reading Research and Instruction*, 40(1), 1–16.

Nieto, S. (2010). *Language, culture, and teaching: Critical perspectives*. New York: Routledge.

Onore, C., & Gildin, B. (2010). Preparing urban teachers as public professionals through a university-community partnership. *Teacher Education Quarterly*, 37(3), 27–44.

Ovando, C. J., & Combs, M. C. (2012). *Bilingual and ESL classrooms* (5th ed.). New York: McGraw-Hill.

Perez, B. (2004). Language, literacy and biliteracy. In B. Perez (Ed.), *Sociocultural contexts of language and literacy* (2nd ed., pp. 21–48). Mahwah, NJ: Lawrence Erlbaum Associates.

Perry, N. J., Kay, S. M., & Brown, A. (2008). Continuity and change in home literacy practices of Hispanic families with preschool children. *Early Child Development and Care*, 178(1), 99–113.

Reyes, I. (2006). Exploring connections between emergent biliteracy and bilingualism. *Journal of Early Childhood Literacy*, 6(3), 267–292.

Reyes, I., & Azuara, P. (2008). Emergent biliteracy in young Mexican immigrant children. *Reading Research Quarterly*, 43(4), 374–398.

Reyes, I., & Guitart, M. E. (2013). Exploring multiple literacies from homes and communities. In K. Hall, T. Cremin, B. Comber, & L. C. Moll (Eds.), *International handbook of research on children's literacy, learning and culture* (pp. 155–171). Somerset, NJ: Wiley-Blackwell.

Reyes, I., Kenner, C., Moll, L., & Orellana, M. (2012). Biliteracy among children and youths. *Reading Research Quarterly*, 47(3), 307–327.

Rodriguez, M. V. (2006). Language and literacy practices in Dominican families in New York City. *Early Child Development and Care*, 176(2), 171–182.

Rueda, R., & DeNeve, C. (1999). Building cultural bridges: The role of paraeducators in diverse classrooms. *Reaching Today's Youth*, 3(2), 53–57.

Short, K. G. (2009). Critically reading the word and the world: Building intercultural understanding through literature. *Bookbird: A Journal of International Children's Literature*, 47(2), 1–10.

Short, K. G. (2012). Story as world-making. *Language Arts*, 90(1), 9–17.Sleeter, C. E. (2001). Preparing teachers for culturally diverse schools: Research and the overwhelming presence of whiteness. *Journal of Teacher Education*, 52(2), 94–106.

Snyder, T.D., & Dillow, S.A. (2015). Digest of Education Statistics 2013 (NCES 2015-011). National Center for Education Statistics, Institute of Education Sciences, U.S. Department of Education. Washington, DC.

Souto-Manning, M. (2013). *Multicultural teaching in the early childhood classroom: Strategies, tools, and approaches, PreK-2nd grade*. New York: Teachers College Press.

Thibault, P. (2004). *Agency and consciousness in discourse: Self-other dynamics as a complex system*. New York: Continuum.

Van Lier, L. (2004). *The ecology and semiotics of language learning: A sociocultural perspective*. Boston: Klwen Academic Press.

Vélez-Ibáñez, C., & Greenberg, J. (1992). Formation and transformation of funds of knowledge among U.S. Mexican households. *Anthropology and Education Quarterly*, 23(4), 313–335.

Voltz, D. L., Collins, L., Patterson, J., & Sims, M. J. (2008, March 1). Chapter 2: Preparing urban educators for the twenty-first century. *Action in Teacher Education*, 29, 25–40.

Vygotsky, L. S. (1978) *Mind in society: The development of higher mental processes* (M. Cole, V. John-Steiner, S. Scribner, & E. Souberman, Eds.). Cambridge, MA: Harvard University Press.

Vygotsky, L. S. (1987). *The collected works of L. S. Vygotsky. V 1. Problems of general psychology: Including the volume thinking and speech* (R. W. Rieber & A. S. Carton, eds.). New York: Plenum.

Vygotsky, L. S. (1997). *The collected works of L.S. Vygotsky. V 3. Problems of the theory and history of psychology* (R. W. Rieber & J. Wollock, eds.). New York: Plenum.

Vygotsky, L. S. (2004). The historical meaning of the crisis in psychology: A methodological investigation. In R. W. Rieber & D. K. Robinson (Eds.), *The essential Vygotsky* (pp. 227–344). New York: Kluwer/Plenum.

Zeichner, K. (2010). Rethinking the connections between campus courses and field experiences in college- and university-based teacher education. *Journal of Teacher Education*, 61(1–2), 89–99.

2 Why Are Critical Perspectives and Ecological Approaches Needed in Early Childhood Teacher Education?

Toward a Trans/contextual Cultural-Ecological Approach

Mariana Souto-Manning

We are living in a new demographic era. White children are no longer the majority in today's U.S. early childhood classrooms, where most young students are of Color (Krogstad, 2014; Maxwell, 2014). This is not a temporary situation as demographic projections predict that the percentage of children of Color in early educational settings is expected to continue rising through at least 2060 (Colby & Ortman, 2015). From 2014 to 2060, the white population under 18 is expected to diminish by 23.4 percent whereas the population of Latinos is expected to increase by 53.6 percent (U.S. Census Bureau, 2014 National Projections). Paradoxically, most early childhood teachers are white (U.S. Bureau of Labor Statistics, 2014). Whereas the percentage of young children of Color in U.S. schools has increased significantly over the past two decades, the percentage of early childhood teachers of Color has declined (Ingersol & May, 2011; Souto-Manning & Cheruvu, 2016; U.S. Bureau of Labor Statistics, 2014). This mismatch often results in *de facto* minoritization; that is, the practices of children of Color—and their very identities—being positioned as "minoritized" (McCarty, 2002) because they are foreign to the dominant cultural and linguistic practices (Paris, 2009) of the overwhelming majority of early childhood teachers. Such minoritization represents capturing "the power relations and processes by which certain groups are socially, economically, and politically marginalized within the larger society" (McCarty, 2002, p. xv).

In light of the growing mismatch between early childhood teachers and young children in U.S. preschools (Ingersol & May, 2011; Krogstad, 2014; Maxwell, 2014; U.S. Bureau of Labor Statistics, 2014), there is a need to rethink and transform early childhood teacher education in ways that recognize that "diversity is the new normal" (Genishi & Dyson, 2009, p. 142) in ways that honor the urgency of developing teachers who question inequities in schools and in society. It is within this context that this chapter explains the need for combining critical perspectives and cultural-ecological approaches in revisioning early childhood teacher education.

On the Opportunity to Reposition Diversities in Early Childhood Teacher Education

These demographic shifts and predictions forecast an exciting time for early childhood education, a time filled with promising possibilities. But for such possibilities to come to life, we must engage in the transformation of early childhood teacher education through the critical problematization of the overwhelming presence and privileging of whiteness, which characterize the field. Yet, overwhelmingly, early educational policies, recommendations, and practices continue to invoke the norm as a "single story" (Adichie, 2009), which continues to promote problematic stereotypes about children of Color, their families, and their communities (Goodwin, Cheruvu, & Genishi, 2008; New & Mallory, 1994).

To move away from a "single story" of how children develop and from the very Eurocentric definitions of normal and appropriate (Goodwin et al., 2008; New & Mallory, 1994), challenging the (problematic) assumption that teacher educators know best, we need to rethink the current approach to early childhood teacher education, coming to fully recognize and regard what Bronfenbrenner (1976; 1977; 1979) titled macrosystem (dominant beliefs, ideologies, discourses, and attitudes) as foundational to early childhood teacher education. Why? Because early childhood teacher education must position itself politically and transform how it prepares teachers, moving away from Whiteified curricula and programs that continue to silence and exclude the expertise, experiences, "funds of knowledge" (Moll, Amanti, Neff, & Gonzalez, 1992), and brilliance of children of Color, their families, and their communities.

With this aim, I propose the need for critical and ecological approaches to inform early childhood teacher education, highlighting the need for—alongside the power and possibility of—a transcontextual cultural-ecological approach to early childhood teacher education. This would involve taking a step back, having a sharper focus on how dominant discourses and ideologies are politically instantiated through the social services provided to young children—the immediate context where early childhood teachers learn how to teach. This is key because a critical approach is predicated on change, and an ecological approach recognizes that multiple factors influence how teachers are prepared—within and across individual, community, and societal realms. But before moving ahead, I reread the world of early childhood teaching and teacher education in hopes of elucidating the urgency of such a shift.

Why Is a Critical Approach Needed in Early Childhood Teaching and Teacher Education?

From a critical perspective, decoding, reading, and rereading realities and situations can unveil the need to transform the world. Freire and Macedo (1987) proposed that critically reading and rereading the world

> enable[s] the people to reflect on their former interpretation of the world before going on to read the word. This more critical reading of

the prior, less critical reading of the world enables them to understand their indigence differently from the fatalistic way they sometimes view injustice.

(p. 36)

It is from this perspective that the critical reading of early childhood teaching and teacher education makes visible the need for transformation. Such transformation is predicated on revisioning teaching and teacher education to honor the expertise and experiences of minoritized populations. It requires critically analyzing, interpreting, and seeking to rewrite early childhood teaching and teacher education, recognizing that they are both firmly grounded in colonialist and whiteified visions of teaching, learning, and the world itself. Thus, they must be transformed to become more democratic, culturally relevant, and inclusive.

Rereading Early Childhood Education

Historically and contemporarily, children of Color are positioned as being "at risk." The very history of early childhood education is rife with inferior and deficit perceptions of children of Color and their families; after all, early childhood education was started to save children of Color from their own families' upbringings, perceived by white middle-class women to be lacking or not as good as what they could offer. Thus, white middle-class women were positioned to fix or to supplement the development of young children of Color, addressing the perceived deficits of their homes (Goodwin et al., 2008).

Throughout its history, the field of early childhood education has framed young children of Color as being inherently inferior, beset with deficits, or different (Goodwin et al., 2008). Inferiority and deficit paradigms framing children of Color persist today and are instantiated through comments such as "her parents don't care" and "he has no language" (Souto-Manning & Martell, 2016). Yet, in critically rereading the world of early childhood education, we early childhood teacher educators have the obligation to reframe the discourse used to frame children of Color and the practices employed to educate them, coming to see young children of Color and their families as being "at promise" (Swadener & Lubeck, 1995) ideologically and pedagogically.

While the pseudo-ideal of homogeneity may appear appealing and attempts to mandate what is "developmentally appropriate" (Copple & Bredekamp, 2010) continue to marginalize the experiences of children of Color and their families, homogeneity is simply an impossibility if we are to engage in equitable and inclusive early education (Souto-Manning & Martell, 2016). As Vivian Paley (2000) posed: "Homogeneity is fine in a bottle of milk, but in the classroom it diminishes the curiosity that ignites discovery" (p. 53). Thus learning from and with children and families of Color becomes a moral imperative in this new demographic era (Ladson-Billings,

2006)—especially in light of the racial mismatch of young children and early childhood teachers.

Without recognizing, for example, the cultural nature of child development (Rogoff, 2003), by regarding development as acultural, early childhood teacher education programs continue to position children of Color according to deficit perspectives (Goodwin et al., 2008), thus focusing on remediating the child. Such remediation rests on whiteification, on the imposition of dominant practices as the norm. Yet, as Rogoff (2003) underscored, "human development is biologically cultural" (p. 32) and thus child development is not standardized; it is cultural.

> Children everywhere learn skills in the context of their use and with the aid of those around them. This is how toddlers in India learn at an early age to distinguish the use of their right and left hands (a difficult distinction for many older children in other communities). The right hand is the "clean" hand used for eating and the left one is the "dirty" hand used for cleaning oneself after defecation.
>
> (pp. 69–70)

As early childhood teacher educators, we must engage in rethinking and problematizing what we know and believe in as unchanged realities. After all, such unchanged realities are key to sustaining an inequitable status quo. And while we each are likely to have a handful of stories of successful, gifted, brilliant early childhood teachers who graduated from our programs, these are exceptions to the larger narratives of teacher stress and lack of job satisfaction. According to the MetLife Survey of the American Teacher (2013), over "half (51 percent) of teachers report feeling under great stress several days a week" (p. 6), an increase of 70 percent from 1985 to 2012. Additionally, teacher job "satisfaction has declined 23 percentage points since 2008, from 62% to 39%" (p. 6). Surely this is not the fault of teacher education programs. Or—perhaps it is.

Contextualizing Early Childhood Teacher Education: On Race, Culture, and Justice

What are we doing in early childhood teacher education? Is what we are doing working? Data pertaining to children in U.S. classrooms and schools unveil the great and disproportional number of children of Color being retained, pushed out of school, and incarcerated, thus suggesting that what we are doing is not working. The brutal murders of African American males Trayvon Martin in Florida, Michael Brown in Ferguson, Missouri, Eric Garner in Staten Island, New York, and Tamir Rice in Cleveland, Ohio (while playing in a park with a toy) are situated representations of a broken system, which criminalizes the children who are now the numeric majority in our (pre)schools—children of Color, enacting what Children's Defense Fund (2007) has titled a cradle-to-prison pipeline.

It is within this context that "I'm not a racist" and "we have a commitment to social justice in our program" are thrown around by early childhood teacher educators, signaling racial privilege and excusing them from any culpability or from the need for reparations in education and in society. Uttering such statements does not position early childhood teacher educators apart from racism and racial privilege. Instead, such statements serve as shields to defend a system that continues to marginalize and silence the perspectives, voices, needs, expertise, and funds of knowledge of children of Color, their families, and their communities. Yet, what hides behind such statements is how early childhood teacher education (an overwhelmingly white profession) continues to position dominant ways of speaking, acting, and interacting as norms against which all children must be scaled and rated (Souto-Manning, 2010a; 2010b). Thus racism and racial privilege hide behind such seemingly innocuous statements.

As Ladson-Billings (2015) explained, we must move away from normalized understandings of "social justice," troubling the very term and engage in "a fundamental rethinking of our work." Ladson-Billings invites us to embrace "justice." She goes on to explain, "social justice is not expansive enough to help us confront the tremendous injustice that has a deafening grip on our society and keeps us so far away from everything we know as right and fair and just." She warns against the fact that social justice has lost its power and become a buzz term in education. This is often instantiated in early childhood teacher education programs, especially in response to accreditation goals, which espouse the use of such a term. We must instead fully engage in "confronting disparity, racism, sexism, heterosexism, ableism, and other forms of human asymmetry and the lack of equity and equality." She underscores the need for moving "from justice as theory to justice as praxis" (Ladson-Billings, 2015).

Defending, Reforming, or Transforming Early Childhood Teacher Education?

Drawing on Zeichner's (2014) conceptualization of teacher educators as defenders, reformers, or transformers, I explain the need to revise and re-envision early childhood teacher education, acknowledging that what is in place often results in teachers who see young children from nondominant and minorized communities as being "culturally deprived" or "inferior" (Goodwin et al., 2008). While I employ Zeichner's framework, I am aware of its limitations as teacher educators' practices, perspectives, and identities may not fit neatly into any one category. I briefly explain each of the teacher educator categories proposed by Zeichner (2014) below.

Zeichner (2014) explained that teacher educators who are defenders are often comprised of those who have been employed in university-based teacher education. They defend what they do without much recognition of how it continues to feed into segregation and educational inequity, without acknowledging the need for teacher education to be transformed in order to better meet the needs of children of Color, their families, and their communities. According to Zeichner (2014), defenders posit: "we are doing a good job, but our work is not being recognized." Defenders do not see a need for significant changes in the way things are now done and want more resources to do these things better.

Zeichner (2014) has documented that university-based teacher education has prepared most teachers in the U.S. over the last 50 years. Yet, policymakers, the mainstream media, university faculty, PreK-12 teachers, and the general public, many of whom were educated by teachers prepared in university-based teacher education programs, have declared that university-based teacher education is indeed a failure, offering alternatives such as the Teaching Academies established by the Every Student Succeeds Act and the well-known Teach for America Program.

Teacher educators who are reformers posit that education schools have failed and that the current system needs to be replaced by an alternative one altogether, one based on deregulation and market competition. They look to profit from education. They glorify practice and demonize theory (as if the two could be conceptualized separately). They put individuals with very little preparation in classrooms—regarding them as technicians who need a script, not as professionals who are culturally and intellectually competent and continue to learn from their practice. They take an economic approach to education, seeing the role of teachers as akin to those of investment bankers. The difference, from my perspective, is that our children are dreams and teachers are dreamkeepers (Ladson-Billings, 1994). Taking a reform approach to teacher education (Zeichner, 2014) implicates deferring dreams.

But what happens if instead of deferring dreams, or defending what we do (which has not worked for children of Color), we develop a vision, a plan, to cultivate the success of children of Color in schools—of America's children, of our children? What would happen if we transformed what we do? These are the questions taken up by those teacher educators Ken Zeichner (2014) labels transformers.

Teacher educators who are transformers are those who see the need for substantive transformation in teacher education, but who do not support blowing the current system up and replacing it with a market economy (as proposed by reformers). Although transformers believe that there are aspects of the current system that are working, they do not support maintaining many key aspects of the current system. Transformers reject the rhetoric of accountability, a global market economy, test scores, and grit (Vossoughi, 2015). They do not place the fault for the systemic failure of children of Color in our nation's (pre)schools on the children themselves. Transformers challenge the disconnect between colleges of education, schools and communities. They act against the traditional system's failure in accessing the expertise that exists in (pre)schools and communities in the education of teachers. They seek to move from remediating children and teachers to remediating teaching(Gutiérrez, Morales & Martinez, 2009). This is the stance I take here.

Transforming Early Childhood Teacher Education

To move away from seeing children of Color as being "at risk," challenge the racialization of the achievement gap (Delpit, 2012), and craft more hopeful possibilities for equitable early childhood teacher education, I employ Freire's critical pedagogical approach (1970). From this approach I engage in a thematic investigation and problematization of the pressing and oppressing issues in early childhood teaching and teacher education. After all, "if you want to understand something, try to change it" (Bronfenbrenner, 1979, p. 37).

Engaging in a thematic investigation of the pressing and oppressing issues in early childhood teacher education is a needed process to identify the generative issues permeating early childhood teacher education—not only in relation to our own worlds, but to the worlds of new, developing, and established master teachers. Once identified, these issues must be troubled within the context of a variety of perspectives and alternatives. This can happen through authentic dialogue as we early childhood teacher educators work to devise a plan for transformation across sites in powerful ways.

After identifying issues that exclude teachers of color from the profession and stances that continue to regard recommended early childhood teaching practices in terms of Eurocentric practices and concepts, we must speak up—not as defenders of what we do, but as a collective committed to transformation—a collective who knows that the very history of early childhood education is a history of positioning children of Color as inferior or deprived, framing them in deficit ways.

In doing so, we have the ethical and moral responsibility to foster a paradigmatic shift in early childhood teacher education—from regarding our preservice and in-service teachers as not being capable (another inferiority perspective) or as having been deprived of certain experiences (from a culturally deprived perspective) to being diverse and unique. This necessitates a rethinking of how we do early childhood teacher education—a necessary reconceptualization if we are to practice what we teach (Picower, 2012). We have the responsibility of developing a new framework from which to transform early childhood teacher education. And if we truly want to understand the ecology of teacher learning and development (Bronfenbrenner,1976; 2004; Zeichner, 1984), we must carefully consider contextual issues in the development of teachers as well as seek to more fully understand complex inter-contextual connections (how one context affects another). The ecological characteristics of learning have been explored by many (Zeichner, 1984) and must be considered by early childhood teacher educators as we seek to prepare teachers who can build on the strengths of diverse children and the funds of knowledge of their families (González, Moll, & Amanti, 2005), we must try to fundamentally change it, theorizing from powerful teacher education practices (Darling-Hammond, 2013) and envisioning a transcontextual cultural-ecological approach to early childhood teacher education. To foster such a framework, I draw on the work of Rogoff (2003), Cole (1998), and Gutiérrez and colleagues (2009), using elements of cultural historical activity theory to inform this framework.

Transforming Who We Are and What We Do as Early Childhood Teacher Educators

But before moving ahead, let's take a moment and recognize that if we are to transform early childhood teacher education, we must start by transforming ourselves—early childhood teacher educators—by recognizing that we are part of the system, and that because the system worked in some (isolated) cases, it is not a great system; it does not promote equity. We must recognize that our identities and beliefs are culturally shaped (Souto-Manning, 2013); so are definitions of best and appropriate in early childhood education (New & Mallory, 1994). This involves a critical analysis of how early childhood teacher education content is built on dominant perspectives and points of view, which are imposed in colonizing ways upon children of Color, their families, and their communities. As early childhood teacher educators, we must recognize our identities as culturally located, not simply and uncritically as "normal." We must problematize the assumption that early education curriculum is free from cultural assumptions.

Additionally, as we look at the demographic shift in schools, we must commit to a demographic shift in early childhood teachers and a demographic shift in early childhood teacher education. University-based early childhood teacher education is predominantly white. And while white allies can educate teachers of Color, there is a dire need to expand the number of early childhood teacher educators of Color and to develop support systems for early childhood educators of Color. Given the common experiences of racialization and isolation experienced by both early childhood teacher educators and early childhood teachers of Color (Cheruvu, Souto-Manning, Lencl, & Chin-Calubaquib, 2015; Souto-Manning & Cheruvu, 2016), it is reasonable to predict that expanding the number of early childhood teacher educators will likely result in improved experiences for early childhood teachers of Color.

As a profession, we are currently preparing an overwhelming majority of white early childhood teachers to teach "other people's children" (Delpit, 1995; 2006). And as Zeichner (2014) proposed, when we do so, we tend to care less and prepare teachers as technicians, as opposed to thinking of them as potential leaders, as entering a profession. Although we early childhood teacher educators may think that we are "doing diversity," early childhood teachers of Color have indicated their perceptions that the curriculum in early childhood teacher education programs often excludes, silences, invisiblizes, or ignores them (Cheruvu et al., 2015; Souto-Manning & Cheruvu, 2016).

Yet, instead of taking a deficit approach toward early childhood teacher education, here I propose we engage in remediation, instead of remediation. That is, teachers of Color have assets that can significantly enrich early childhood teacher education programs.

> In contrast to the traditional remedial approaches to instruction [which seek to fix the individual] . . . the notion of re-mediation—with its focus on the sociohistorical influences on students' learning and the context of their development—involves a more robust notion of learning and thus disrupts the ideology of pathology linked with most approaches to remediation. Instead of emphasizing basic skills and problems as located in the individual, remediation involves a reorganization of the entire ecology for learning.
>
> (Gutiérrez & Vossoughi, 2010, p. 102)

We must engage in the development of early childhood teacher education programs in ways that offer promise and possibility to educating young children and early childhood teachers of Color, in ways that reorganize the ecology of their learning. From this perspective, such a redesign necessitates a "social system's reorganization" (Cole & Griffin, 1983, p. 73). From this perspective, "remediation constitutes a framework for the development of rich learning ecologies, in which all students can expand their repertoires of practice and rupture the encapsulating practices of schooling" (Gutiérrez & Vossoughi, 2010, p. 102).

Such an approach to transformation through systems reorganization is especially important as many teacher education programs operate as if they were not members of larger communities and did not have responsibilities to preschools, schools, and communities. They use schools for placements but do not systematically invest in developing mutually beneficial critical partnerships. They effectively behave as parasites. Instead of finding a remedy for the approach that currently reigns in early childhood teacher education, I invite you to problematize, trouble, re-envision, revision, and transform it, focusing on remediation, within and across the multiple contexts that shape and are shaped by early childhood teaching and teacher education. The following section explains theories informing a transcontextual cultural-ecological approach and its affordances.

From Remediation to Remediation in Early Childhood Teacher Education

Well-known notions of remediation fail to document, value, and build on the rich contexts of early childhood teaching and teacher education and instead see educational failure as the result of individual teachers, or groups of teachers, rather than the educational practices of institutions themselves (Gutiérrez et al., 2009). And blaming the teacher, according to Kumashiro (2012), distorts the bigger picture. Focusing on the bigger picture, Griffin and Cole (1984) proposed the notion of remediation to put forth the idea that perhaps it is the tools and artifacts, and/or the learning environments that must be reorganized in ways to encourage deep learning; our own roles and programs must be reorganized, instead of blaming teachers—pre- and in-service—for not changing educational inequities.

Drawing on theoretical perspectives from cultural historical activity, I take up the notion of remediation introduced by Griffin and Cole (1984) for transforming early childhood teacher education. Arguing against reductive educational practices that seek to "remediate" learners (in this case, pre- and in-service early childhood teachers), instead this approach urges us to remediate learning environments; that is, transform early childhood teacher education, mediating or reconciling its relationships with multiple contexts that are currently seen outside of its purview.

Cultural historical activity theory requires researchers

> to focus on the social/spatial ecology of the activities they study-the relation of activities to their institutional arrangements. With respect to formal education, for example, instructional interactions are constitutive of lessons, which along with other forms of activity, are constitutive of classrooms that are constitutive of schools that are parts of communities, and so on.
>
> (Cole, 1998, p. 292)

In offering a framework for early childhood teacher education, remediation invites us to saturate learning environments with robust culturally and linguistically meaningful tools from multiple contexts, remediating them in productive ways. This approach views the activity settings—including the tools available in the learning environment—as problematic and in need of reorganization rather than placing all responsibility (and often blame) on the learner. It is from this perspective that I propose that we remediate early childhood teacher education, developing a transcontextual approach.

Toward a Transcontextual Approach to Early Childhood Teacher Education

Theoretically, we need to stop talking about remediating early childhood teaching and teacher education as if we alone (early childhood teacher educators) have the solutions. We don't. We are not working with young children every day. We are not living in the communities in which we are educating our teachers to work. We are not privy to the intentions behind new policies, mandates, and compliance measures. We need to acknowledge that we ourselves are cultural beings who, by and large, succeeded in the current system. Thus, we are likely to return to what is familiar to us and to what has worked for us in the past. In doing so, we are taking the same "fix it" approach we so vehemently condemn—a deficit approach; an approach that assumes that we know what is best; an approach that assumes a singular definition of best will work in every setting. I question this and propose that the first step to doing this transcontextual work is acknowledging our cultural positionings and our histories. We must acknowledge how our beliefs about early childhood teacher education are grounded in our very experiences (Goodwin, 2010; Goodwin & Genor, 2008), troubling them.

We need to move away from ethnocentric positionings that judge others against our own experiences, as if our lived experiences comprised the norms against which all should be scaled and rated (Rogoff, 2003). We need to humbly position ourselves as learners—acknowledging the "obvious truth; no one knows it all, no one is ignorant of everything" (Freire, 1998, p. 39). In doing so, we must strive to become learners and better understand how we can support the development of early childhood teachers, thus reorganizing the ecology of early childhood teacher education in order to actualize early childhood teachers' potentialities.

Remediating Early Childhood Teacher Education's Concerns, Influence, Commitments

In acknowledging this, our next step is to remediate what our current concerns are, how we exert our influence, and what we committed to (re)doing in early childhood teacher education. As explained earlier, while our concerns with education (especially regarding equity) may be multiple, we often see our influence as very small and thus commit to change little. Instead of spending time deeming our concerns inadequate, I suggest we take on this opportunity to remediate our areas (or what Covey, 2004, labels circles) of concern, influence, and commitment.

Covey's (2004) circles of concern, influence, and commitment can offer a helpful heuristic here. Typically, the practices of teachers are ignored or positioned inside the circle of concern (which includes all one cares about, personally, socially, and globally) of early childhood teacher education, but not fully within the circle of influence (which includes those things we can affect; being positioned within the circle of concern, but being much smaller) of early childhood teacher education programs. They are commonly positioned completely outside our circle of commitment—those things we can affect and are committed to change (Covey, 2004).

In early childhood teacher education, there is a focus on the programmatic matters, content of syllabi, scope, sequence, and standards. This concern (further reinscribed by accrediting agencies) takes us away from the humanity of teachers. Thus, in remediating our concerns, influence, and commitment, we may engage in an expansive reorganization of the learning environment and possibilities of early childhood teachers. To do so, Covey's notion of circle of concern, circle of influence, and circle of commitment as concentric, predetermined, and fixed ecological spaces (Figure 2.1) must be reread and troubled. After all, if we aim to transform early childhood teacher education, we must fight against this notion (that our commitments are infinitely smaller than our concerns, positioning ourselves as objects) and acknowledge our potential impact on and responsibilities within and across multiple contexts (repositioning ourselves as capable agents, as subjects of change). This agentive (re)positioning (Souto-Manning, 2014) can expand not only our commitments, but develop our influence. Covey's (2004) framework can thus be re-envisioned and expanded to cut across contexts, dialogically blurring universities, schools, communities, and policies; breaking down the artificial dividers between theory and practice; benefitting all realms and stopping the blame game that currently dominates educational policy discourses. In such a way, this framework rooted in

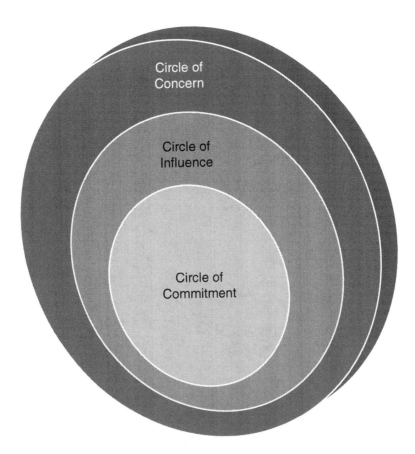

Figure 2.1 Covey's Circles

building caring and committed relationships is based on critical and authentic dialogue transcontextually.

Here, Covey's circles serve as frames from which to take a closer look at the transcontextual ecology of early childhood teacher education. To do so, I call for concerns, influences, and commitments to stop being conceptualized as differing and diminishing areas and affirm that if we are to change what is (comprised of our concerns), we must expand our influence and commitments. Not doing so would result in mistakenly conceptualizing and defending what is as if it were an equitable status quo. These concentric circles thus become one and the same frame of a magnifying glass through which we examine early childhood teacher development, from a transcontextual cultural-ecological framework (Figure 2.2).

Envisioning a Transcontextual Cultural-Ecological Framework

If we truly want to understand the ecology of teacher development, we must endeavor to fundamentally change the way we perceive it (Bronfenbrenner, 1979). Given the issues outlined earlier, and knowing that teacher

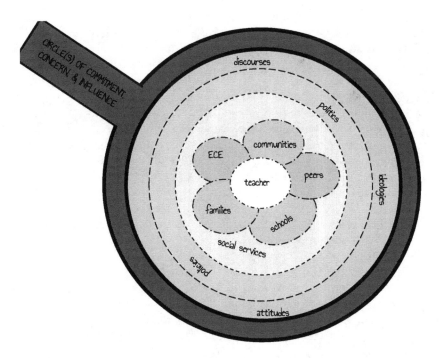

Figure 2.2 A Transcontextual Cultural-Ecological Approach to EC Teacher Development

development is influenced by culture and history, through participation in a variety of communities, I propose taking a transcontextual cultural-ecological approach to early childhood teacher education. While I could simply have referred to this stance as a cultural-ecological approach, I avoid doing so to emphasize the cross-contextual nature of the ecological model, which proposes that development is inherently cultural, thus moving away from concentric (yet impermeable) systems as initially proposed by Bronfen-brenner (1976; 1977; 1979).

Such a framework (represented by Figure 2.2) starts by acknowledging that macro discourses, ideologies, and attitudes (akin to what Bronfen-brenner titled macrosystem) frame teacher development and thus must be considered in transforming early childhood teacher education. These are instantiated through politics and policies, which frame and determine the social services available, at times instantiating arid zones with sparse educational resources for minoritized populations (daSilva Iddings, Combs, & Moll, 2012). These social services, instantiated by macro discourses, ideologies, and attitudes and mediated by politics, delineate the contexts that inform teacher (human) development—namely, schools, peers, families, communities, and early childhood education.

The frameworks' dotted lines indicate the permeability of multiple components of such a system for rethinking and transforming early childhood teacher education. But these permeable lines also indicate how movement happens from macro to micro systems as well as from micro to macro systems. This serves to analytically divide the ecology of early childhood teacher development into multiple components of a system, all of which influence teacher development. While Bronfenbrenner (1979; 1992) posed that the closer the relationship, the more influential a system is, I am unsure of such a claim. After all, each level, or each realm influences the other in such a complex system. And from a systems perspective, if any of these pieces are not in place, then change cannot effectively occur.

I propose the need to expand our concern in early childhood teacher education from preparing teachers who engage in "developmentally appropriate practice" (Copple & Bredekamp, 2010), from positioning early childhood teachers as their sole context, to understanding how teachers develop within the complex context of communities, social services, politics, macro discourses, and ideologies. Expanding our circle of commitment from the teacher to the system, which informs, influences, and shapes the development of early childhood teachers, is a first step.

A transcontextual cultural-ecological approach to early childhood teacher education is informed by the work of Rogoff (2003), who affirms that development is biologically cultural. That is, human development is culturally shaped. Such an approach is also informed by the work of Cole (1998) and Gutiérrez and colleagues (2009), who call for a powerful and expansive reorganization of learning environments, such as teacher education, remediating multiple realms, which directly and indirectly affect the preparation, education, development, and practice of teachers. It draws on the calls issued by Freire (1970), to transform what is in hopeful and powerful ways. It revises Bronfenbrenner's bioecological framework of understanding child development (1977; 1992), which features an ecology comprised of multiple systems influencing development. In remediating Bronfenbrenner's framework, I specifically draw on his newer work, in which he moved away from discrete systems (Bronfenbrenner, 1976; 1977; 1979) and acknowledged the need for the recognition of the interconnectedness of multiple contexts (Bronfenbrenner, 1994; 1999; 2005). This is an important distinction as Bronfenbrenner (1999) himself stated that "it is useful to distinguish two periods: the first ending with the publication of the *Ecology of Human Development* (Bronfenbrenner, 1979), and the second characterized by a series of papers that call the original model into question" (p. 4). He initially proposed the levels he labeled microsystem, mesosystem, exosystem, and macrosystem as separate. Later, he questioned such a focus on distinct and separate levels, acknowledging their interplay (Bronfenbrenner, 1989).

I propose, for early childhood teacher education, that a framework on early childhood education teacher development must acknowledge the teacher centrally. But in taking a close and careful look, through a magnifying glass comprised of overlapping circles of concern, influence, and commitment, it is impossible to consider teachers as individuals without considering their early educational and schooling experiences, peers, communities, and families. It is also impossible to fully consider these contexts apart from larger social services and public policies, which are shaped by politics (at the local, state, national, and international levels). These influence and inform (and are influenced and informed by) attitudes, ideologies, and discourses. That is, ideologies framing children of Color impact how politics mediates the social services available to them.

As teacher educators, I propose that we position early childhood teacher education's circles of concern, influence, and commitment as one and the same. And to do so, we must expand our influence by partnering with policymakers, social service providers, teachers, administrators, community members, family members, and university faculty. Only then will these circles start to overlap. This is imperative if we are to engage in transformation through inter- and cross-disciplinarity.

While we must recognize the need for us to expand our circle of influence and our circle of commitment to match our circle of concern, making them one and the same, we must also recognize the need to do away with a panoptical (Lesko, 2012) approach to early childhood teacher education—an approach that expects teachers to develop according to societal timelines (and/or according to teacher education program timelines). Pressuring and watching and measuring will not result in better teachers. A re-envisioned system for early childhood teacher education will.

But how do we remediate what is? A commitment to cultivating teachers as lifelong learners, as members of a profession; re-envisioning the entry of teachers into the profession as just that, the first step (Ellis, 2014) is a necessity. We must acknowledge this momentous occasion with hope and not with fear. It should not be a moment to jump off the cliff, to sink or swim, but a moment to enter the profession and to continue learning, as part of a collective. After all, teaching is the only profession where novices are expected to perform as experts. As Goodwin (2013) explains: "For some reason, we think that teachers . . . should be able to come out of . . . program and . . . from day one behave the same way as someone who's been teaching for five or ten years. We don't expect that of any other profession." A teacher's entry into the profession should instead signal that the person is becoming part of a profession (Ellis, 2014). This is an imperative revisioning if we are to cultivate teachers and their professional development.

The panopticon (Foucault, 1977) that early childhood teacher education has become, grounded in reform discourses and conceptions, such as accountability, testing, and grit, needs to be problematized. This panoptical framework leads us educators not to question or contest rules and regulations—but to follow them even when they are oppressing and disempowering. Our preservice teachers learn to do the same. We must contest the rules of the current system if we are to transform early childhood teaching and teacher education, challenging ideas of "normal" that exclude diversities. We must transform surveillance into collaboration and inquiry—for example, instead of the consequential rating of videos of teachers by strangers (in the case of assessments such as edTPA and CLASS), engagement in self-analysis and reflection as a result of video recordings is warranted.

Currently, the system in place (over)values bureaucracy (turning individuals into statistics and paperwork) and efficiency (placing a value on more and more work, goods, etc., even as it fosters injustice), at the expense of humanity. We must question, appropriate, and dismantle such a colonialist system, which continues to oppress and deprofessionalize teachers. Preservice teachers don't need to develop grit (code for the inhuman or subhuman struggle for efficiency) by engaging in high-stakes processes that add little to their professional repertoire. They need nurturing, preparation, and support as they develop within and beyond what we have come to call their "teacher preparation."

We must promote the recognition that human development, and thus teacher development, is inherently cultural. Teacher development is a cultural process. It is influenced by prior experiences in and with schooling. As such, teachers' developmental timelines will vary and cannot be comprised in a fixed (often two-year) window of time in standardized ways. As a field, we need to expand teacher education in ways that are supportive and flexible and regard teachers as lifelong learners. This expansion needs to go beyond a more flexible and nuanced timeline. Remediation must be at its core.

Note

I thank Lucas Souto-Manning for his graphic skills in designing Figure 2.2.

Bibliography

Adichie, C. (2009). *The danger of a single story*. Retrieved from http://www.ted. com/talks/chimamanda_adichie_the_danger_of_a_single_story.html

Bronfenbrenner, U. (1976). The experimental ecology of education. *Educational Researcher, 5*(9), 5–15.

Bronfenbrenner, U. (1977). Toward an experimental ecology of human development. *American Psychologist, 32*(7), 513–531.

Bronfenbrenner, U. (1979). *The ecology of human development: Experiments by nature and design*. Cambridge, MA: Harvard University Press.

Bronfenbrenner, U. (1989). Ecological systems theory. In R. Vasta (Ed.), *Annals of child development* (Vol. 6, pp. 187–249). Greenwich, CT: JAI Press.

Bronfenbrenner, U. (1992). Ecological systems theory. In R. Vasta (Ed.), *Six theories of child development: Revised formulations and current issues* (pp. 187–249). London: Jessica Kingsley Publishers.

Bronfenbrenner, U. (1994). Ecological models of human development. In M. Gauvain & M. Cole (Eds.), *Readings on the development of children* (pp. 3–8). New York: Worth Publishers.

Bronfenbrenner, U. (1999). Environments in developmental perspective: Theoretical and operational models. In S. L. Friedman & T. D. Wachs (Eds.), *Measuring environment across the life span: Emerging methods and concepts* (pp. 3–28). Washington, DC: American Psychological Association Press.

Bronfenbrenner, U. (2005). The bioecological theory of human development. In U. Bronfenbrenner (Ed.), *Making human beings human: Bioecological perspectives on human development* (pp. 3–15). Thousand Oaks, CA: Sage.

Cheruvu, R., Souto-Manning, M., Lencl, T., & Chin-Calubaquib, M. (2015). Race, isolation, and exclusion: What early childhood teacher educators need to know about the experiences of preservice teachers of color. *The Urban Review, 47*(2), 237–265.

Children's Defense Fund. (2007). *America's cradle to prison pipeline report: A report of the Children's Defense Fund*. Washington, DC: Children's Defense Fund. Retrieved from http://www.childrensdefense.org/library/data/cradle-prison-pipe line-report-2007-full-lowres.pdf

Colby, S., & Ortman, J. (2015). *Projections of the size and composition of the U.S. population: 2014 to 2060*. Washington, DC: U.S. Census Bureau. Retrieved from https://www.census.gov/content/dam/Census/library/publications/2015/demo/ p25-1143.pdf

Cole, M. (1998). Can cultural psychology help us think about diversity? *Mind, Culture, and Activity, 5*(4), 291–304. DOI: 10.1207/s15327884mca0504_4

Cole, M., & Griffin, P. (1983). A socio-historical approach to re-mediation. *Quarterly Newsletter of the Laboratory of Comparative Human Cognition, 5*(4), 69–74.

Copple, C., & Bredekamp, S. (2010). *Developmentally appropriate practice in early childhood programs serving children from birth through age 8* (3rd ed.). Washington, DC: NAEYC.

Covey, S. (2004). *The 7 habits of highly effective people: Powerful lessons in personal change*. New York: Simon & Schuster.

Darling-Hammond, L. (2013). *Powerful teacher education: Lessons from exemplary programs*. San Francisco, CA: Jossey Bass.

da Silva Iddings, A. C., Combs, M. C., & Moll, L. (2012). In the arid zone: Drying out educational resources for English language learners through policy and practice. *Urban Education, 47*(2), 495–514.

Delpit, L. (1995/2006). *Other people's children: Cultural conflict in the classroom.* New York: The New Press.

Delpit, L. (2012). *"Multiplication is for White people": Raising expectations for other people's children.* New York: The New Press.

Ellis, V. (2014, November). *Transforming the landscape of teacher education: Possible futures for the profession and universities working together.* Sachs Lecture, Teachers College, Columbia University, New York, NY.

Foucault, M. (1977). *Discipline & punish: The birth of the prison.* London: Penguin.

Freire, P. (1970). *Pedagogy of the oppressed.* New York: Continuum.

Freire, P. (1998). *Teachers as cultural workers: Letters to those who dare teach.* Boulder, CO: Westview Press.

Freire, P., & Macedo, D. (1987). *Literacy: Reading the word and the world.* Westport, CT: Bergin & Garvey.

Genishi, C., & Dyson, A. H. (2009). *Children, language, and literacy: Diverse learners in diverse times.* New York and Washington, DC: Teachers College Press and National Association for the Education of Young Children.

González, N., Moll, L., & Amanti, C. (2005). *Funds of knowledge: Theorizing practices in households, communities and classrooms.* Mahwah, NJ: Lawrence Erlbaum Associates.

Goodwin, A. L. (2010). Globalization and the preparation of quality teachers: Rethinking knowledge domains for teaching. *Teaching Education, 21*(1), 19–32.

Goodwin, A. L. (2013). *Mini moments with big thinkers: A. Lin Goodwin.* Retrieved from http://www.tc.columbia.edu/admin/125/moments.asp?id=9191

Goodwin, A. L., Cheruvu, R., & Genishi, C. (2008). Responding to multiple diversities in early childhood education. In C. Genishi & A. L. Goodwin (Eds.), *Diversities in early childhood education: Rethinking and doing* (pp. 3–10). New York: Routledge.

Goodwin, A. L., & Genor, M. (2008). Disrupting the taken-for-granted: Autobiographical analysis in preservice teacher education. In C. Genishi & A. L. Goodwin (Eds.), *Diversities in early childhood education: Rethinking and doing* (pp. 201–218). New York: Routledge.

Griffin, P., & Cole, M. (1984). Current activity for the future. In B. Rogoff & J. Wertsch (Eds.), *Children's learning in the "zone of proximal development": New directions for child development* (pp. 45–63). San Francisco, CA: Jossey-Bass.

Gutiérrez, K., Morales, P., & Martínez, D. (2009). Re-mediating literacy: Culture, difference, and learning for students from nondominant communities. *Review of Research in Education, 33,* 212–245.

Gutiérrez, K., & Vossoughi, S. (2010). Lifting off the ground to return anew: Mediated praxis, transformative learning, and social design experiments. *Journal of Teacher Education, 61*(1–2), 100–117.

Ingersoll, R., & May, H. (2011). *Recruitment, retention and the minority teacher shortage.* Philadelphia, PA: Consortium for Policy Research in Education.

Krogstad, J. (2014). *A view of the future through kindergarten demographics.* Retrieved from http://www.pewresearch.org/fact-tank/2014/07/08/a-view-of-the-future-through-kindergarten-demographics/

Kumashiro, K. (2012). *Bad teacher! How blaming teachers distorts the bigger picture.* New York: Teachers College Press.

Ladson-Billings, G. (1994). *Dreamkeepers: Successful teachers of African American children.* San Francisco, CA: Jossey-Bass.

Ladson-Billings, G. (2006). From the achievement gap to the education debt: Understanding achievement in U.S. schools. *Educational Researcher, 35*(7), 3–12.

Ladson-Billings, G. (2015, April). *Justice . . . Just, justice!* Social Justice in Education Award Lecture, American Educational Research Association Annual Meeting, Chicago, IL. Retrieved from http://www.aera.net/EventsMeetings/AnnualMeeting/PreviousAnnualMeetings/2015AnnualMeeting/2015AnnualMeetingWebcasts/SocialJusticeinEducationAward(2015)LectureGloriaJLadson-Billings/tabid/15943/Default.aspx

Lesko, N. (2012). *Act your age! A cultural construction of adolescence* (2nd ed.). New York: Routledge.

Maxwell, L. A. (2014). U.S. school enrollment hits majority-minority milestone. *Education Week.* Retrieved from http://www.edweek.org/ew/articles/2014/08/20/01demographics.h34.html

McCarty, T. (2002). *A place to be Navajo: Rough Rock and the struggle for self-determination in indigenous schooling.* New York: Routledge.

MetLife. (2013). *MetLife survey of the American teacher: Challenges for school leadership.* New York: MetLife. Retrieved from https://www.metlife.com/assets/cao/foundation/MetLife-Teacher-Survey-2012.pdf

Moll, L., Amanti, C., Neff, D., & Gonzalez, N. (1992). Funds of knowledge for teaching: Using a qualitative approach to connect homes and classrooms. *Theory into Practice, 31*(2), 132–141.

New, R. S., & Mallory, B. L. (1994). Introduction: The ethics of inclusion. In B. Mallory and R. New (Eds.), *Diversity and developmentally appropriate practices: Challenges for early childhood curriculum* (pp. 1–13). New York: Teachers College Press.

Paley, V. G. (2000). *White teacher* (2nd ed.). Cambridge, MA: Harvard University Press.

Paris, D. (2009). "They're in my culture, they speak the same way": African American language in multiethnic high schools. *Harvard Educational Review, 79*(3), 428–447.

Picower, B. (2012). *Practice what you teach: Social justice education in the classroom and the streets.* New York: Routledge.

Rogoff, B. (2003). *The cultural nature of human development.* Oxford: Oxford University Press.

Souto-Manning, M. (2010a). Challenging ethnocentric literacy practices: (Re)Positioning home literacies in a Head Start classroom. *Research in the Teaching of English, 45*(2), 150–178.

Souto-Manning, M. (2010b). Teaching English learners: Building on cultural and linguistic strengths. *English Education, 42*(3), 249–263.

Souto-Manning, M. (2013). *Multicultural teaching in the early childhood classroom: Strategies, tools, and approaches, Preschool-2nd grade.* Washington, DC: Association for Childhood Education International and New York: Teachers College Press.

Souto-Manning, M. (2014). Critical narrative analysis: The interplay of critical discourse and narrative analyses. *International Journal of Qualitative Studies in Education, 27*(2), 159–180.

Souto-Manning, M., & Cheruvu, R. (2016). Challenging and appropriating discourses of power: Listening to and learning from successful early-career early childhood teachers of color. *Equity and Excellence in Education, 49*(1), 9–16.

Souto-Manning, M., & Martell, J. (2016). *Reading, writing, and talk: Inclusive teaching strategies for diverse learners, K-2.* New York: Teachers College Press.

Swadener, B., & Lubeck, S. (Eds.). (1995). *Children and families "at promise": Deconstructing the discourse of risk.* Albany, NY: State University of New York Press.

U.S. Bureau of Labor Statistics. (2014). Labor force characteristics by race and ethnicity, 2013. *BLS Reports*, 1050, 1–59.

U.S. Census Bureau. (2014). *2014 National population projections.* Retrieved from https://www.census.gov/population/projections/data/national/2014.html

Vossoughi, S. (2015). Intellectual respect: Envisioning alternative educational possibilities. *Equity Alliance Blog.* Retrieved from http://www.niusileadscape.org/bl/shirin-vossoughi/#more-1810

Zeichner, K. (1984, February). *The ecology of field experience: Toward an understanding of the role of field experiences in teacher development.* Paper presented at the 64th Annual Meeting of the Association of Teacher Educators, New Orleans, LA. Retrieved from http://files.eric.ed.gov/fulltext/ED240111.pdf

Zeichner, K. (2014, October). *The struggle for the soul of teaching and teacher education: Imagining a more democratic future for teacher preparation in the U.S.* Sachs Lecture, Teachers College, Columbia University, New York, NY.

3 Using a Design-based Research Approach

Educating Early Childhood Teachers to Understand, Engage, and Teach the Culturally and Linguistically Diverse Child

Donna Jurich, Ana Christina daSilva Iddings, and Renée Tipton Clift

Design-based research is frequently traced back to the work of Ann Brown (1992) and Alan Collins (1992). Since then, many researchers have employed this research methodology to investigate learning in context (e.g., Cobb, 2000; Lehrer & Schauble, 2000; Simon, 2000). Design-based research methodology is distinguished from traditional experimental research in its treatment of the participants, learners, their localities, and their communities. It addresses problems in real-world settings and has two primary goals: to develop knowledge and to develop solutions. This involves empirical investigations conducted in naturalistic contexts, many of which are designed and systematically changed by the researcher. As such, it can offer researchers and practitioners the opportunity to generate evidence-based claims about learning and to produce interventions that can be readily useable. To this end, Cobb, diSessa, Lehrer, and Schauble (2003, p. 9) affirmed:

> Prototypically, design experiments entail both "engineering" particular forms of learning and systematically studying those forms of learning within the context defined by the means of supporting them. This designed context is subject to test and revision, and the successive iterations that result play a role similar to that of systematic variation in experiment.

Cobb, Confrey, diSessa, Lehrer, and Schauble (2003), and more recently Reinking and Bradley (2008), further explain that there are five features central to the methodology of design-based research. First, this paradigm aims to derive theories relating to the process of learning as well as the means by which this process is supported. Second, design-based research methodology relies upon intervention. "The intent is to investigate the possibilities for educational improvement by bringing about new forms of learning in order to study them" (Cobb et al., 2003, p. 10). Third, design-based research has two complementary faces: prospective and reflective. Prospectively, hypotheses are created about a specific form of learning and the means of supporting it. Reflectively, these conjectures are implemented, exposed to scrutiny, accepted, or refuted. Researchers may need to refine their initial hypotheses in light of newly collected data. Fourth, the methodology requires that researchers engage in repeated cycles of hypothesis creation and analysis. Last, as design-based research is heavily reliant on theory, the work done within this paradigm tends to focus on directing the application of seemingly abstract theoretical concepts onto a specific context. In other words, the theories employed within the experiment are useful to impel not only thinking but also practice.

The Design-Based Research Collective (2003) contends that this type of research is "of value in addressing research questions related to the enactment of interventions in varying contexts" (p. 8). Through detailed description and analysis of these interventions, researchers, in collaboration with practitioners in the field, can expand the base of *useable knowledge* (Lagemann, 2002)—that is, knowledge that could be directly applicable to their classrooms' contexts and the circumstances of their students. In these ways, researchers take the role of curriculum designers, and implicitly, curriculum theorists who are directly positioned in social and political contexts of educational practice and who are ultimately accountable for the learning that occurs (cf. diSessa & Cobb, 2004).

A fundamental assumption of design-based research is that learning is not located within the individual's head but is a process that is distributed across the knower, the environment in which knowing occurs, and the activity in which the learner participates. In other words, learning, knowing, and context are irreducibly co-constituted and cannot be treated as isolated entities or processes (Barab & Squire, 2004). Thus, the focus of this research paradigm is not placed on the individual learner, but instead, on the *ecology* of learning, or the idea that multiple contexts interact on various levels in such a way as to impact learning (daSilva Iddings & Rose, 2012). This research paradigm then considers the learning process as an intricate system of relations as opposed to a mere set of practices that work in isolation. As such, one challenging component of doing educational design-based research is to characterize the complexity, fragility, messiness, and eventual solidity of the design and doing so in a way that will be valuable to others. Using a design-based research methodology with the overarching intent to improve the educational circumstances of young culturally and linguistically diverse children for the past five years, the CREATE team (Clift, daSilva Iddings, Jurich, Reyes, & Short 2011–2015) has been working on a comprehensive redesign of the early childhood teacher education curriculum. Our goal was to reform the course content and field experiences we provided our pre- and in-service teachers to create opportunities where early childhood educators, university students, families, and children would be engaging together in exploring the ways diverse linguistic, cultural, and community backgrounds can interact to enhance literacy development for young children and for English learners, in particular. We began by identifying the need for change, then designing the new program, and finally engaging in the change process. The following paragraphs describe these experiences.

Identifying the Need for Change

In 2007 in response to certification changes being implemented by the Arizona Department of Education (ADE), faculty in the Department of Teaching, Learning, and Sociocultural Studies began developing a Bachelor of Arts in Early Childhood Education that would meet the requirements for an Early Childhood Education certificate. Faculty were working swiftly because ADE initially set 2009 as the implementation year for all kindergarten teachers to have an Early Childhood Education Certificate or an Early Childhood Endorsement. School districts knew they would need to have additional qualified kindergarten teachers, and the faculty wanted to ensure that teacher candidates who planned to teach kindergarten were qualified. As a result, to expedite the process of developing a new program with 60 credits of coursework, the faculty designed the Early Child Program based on the existing Elementary Education Program. This meant that the courses in the initial version of the Early Childhood Program mirrored those in the Elementary Education Program with modifications made to address teaching and learning from birth to age eight. In addition, two courses were added to the program of study: one course on early language acquisition and literacy development and one course on cultural pluralism.

Key features of the Elementary Program were also replicated in the new Early Childhood Program. Like the Elementary Education Program, Early Childhood Education students were admitted to the university as pre-education majors. After completing the general education and pre-education requirements, students applied to the program and, if accepted, completed two years of upper division coursework. The two years of programmatic coursework began on-campus in the first year with little field experience and then moved off campus in the last year with extensive fieldwork designed to provide teacher candidates with a wide variety of experiences.

During the first year of the Early Childhood Program, the on-campus courses focused on the foundations of early childhood education: social, cultural, historical, and philosophical contexts of early childhood education; child development; assessment; classroom processes; inclusion; early literacy; and structured English immersion, state-required courses on teaching English language learners. The on-campus foundation courses were sequenced; however in practice, students often took them in an order that best met their scheduling needs. In addition, the fieldwork component that was to be completed in the second semester often focused on kindergarten and first grade classrooms.

In the first semester of the second year of the original Early Childhood Program, courses moved off-campus to an elementary school. In this semester, the "methods" courses covered teaching the content areas: mathematics, science, social studies, language arts, reading, and art. In addition, during this semester, students completed two eight-week placements: one in a birth to pre-kindergarten classroom and one in a kindergarten through third grade classroom. The last semester was comprised of two eight-week student teaching placements. The first student teaching placement was in a kindergarten through second grade classroom, often with a new teacher at a new school site. The second student teaching placement was in a birth to pre-kindergarten classroom, again often with a new teacher at a new school site.

No one was happy. While the first year allowed teacher candidates some freedom in choosing their coursework, faculty found it difficult to address the varying knowledge bases of the teacher candidates. The first year also included very limited field experiences. Faculty found that some assignments were challenging because teacher candidates could not enact or observe practices with young children. Often, teacher candidates had completed assignments with young children in their own families or their peers' families, not in early learning centers.

By the end of the first year, teacher candidates had had few or no experiences with young children prior to entering kindergarten. In the second year of the original program, with their first placement in toddler or four-year-old classrooms, teacher candidates felt unprepared and overwhelmed. Although the program director and Office of Field Experiences were slowly building relationships with public and private early childhood centers, the centers were reticent to have teacher candidates placed at their schools for only eight weeks. Early childhood center directors were concerned that the teacher candidates had little time to develop relationships with the children and their families, let alone plan instruction for the children that was developmentally appropriate. Teacher candidates realized that planning for classrooms for very young children was different from planning for first graders. Instructors who supervised during student teaching were unsure how to coach students in the second eight weeks of student teaching in pre-kindergarten classrooms. Data collected from teacher candidates, mentor teachers, and faculty provided insights into the development of the new program.

Designing the New Program

We began this phase by generating a wish list, or a set of desirable design features that we believed would be particularly relevant to guide our work toward the broader vision for the program. These features were:

- A design-based research approach to curriculum
- A problem-posing approach situated in local knowledge and contextualized in the local communities
- An understanding of families' and communities' funds of knowledge

- A participatory and action-based approach to community engagement
- Integrated experiences that involved multiple stakeholders
- The creation of places and spaces for community integration
- Long-term engagement in the various partnering sites and communities
- Emphasis on language and literacy
- Plan for sustainability

These features were helpful in our developing a program model to represent our vision and the application of the CREATE principles (i.e., valuing the funds of knowledge within diverse cultural communities; encouraging story as a meaning-making process to understand self and the world; celebrating the significance of family and community literacies in literacy learning; providing professional learning opportunities for educators across community, school, and university settings) as described earlier in this volume. The program model makes evident the ways these principles permeated our work with the different stakeholders, keeping the commitment to community development at the core of our work in teacher education.

Project Model

In addition (and in accordance with the design-based research approach), we wished to closely observe the ways we progressed through the prospective and reflective cycles of implementation of the model. To do so, we developed an inquiry model to systematically document these cycles as we worked to reconceptualize our courses and field experiences and also as we worked with in-service teachers, families, and communities, creating opportunities for contextual change through action-oriented projects (Figure 3.1).

Inquiry Model

Using this inquiry model, we sought to address the following questions through the curricular experiences we provided our teacher candidates:

- How do we educate teachers to serve culturally and linguistically diverse children?
- How do we support teachers to engage in the communities?
- How do we work directly on community engagement?
- How do we work with current teachers to implement a culturally sustainable (Paris & Alim, 2014) curriculum in their schools?
- How do we transform our own teacher education program?
- How do community members come together and develop a sense of agency and engage in decision-making in their school communities?
- How do we understand families' multiple linguistic and cultural resources, and how do we draw on these resources to leverage them in their children's schooling?

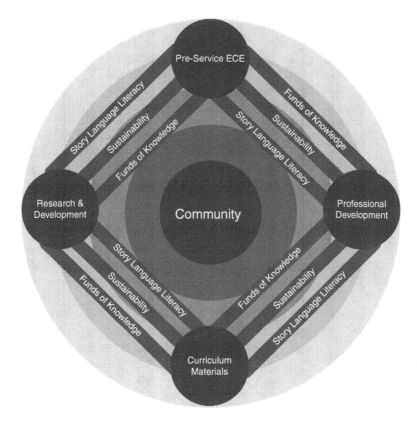

Figure 3.1

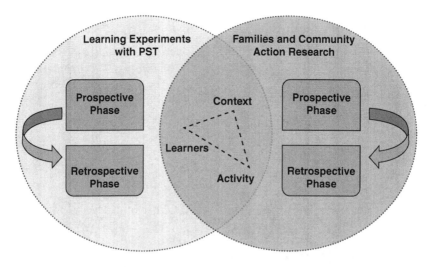

Figure 3.2

- How do we challenge our own assumptions and understandings regarding the families and communities with whom we work?

With these and other related questions in mind, we began to conceptualize an early childhood teacher education curriculum that was not just another version of what we had in place but that instead would be fundamentally reformed.

Curriculum considerations

We intended that our new curriculum reinforce our commitment to knowledge of and engagement in community and family relationships that extended beyond *knowing that* or *knowing about who* to *knowing with*, focusing on actual relational knowledge. In addition, our focus on stories would allow us to illuminate historical knowledge comparatively through different variants of cultural practices coming into contact. So, cultural knowledge funds were not conceived as monolithic but instead, developed relationally by culture-to-culture contact and in the context of actual relationship, in its lived affective, cognitive, embodied, and cultural dimensions.

The procedural steps of creating a new curriculum to attend to our roughly entailed (for more detailed information, refer to Appendix A):

- Mapping the courses
- Interviewing the faculty
- Incorporating the CREATE principles into the assignments
- Analyzing course syllabi to discover gaps and redundancies of content
- Creating an expected learning progression of experiences across courses and field experiences
- Providing communication opportunities among constituents—community, families, instructors, students, mentor teachers, and children.
- Establishing and sustaining community partnerships
- In the paragraphs that follow, we describe some of our experiences in engaging in the process of change as we began to advance the CREATE program.

Engaging in the Process of Change

> *No matter how honorable the motives, each and every individual who is necessary for effective implementation will experience some concerns about the meaning of new practices, goals, beliefs, and means of implementation.*
> (Fullan, 2007, p. 39)

The fourth edition of Fullan's (2007) discussion of change and change processes guided our actions as we began to redesign the early childhood curriculum, including field experiences. Although much of his text concerned change in schools and school districts, we found that several key concepts were relevant to working within our department and between our department and our cooperating schools and districts: involvement and buy-in from stakeholders, concerns about meaning, and program coherence. Early in the process, as the funding proposal was being written, the co-principal investigators began to identify the relevant stakeholders key to the first stages of implementation. We built strong and positive relationships with the surrounding school districts, including individual schools, and we have the same kind of relationship with the Arizona Department of Education (ADE). Our potential funder, the Helios Education Foundation, was and is committed to projects serving low-income populations, as well as to children whose first language is not English. The first level of stakeholder negotiation, therefore, was to ask the three local districts whose populations met the parameters if they were interested in being partners. We explained that we would be revamping the entire program and that it would involve a greater UA presence in the schools and that our students would be reaching out to families. We also explained that although we would have an overall plan, this plan would be revised based on our ongoing data collection and based on their feedback. In addition, because the project would be relying on data, we explained that there was a strong research component that would complement the curriculum design and ongoing modifications.

All three districts agreed to participate, and all three agreed to host UA classes onsite in their early learning centers. One district even dedicated a room for our use and placed the UA logo on the building exterior. We return to district-level negotiation later in this section, but their original commitment was important (and their commitment and support continues today). The second stakeholder from whom we needed commitment was the Arizona Department of Education. We asked that we not be reviewed by the state until the design was fully implemented, a task we knew would take four years. In addition, we asked that an ADE early childhood staff person serve on our advisory board, so that our changes would receive ongoing monitoring. In asking for support from both the schools and the department, it is important to note that we did not also need to negotiate or ask permission from the deans' office because that office was represented by one of the co-principal investigators. Because the four additional co-principal investigators were directly involved in departmental instruction and leadership, and because the department head was supportive of curricular change, the early negotiations at this level were minimal, as well. That said, even though both units (department and deans' office) were involved and on board early, it would be a mistake to deny the power dimensions inherent in the initial discussions and throughout the change process, something we return to later in this section.

Writing the proposal (all twenty drafts) included input from each of the co-principal investigators, the dean, and the department head. Each contributed thoughts, ideas, and concepts. Our program officer at the Helios

Education Foundation was also instrumental in shaping our proposal. We began by sharing concepts based on our individual areas of expertise, obtained feedback, rewrote, and went through the process again. Once our program officer was assured that there were theories and data relevant to our proposed changes, she asked us to take out all of the academic language and to prepare a final proposal that was accessible to a broad audience, which we did. These iterations served two important purposes. The first was the constant challenge to be articulate and coherent; the second was to ensure that the five co-principal investigators could work together, something that would be tested as those inevitable concerns arose.

Once the project was funded, negotiating assumed a new level of intensity as the project was introduced to our faculty colleagues, our collaborating school administrators, the incredible teachers who agreed to serve as our teacher preparation partners, and (of course) our teacher preparation students. These stakeholders would either support the changes or would scuttle them. Inherent in working across stakeholders within and across institutions are elements of power, differences in cultural backgrounds, nuances of language, and disparate job requirements. As an example of this last point, many of our school-based partners are expected to follow a given curriculum for literacy development—curricula that are generic and not amenable to customizing to students' funds of knowledge, nor to inviting parents into the classroom. While this situation is typically more prevalent in kindergarten through third grade, we see it in some early learning centers as well. Examples of the other three points include the power disparity between faculty who are in tenured positions, faculty who are pre-tenure, and faculty who are not tenure track; cultural mixes that include (but are not limited to) white European-Americans, Latinas, upper middle class, and working class backgrounds; and academic languages that are replete with critiques of the status quo (not to mention acronyms) mixed with languages of practice that by law must be languages of compliance (and a whole other set of acronyms). Many of the chapters in this volume document the process of change through the different activities our preservice teachers engaged in and the impact on participants and on further changes, change that is ongoing as we continue to improve CRE-ATE. Indeed, even though the funding from the grant has subsided, data collection and analysis have been and will continue to be important, and we continue to work on finding ways to sustain the program that do not rely on external funds.

At the beginning of this section, we mentioned that ongoing relationships enabled us to reach out successfully to our partner districts. We also mentioned that the writing and rewriting of proposal drafts created a relationship among the co-principal investigators that had not existed previously. The change process for us has been dependent on continuously building and sustaining relationships. Three examples illustrate this process: Establishing Relationships at the School and District Levels, the Family and Community Welcome Centers, and the Professional Learning Opportunities (PLOs).

Establishing Relationships at the School and District Levels

We have long worked with the three school districts in whose early learning centers we began CREATE because virtually all of our teacher preparation programs place University of Arizona students in schools. It was quite easy to pick up the telephone and ask for a letter of support. Indeed, one of our districts was opening a new center for children from three to five years old and built a classroom for us. This district agreed that they would be the Year One test case for CREATE. The director of the center concurred. We set our prospective teachers' class schedule around center events, and we hired a parent who worked with the school to serve as a community liaison. The research team discussed above conducted end-of-year interviews with the district and center administrators in each of the first two years, although we did not discuss in that section.

Over the first year we quickly learned that the norms of the university-based faculty and the norms of the center-based faculty often conflicted. Issues of timely attendance at meetings, of respect for curricula that had been in place long before CREATE began, of fair compensation for time, and of ongoing communication surfaced numerous time throughout the first year. Often, one of the co-principal investigators would get a call from the district, and a different co-principal investigator would get a call from the director.

In working through all of the issues (and we did) found that three particular actions enabled success:

- Timely response, in person, to discuss the issues face-to-face.
- Respectful and non-defensive conversations that focused on resolving the specific issue and on ways to prevent any recurrence.
- Verbal and frequent acknowledgment of the importance of everyone's time and work and of the collaboration.

As we began to add additional early learning centers, we drew on what we had learned from the first one, and because of the tolerance and patience of that district, we did not experience the same concerns moving forward. Additionally, we were able to work directly with the newly added schools, and because there were many fewer details concerning CREATE implementation, district administrators in the second and third districts were less likely to be involved. Our interview data indicate that CREATE was a source of pride for the district-based early learning centers.

The Family and Community Welcome Centers as a Place for Building and Sustaining Relationships

In order to promote the inclusivity of culturally and linguistically diverse families in the life of schools and continuous interactions between families, teachers, and children, we designed Family and Community Welcome Centers in the three partnering districts. Our work in this area was aimed toward developing infrastructures for family participation in the life and culture of schools, not merely as passive observers, but as active decision makers. To that effect, we have transformed empty classrooms into documentation rooms, family-run kitchens, meeting rooms, or art rooms, according to the needs and desires of the different constituents and also in accord with the different histories and geographies of each district where the individual partnering center was located. Together with school officials, teachers, families, and community members (e.g., school custodians and bus drivers), we aimed to shift traditional power relations and deficit-oriented educational models in the institutional settings of schools. In addition, we utilized these spaces for literacy activities involving connections between family, community, school, and university through the use of a transportable curriculum (i.e., Children's Photobooks, Family Story Backpacks, and Community Canastas), further explained in the various chapters in this volume. These activities fostered caring relationships and dialogue as well as shifted perceptions of the role of parents, primary caregivers, and teachers to protagonists of children's literacy education. In addition, these designed community engagements and the transportable curriculum activities facilitated the rupture of some prevalent institutional patterns of exclusion of culturally and linguistically diverse populations from schools, an increased appreciation and respect for the values, needs, and aspirations of these families by school and university faculty; a greater understanding about their households as places that hold valuable knowledge that foster and support the literacy development of young children (as opposed to common misconceptions about immigrant homes as places from which children need rescued from); and a growing awareness that literacy is fundamentally related to cultural identity and shaped by ethnicity, primary language, and social class.

Professional Learning Opportunities (PLOs)

As we crafted the four principles guiding the curriculum revision, we purposefully included a principle that would support the development of a professional learning community that involved the faculty, mentor teachers, and teacher candidates. Knowing that the teacher candidates would be taking courses and completing field experiences at the same time, we thought it important to bring the faculty, mentor teachers, and teacher candidates together to discuss theory and practice in early childhood education and teacher preparation as well as all the structural changes taking place in the Early Childhood Program. We believe that it takes a community—family members, mentor teachers; faculty, including university supervisors—to educate and support teacher candidates. This community needed to meet regularly, and we named those community meetings Professional Learning Opportunities (PLOs).

During the initial semesters as curriculum changes began, the PLOs provided an opportunity to discuss the CREATE principles and the subsequent curriculum changes that were occurring. For example, the Family Story Backpacks, which will be discussed later in this volume, are a part of the transportable curriculum and are a part of the curriculum taught by the teacher candidates during their field experiences in the second year. The Family Story Backpacks were new to everyone involved with the Early Childhood Program. Faculty, mentor teachers, and teacher candidates needed to be introduced to the concept of "transportable curriculum," curriculum that travels from classroom to families and then back to classroom and families. In addition, the mentor teachers, teacher candidates, and university supervisors needed to be able to discuss and plan for the Family Story Backpacks with the faculty who were teaching the courses that incorporated the Family Story Backpacks into the assignments.

The PLOs have also been important to our steady movement toward co-teaching as the framework for the field experiences, including student teaching. Mentor teachers have expressed the following assumptions about field experiences, especially student teaching:

- Teacher candidates can implement "assignments" from coursework in the mentor teachers' classroom. The assignments are not part of the mentor teachers' curriculum.
- Student teaching is a semester standalone experience that does not include connection to earlier fieldwork experiences or supporting coursework.
- Student teaching should follow a "phase in, full takeover, phase out" schedule.

The PLOs provide a space to disrupt these assumptions about teacher preparation and the coursework-field experience assumptions. Through the PLOs, faculty, mentor teachers, and teacher candidates work to weave together the coursework and field experiences and to validate the roles each plays in the process of teacher preparation.

In addition to introducing and deepening understanding of the CREATE principles and related curriculum innovations, the PLOs in later semesters have progressively provided professional development in areas that mentor teachers and teacher candidates have wanted to explore. PLOs have addressed teacher assessment tools in the program and in school districts as well as gender identity in early childhood education. In the future, as the more mentor teachers are familiar with the Early Childhood Education Program, the PLOs will continue to develop common, shared professional opportunities with all participants creating the agendas.

Affordances and Challenges of a Design-based Research Approach to Program Reform

Overall, in developing and designing new curricular and community project activities, programmatic engagements for our teacher candidates, and PLOs for mentor teachers, we have aimed to systematically contest deficit views of diverse families. In so doing, our goal has been to incorporate the local knowledge that both families and their early childhood educators can use as resources (e.g., native language), and are not seen as obstacles to learning. However, major challenges we have consistently faced in shifting educational views for teaching practices that attend to the needs to diverse populations are the continuous and exaggerated emphases on prescribed curriculum, standardization, and high-stakes testing. These challenges are also addressed in other various chapters within this volume.

Appendix A

Initial Program of Study

Cohort 3: Fall 2009 - Spring 2011			
Semesters	Fall 2009	Spring 2010	Fall 2010	Spring 2011
Courses	LRC 411 Cultural Pluralism (3) LRC 480C Children's Literature (3) TTE 300C Classroom Processes (4) TTE 350D Schooling in America(3)	SERP 301C Inclusion (2) EDP 301C Child Development (3) EDP 358C Assessment (3) LRC 416 SEI (3) LRC 312C Early Language Acquisition and Literacy Development (3)	TTE 312,Reading & language arts TTE 314, Science (3) TTE 316, Math (3) TTE 317, Social Studies (3) TTE 321C, Art (1)	TTE 493D Student Teaching
Locations	On campus	On campus	On site	On site
Fieldwork	45 hours of field work birth-grade 3. Students located sites	No fieldwork hours. Courses have field based assignments. Student located sites.	8 weeks birth through prek placement 8 weeks K-3 placement	8 weeks birth through prek placement 8 weeks K-3 placement

CREATE

Figure 3.3

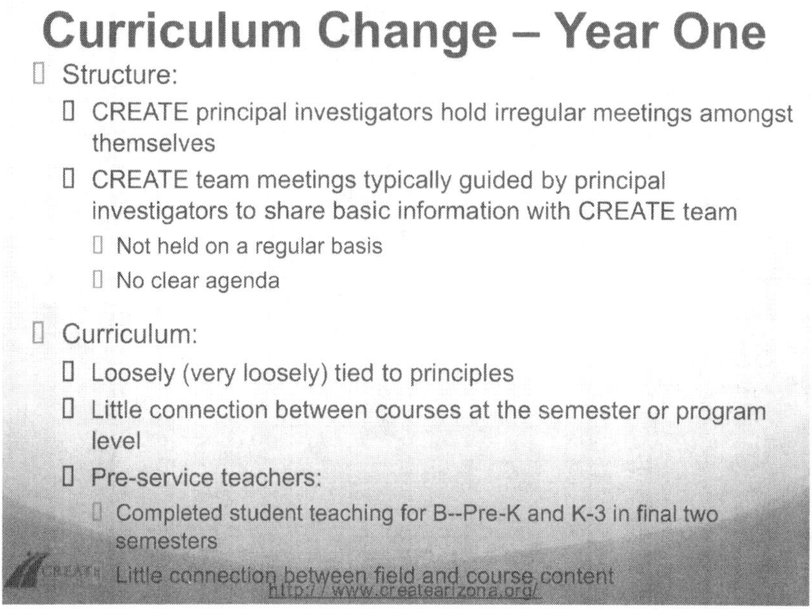

Curriculum Change – Year One

- Structure:
  - CREATE principal investigators hold irregular meetings amongst themselves
  - CREATE team meetings typically guided by principal investigators to share basic information with CREATE team
    - Not held on a regular basis
    - No clear agenda

- Curriculum:
  - Loosely (very loosely) tied to principles
  - Little connection between courses at the semester or program level
  - Pre-service teachers:
    - Completed student teaching for B--Pre-K and K-3 in final two semesters
    - Little connection between field and course content

http://www.createarizona.org/

Figure 3.4

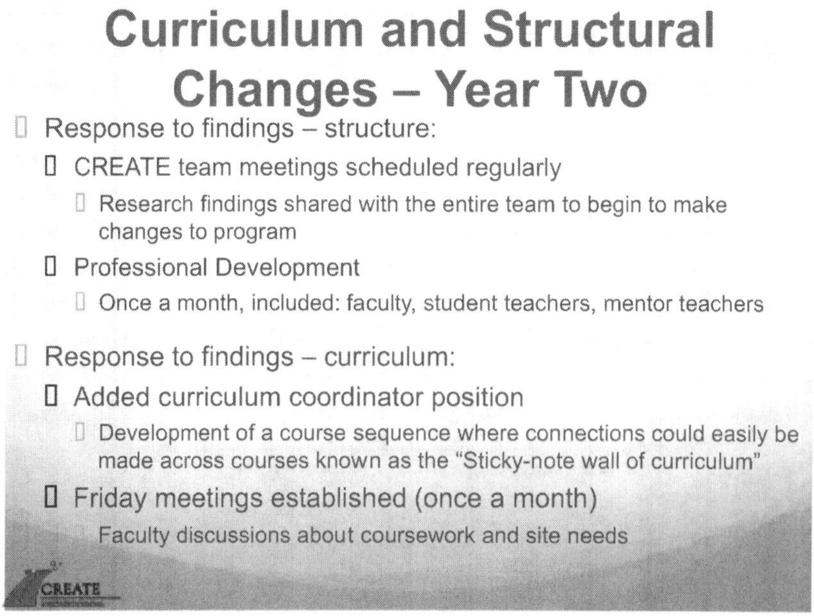

Curriculum and Structural Changes – Year Two

- Response to findings – structure:
  - CREATE team meetings scheduled regularly
    - Research findings shared with the entire team to begin to make changes to program
  - Professional Development
    - Once a month, included: faculty, student teachers, mentor teachers

- Response to findings – curriculum:
  - Added curriculum coordinator position
    - Development of a course sequence where connections could easily be made across courses known as the "Sticky-note wall of curriculum"
  - Friday meetings established (once a month)
    - Faculty discussions about coursework and site needs

CREATE

Figure 3.5

Curriculum and Structural Changes – Year Three

- Response to findings – curriculum:
  - Continuing:
    - Curriculum coordinator
    - Friday Meetings
    - Professional Development – Now Professional Learning Opportunities
  - New:
    - Instructional team meeting (minimum once a month beginning *prior* to Fall semester)
      - Faculty discussions focused on curriculum and assignment connections across courses
    - Pre-service teachers – student teach and take coursework concurrently – each area = one full year
      - B--Pre-K junior year
      - K-3 senior year

CREATE

http://www.createarizona.org/

Figure 3.6

Curriculum and Structural Changes – Year Four

- Continuing:
  - Curriculum coordinator aligns curriculum:
    - CREATE principles
    - State standards (InTASC standards)
    - ISTE standards
    - NAEYC standards
  - Friday meetings:
    - Faculty discussions by site focused on aligning curriculum and performance-based benchmark assignments across courses
  - Pre-service teachers – student teach and take coursework concurrently – each area a full year

CREATE

http://www.createarizona.org/

Figure 3.7

Evolved Program of Study

	Year 1		Current	
Semesters	Fall	Spring	Fall	Spring
Courses	Reading & Language Arts Science Math Social Studies Art	Student Teaching	Using Data to Guide Instruction: Birth to Age 8 Structured English Immersion I Inclusion Teaching Math Language Arts and Literacy Practices for the Young Child Internship	Structured English Immersion II (3) Reflective Professionalism and Leadership in Early Childhood Education Teaching Science Student Teaching K-3

Figure 3.8

Benchmark Assignments

Fall	Spring	Fall	Spring
Cultural Story Boxes Family Story Back Packs Funds of Knowledge-Family Story Interactions in Homes	Cultural Story Boxes Community Literacy Canastas	Family Story Back Packs Community Map Funds of Knowledge Digital Stories	Family Story Back Packs

CREATE

http://www.createarizona.org/

Figure 3.9

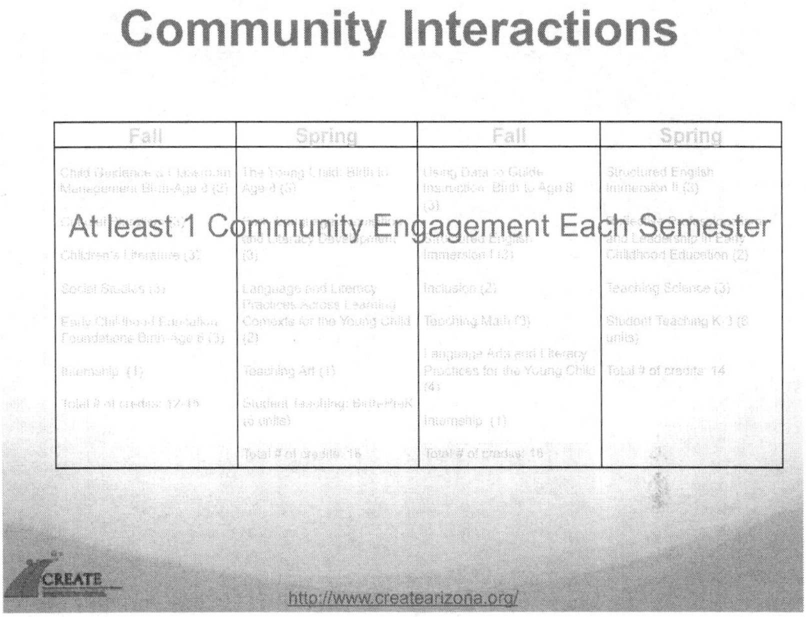
Community Interactions
Fall
Spring
Fall
Spring
At least 1 Community Engagement Each Semester
CREATE
http://www.createarizona.org/

Figure 3.10

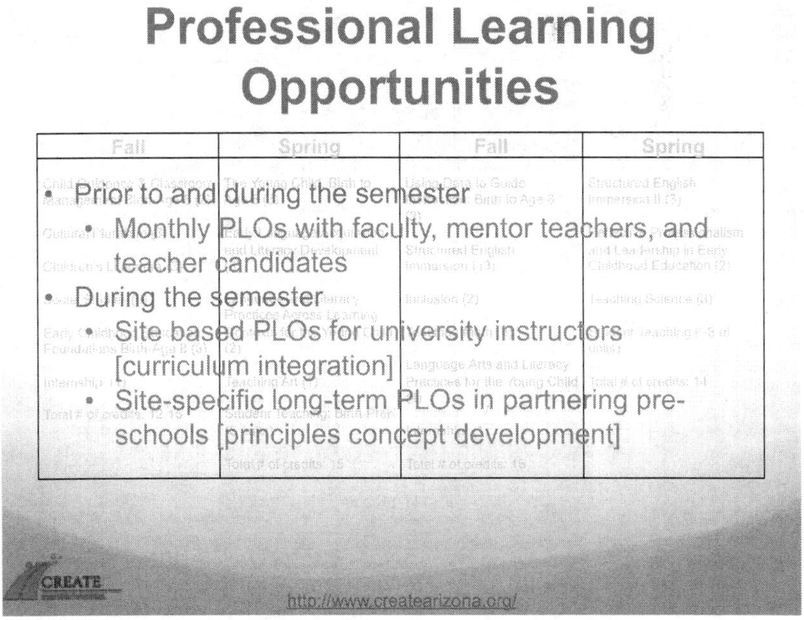
Professional Learning Opportunities
Fall
Spring
Fall
Spring
• Prior to and during the semester
• Monthly PLOs with faculty, mentor teachers, and teacher candidates
• During the semester
• Site based PLOs for university instructors [curriculum integration]
• Site-specific long-term PLOs in partnering pre-schools [principles concept development]
CREATE
http://www.createarizona.org/

Figure 3.11

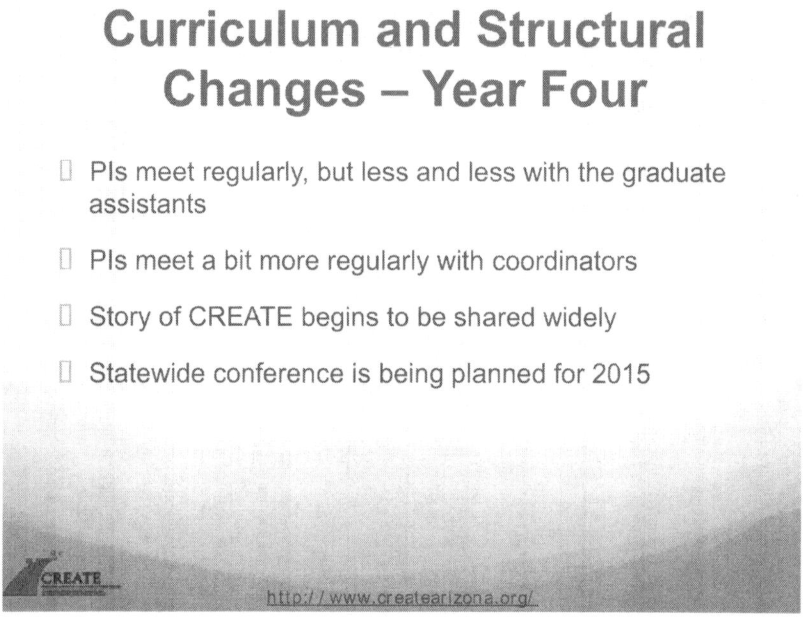

Curriculum and Structural Changes – Year Four

☐ PIs meet regularly, but less and less with the graduate assistants

☐ PIs meet a bit more regularly with coordinators

☐ Story of CREATE begins to be shared widely

☐ Statewide conference is being planned for 2015

Figure 3.12

Bibliography

Barab, S., & Squire, K. (2004). Design-based research: Putting a stake in the ground. *The Journal of the Learning Sciences*, 13(1), 1–14.

Brown, A. L. (1992). Design experiments: Theoretical and methodological challenges in creating complex interventions in classroom settings. *Journal of the Learning Sciences*, 2, 141–178.

Cobb, P. (2000). Conducting teaching experiments in collaboration with teachers. In A. E. Kelly & R. A. Lesh (Eds.), *Handbook of research design in mathematics and science education* (pp. 307–333). Mahwah, NJ: Lawrence Erlbaum Associates.

Cobb, P., Confrey, J., diSessa, A., Leher, R., & Schauble, L. (2003). Design experiments in research. *Educational Researcher*, 32 (1), 9–13.

Collins, A. (1992). Toward a design science of education. In E. Scanlon & T. O'Shea (Eds.), *New directions in education technology* (pp. 15–22). New York: Springer-Verlag.

Collins, A. (2004). Design research: Theoretical and methodological issues. *Journal of the Learning Sciences*, 13(1), 15–42.

daSilva Iddings, A. C., & Rose, B. C. (2012). Developing pedagogical practices for English-language learners: A design-based approach, *Pedagogies: An International Journal*, 7(1), 32–51.

diSessa, A. A., & Cobb, P. (2004). Ontological innovation and the role of theory in design experiments. *Journal of the Learning Sciences*, 13(1), 77–103.

Fullan, M. (2007). *The new meaning of educational change.* New York, NY: Routledge.

Lagemann, E.C. (2002). Usable knowledge in education: A memorandum for the Spencer Foundation board of directors [Memorandum]. Chicago, IL: Spencer Foundation.

Lagemann, E. C. (2012, January 24). *Usable knowledge in education: A memorandum for the Spencer Foundation board of directors* [Memorandum]. Chicago: Spencer Foundation. Retrieved from http://www.spencer.org/publications/usable_knowledge_report_ecl_a.htm

Lehrer, R., & Schauble, L. (2000). Modeling in mathematics and science. In R. Glaser (Ed.), *Advances in instructional psychology: Educational design and cognitive science* (pp. 101–159). Mahwah, NJ: Lawrence Erlbaum Associates.

National Research Council. (2002). Scientific research in education. In R. J. Shavelson & L. Towne (Eds.), *Committee on scientific principles for education research* (pp. 50–79). Washington, DC: National Academy Press.

Paris, D., & Alim, H. S. (2014). What are we seeking to sustain through culturally sustaining pedagogy? A loving critique forward. *Harvard Educational Review*, 84(1), 85–100.

Reinking, D., & Bradley, B. A. (2008). *Formative and design experiments: Approaches to language and literacy research.* New York: Teachers College.

Simon, M. A. (2000). Research on the development of mathematics teacher: The teacher development experiment. In A. E. Kelly & R. A. Lesh (Eds.), *Handbook of research design in mathematics and science education* (pp. 307–333). Mahwah, NJ: Lawrence Erlbaum Associates.

Vygotsky, L. S. (1978). *Mind in society: The development of higher psychological processes.* Cambridge, MA: MIT Press.

Westheimer, J. (1998). *Among schoolteachers: Community, autonomy, and ideology in teachers' work.* New York: Teachers College.

4 Engaging Teacher Educators' Commitment to the Principles of CREATE over Time

Sheri Robbins, Kimberly S. Reinhardt, and Renée Tipton Clift

Redesigning a teacher education program does not happen without all stakeholders understanding, embracing, and then striving to implement change in a way that is practical (Doyle & Ponder, 1977) and meaningful (Fullan, 2001). In this chapter we report on three years of data documenting the evolution of a curriculum redesign aimed at alignment with conceptual and philosophical principles, increased collaboration among faculty members, and encouragement of student and faculty interaction with families and communities. We investigated the ways in which university-based teacher education stakeholders' understanding of and engagement with the principles of the Communities as Resources for Early Childhood Teacher Education (CREATE) evolved. Our ongoing research also contributed to program changes over the three years, which we also discuss in this chapter.

As described in detail in the introductory chapter of this book (daSilva Iddings), the CREATE curriculum was redesigned to ensure that our college's commitment to working with culturally and linguistically diverse populations was embedded in the early childhood curriculum and grounded in four fundamental principles:

Principle 1: Valuing the funds of knowledge within diverse cultural communities.
Principle 2: Encouraging story as a meaning-making process to understand self and world.
Principle 3: Celebrating the significance of family literacies in literacy learning.
Principle 4: Providing professional learning opportunities for educators across community, school, and university settings.

We began our research in order to understand the ways in which our colleagues learned about, embraced (or did not embrace), and enacted (or did not enact) the CREATE principles throughout the first three years of the change process. CREATE was (and still is) an ever-evolving endeavor in which teacher educators' understandings of the principles are crucial to the success of the redesign, as are the ways in which they began and continued to enact the principles in their own teaching. We knew that if teacher educators could not implement the principles, the change effort would be doomed to failure. As we collected and reflected on our data, we shared our interpretations with the leadership team in order to identify areas for growth and to implement changes based on our findings (Kelly, Baek, Lesh, & Bannan-Ritland, 2008). We also knew our research would, by design, impact the ongoing changes. Therefore, our research was design-based (Cobb, Confrey, diSessa, Leher, & Schauble, 2003) in that it was shaped by the data we collected and the discussions we had based on our interpretations of those data.

CREATE is a complex, systemic curriculum change that involves many teacher educators on our campus, many of whom are not full-time, tenure-line, or practice track faculty member. In other words, a number of different role groups were a part of the system. On our campus, CREATE involved negotiations with deans and department-level administrators, field experience directors, field supervisors, graduate assistants who taught, graduate assistants who only conducted research, teachers-in-residence, tenure-line professors, professors of practice, temporary instructors, administrative assistants, and CREATE coordinators who worked for but did not teach within the program. The term *teacher educator* can refer to any of the above role groups (as well as to classroom-based mentor teachers and school- or district-based administrators and community-based program participants). In our research, we defined anyone as a teacher educator who worked directly with CREATE in any capacity that directly affected curriculum, instructional processes, or policies. The CREATE leadership team represented some of this complexity—a college administrator, a professor of practice with responsibilities for program administration, and three tenure-line professors. The leadership team, which had written the original proposal for funding, possessed a working knowledge of the principles and were able to articulate their meaning to one another; however, as our data show, sharing this knowledge with others took planning, time, and workable structures.

Methodology

Because our work is design-based and because each of the co-authors was a part of the project, it is important to discuss our involvement with CREATE and the ways in which we apportioned our research tasks. The first author occupied three roles, in addition to that of researcher: site coordinator, graduate assistant, and student teaching supervisor. The second author's role was only as a research assistant conducting the data collection and analysis for the line of research reported in this chapter. The third author served as a part of the leadership team and therefore, as an advisor to curriculum change and partnerships with the schools. The first and second authors of this paper conducted the interviews and therefore, were the only ones who could link data directly to participants. We felt that since the last author was a college administrator, it was important to remove her from any situations in which her position might influence other participants' responses. As a member of the leadership team, however, her position and participation gave us access to decisions about how the data were received by the team and any subsequent actions as a result of sharing the data. Collaboratively, the authors drew on their knowledge stores to both interpret the data and to share interpretations with the relevant members of the CREATE leadership team in order to feed important information back to the team.

Participants

Five co-principal investigators (who comprised the leadership team) monitored program development and implementation, and four either taught early childhood courses or directly supervised graduate teaching assistants (instructors) who taught courses. Tenure-line professors or professors of practice (instructors) taught the early childhood courses and participated in implementing the CREATE principles. University student teaching supervisors evaluated prospective students' progress and over time, also participated in implementing the CREATE principles. University-based field site coordinators and supervisors provided support for working with families, schools, and project documentation.

Over the three years of data collection, the number of participants increased because the students in the program doubled in the second year of CREATE (and therefore in the second and third years of data collection). In the third year of data collection, teacher education participants included five co-principal investigators, three administrators, eight instructors, three coordinators, six graduate assistants, three supervisors, and one administrative assistant. As we noted above, across the three years some participants held more than one position on the project. For the first and second year of data collection, our analysis included all participants. However, in the third year, although we interviewed all role groups, we chose not to include any person who did not work directly with students when analyzing for enactment of the principles. We also chose not to include the principal investigators in our analysis, even though some were also instructors, because of their inside knowledge of the principles and our research. Therefore, our analysis of data and findings for Year One and Year Two included all participants, and our analysis of data and findings for Year Three included only the teacher educators who worked directly with student teachers.

Data Collection

Year One data comprised interviews with the following role groups: co-principal investigators, administrators, instructors, coordinators, and graduate assistants/graduate teaching assistants. We designed the Year One interview protocol to elicit participants' perceptions of their experiences throughout the year and also, their perceptions of the value of CREATE. When we shared our analysis of the data from Year One, team members noted that the CREATE principles were not mentioned by anyone, other than the five principal investigators. In Year Two, at the request of the leadership team, we added specific questions about each of the principles. As we began analyzing the Year Two data, we realized that student teacher supervisors had not been a part of our original data collection plan, yet they were a primary source for our students' abilities to apply their learning in classroom settings (see Acevedo, Klecker, Pangle & Short, this volume). We also realized that many participants occupied more than one role in a given year and across years. This led us to wonder whether there were differences in perceptions of people who had multiple roles on the project. In Year Three we modified the protocol, asking participants to speak about the principles based each role they occupied on the project. We also altered the Year Three protocol to ask how participants saw others using the principles (Appendix A).

Data Analysis

Each year we created codes based on key words from the protocol questions and kept copious notes about repeated phrases or key words that were not part of our original codes as we transcribed the interviews. Then, as a research team, we collaboratively established the final codes for each year and reanalyzed the data based on our co-constructed agreements. In Year One, for example, we noted that many participants discussed the area of communication; therefore, we established a code for that theme. In Year Two we used the same coding system, adding codes for recurring phrases or words that were new because of the revised protocol. In Year Three we again looked back at the previous year and used the same coding system, collaborating to add codes when needed. Upon completion of the final years of interviews, we created a final list of codes that were representative of all the data collection (Appendix B) and using qualitative analysis software, Dedoose (Version 5.0.11, 2014), recoded all years, using the final list of codes.

Findings

In this section we first describe participants' perceptions of the challenges and strengths of CREATE and of understanding and working with the CRE-ATE principles for each year of the project.

Year One Challenges

The first year can best be described as working through confusion and struggling toward effective communication within and across role groups. Participants did not understand how to maneuver within the project's daily operation. The many and varied evolving components discussed in daSilva Iddings, Jurich, and Clift (this volume) often overwhelmed and challenged every role group. As one participant noted, there was no shared understanding of what the principles meant, nor of how they should be implemented in practice:

> We all operate and bring different funds of knowledge, and although we are all working from the principles, we are not always working from the same four principles—you know, [with] how they get interpreted. We are moving quickly, and so sometimes we think everybody agrees, and [then] find out, no, we don't.
>
> (Interview Response, 2011)

Another participant spoke to the fact that communication was an area that needed to be reevaluated and was a source of confusion for everyone, especially the university students.

> I feel like there is a lack of communication, because everyone has different goals, and we're trying to merge them altogether. I see that reflected in the preservice teachers, where they kind of, they show frustration, because they see that there is a lack of communication and not a real consensus of where the project is going, and what the ultimate goal of the project is.
>
> (Interview Response, 2011)

Meetings across role groups in Year One that took place were typically guided by the principal investigators, in an effort to share information, not as a way to connect instructors, their coursework, and the CREATE principles.

> I think that the meetings try to touch on too many things at the same time. Maybe create subcommittees and small meetings that you do not all have to go to. Or yeah, maybe create committees and maybe once a month or every other week have a big meeting to share and report back, but the subcommittees can meet.
>
> (Interview Response, 2011)

Although instructors of the courses were asked to use the CREATE principles to develop their curriculum, there were very few connections between courses within and across semesters. The participants were aware of this and were also aware that coordination was beginning; there just was not time in the first year to achieve such coordination. "[F]or example, the 312C [class] and the 480C [class] . . . those two courses I think really worked together strongly . . . we were hoping that those strands would be fully woven into all of the courses in spring, and they got woven into some and not into others" (Interview Response, 2011). Another participant identified the need for a curriculum coordinator to help pull things together:

> . . . the whole idea that you take an assignment done in one course and it connects to an assignment, that, you then use that to do an assignment in another class . . . I think that is a model that we need to look at across, and I hope when we get this curriculum person, it's possible to really sit down with that person and say, you're the one that's going to have to look for those opportunities.
>
> (Interview Response, 2011)

Year One Strengths

No matter what the challenges, it was clear that participants were committed to and clearly believed in the strengths of the project, and they were excited about what they were seeing. One strength was the diverse roles and funds of knowledge of the leadership team: ". . . this project could not happen without the team, there's just no way. The levels of knowledge that are required for this, the breadth, the depth of knowledge that is required for this, it has to have the team" (Interview Response, 2011).

Another strength was the benefit of working with the schools, the families, and the community. "The critical aspect is that we are seeing more of a reciprocal relationship with the sites and the teachers we are working with and I think that is a real benefit" (Interview Response, 2011). The connection developed between the teacher educators, the preservice teachers, the mentor teachers, and the community was crucial to the project. "I think what [the students] are learning as a partnership with families, they're also learning how to assess what the resources are . . . that they can then pull from to make their classrooms stronger" (Interview Response, 2011), and another participant noted, "To see them [in-service teachers] shift from one paradigm to another was very exciting. We need to listen to teachers and what they need" (Interview Response, 2011). Our data show that although there were many challenges, there were many accomplishments to be celebrated.

To work through the curricular and communication challenges, in the summer between Year One and Year Two, three of the co-principal investigators and the director of field experiences began mapping the curriculum—aligning all courses to both state-mandated standards and to the CREATE principles. The project also hired a curriculum coordinator, who helped instructors embed the principles in all courses and assisted with ongoing professional development for faculty, graduate students, and instructors within and across courses and semesters.

Year Two Challenges

As Year Two began, the five principal investigators, informed in part by our Year One research, designated each Wednesday morning as a time for project meetings. In addition, the instructors for each cohort began to meet biweekly with one another to discuss their courses and to examine the connections among courses and CREATE principles. The newly hired curriculum coordinator helped to

> . . . map out the curriculum, to identify the assignments that are being done, also the topics that are being taught, how they coordinate with all the other subjects that are being taught that semester, and how they flow into each other throughout the courses during their time here.
> (Interview Response, 2012)

She created what people referred to as the "sticky note wall of curriculum," which encircled the entire project office. Based on the wall, the instructors worked across the courses to build upon each other's content and activities. "It is not just a onetime thing, but to make sure [the principles] are there throughout the semester. Making sure those messages are constant and consistent" (Interview Response, 2012).

Year Two Strengths

The principles began to assume more prominence in Year Two, particularly the first principle, Funds of Knowledge. Instructors perceived that the pre-service teachers began to better understand themselves as cultural beings, which helped them better appreciate the opportunity to work in diverse, urban schools.

> We're teaching the preservice teachers and the in-service teachers both about how to look differently at the community that they are teaching in and the parents and families in their community . . . looking at it in a positive way and trying to see what those different families and the community can bring to the classroom.
> (Interview Response, 2012)

Faculty, instructors, and graduate assistants made deliberate efforts to recognize and address a deficit view of families and cultures different from their own by, "honoring and valuing family's practices, their home practices, and their dynamic ways of living and operating and being part of their community and seeing that as valid knowledge to be brought into the classroom, to be drawn upon" (Interview Response, 2012).

The second principle, story as way of knowing and sharing culture and knowledge, slowly began to be understood as a dynamic, living part of the curriculum.

> Books and stories that they [the students] wouldn't necessarily see in their placement or observation classes . . . [are] expanding the idea of

what's available. But also, through that, encouraging the oral stories as a way of helping students understand themselves and [their] community, as students, as well as the broader community.

(Interview Response, 2012)

Literature was a resource tool to foster storying. Therefore, the two work together to establish meaningful spaces for children and families to share their specific funds of knowledge.

By the end of the first year, we saw the focus shift away from communication challenges and time constraints. At the same time, participants began to discuss the first principle in more depth and provided a few examples of enactment. Our data suggested that the teacher educators felt more comfortable with the concept of funds of knowledge but did not fully understand the concept of story. The professional development sessions, therefore, began to address the second and third principles in more detail. Summer professional development sessions and ongoing Friday sessions (daSilva Iddings & Jurich, this volume) included more discussions of both of these principles. Additionally, the family and community liaison's role assumed even greater responsibilities for connecting family and community events to courses.

Year Three Challenges

The challenges of sustaining the CREATE curriculum and engagements with all of the changes in faculty from year to year, and of working more effectively with mentor teachers as they face increasing pressures for their students' performance on state tests, were predominant in Year Three. As the following quote illustrates, faculty members, instructors, and graduate students changed every year, and therefore the process of gaining a deep understanding of the principles and their implementation began over and over again.

I think we have a really strong curriculum, and . . . our courses are taught once a year, and we have a turnover in faculty sometimes, so when somebody finally gets it, they may not get it again, and it's like, oh God. So, that to me is a challenge. And, then the challenge is [maintaining] that sense of collaboration.

(Interview Response, 2013)

The institutional knowledge of veteran members of the instructional team was crucial for continuing to move the CREATE curriculum forward. Equally important, the program leadership would need to provide professional development for instructors and mentor teachers new to the program.

Another important key to sustainability was the Family Community Liaison, described in more detail in earlier chapters in this volume. This position, the only CREATE position that was totally dependent on grant funding, was responsible for organizing family events at school sites, projects with community centers, and family visits. Many participants agreed with the sentiments expressed below.

> I also think for sustainability that you cannot get rid of the [Family Community Liaison's] position. I think [she] is integral to the whole process. When you think about her job and . . . I think that a lot of people think, 'Oh, well, she goes out and she . . .' you know, 'She goes to all these fun things,' but what they don't realize is she's establishing relationships with directors, with the preservice teachers, with instructors, with mentor teachers, with families, and she is that one connection between here and . . . maybe there needs to be more of her as I don't know if she can continue to do it all, but I think that by having these connections or by knowing where to go for this resource or . . . knowing the community well, it has to be someone who knows the community well to do that job.
> (Interview Response, 2013)

Equally important to sustainability were mentor teachers who understood and supported the CREATE principles and fostered these principles with their students teachers. Just as it took time to develop an understanding of the principles with university-based teacher educators, it would take ongoing professional development to mentor teachers. Therefore, in selected field sites, mentors, student teachers, and CREATE staff met once a month in what they termed professional learning opportunities or PLOs.

> They had a lot of time to reflect together, just in terms of, I think those opportunities were helpful for the teachers to understand what the students were going through, to kind of see the students working at a different level. And giving them a chance to talk together and look at kind of the bigger picture, where they were interacting with each other in a broader sense, with other professionals, not just in their own school setting, which can be a microcosm. Then, when you go, 'Oh, you're doing that, and you're doing that.' Kind of heads up looking around seeing what's different in different areas. I thought that was pretty powerful to give them a chance to talk to each other. . . .
> (Interview Response, 2013)

Mentor teachers, student teachers, and faculty were able to develop a deeper understanding of the principles in practice through working and reflecting together during professional learning opportunities held once a month.

Year Three Strengths

By Year Three, the basic curriculum structure for CREATE was set (http://createarizona.org/ua-program/resources/copy_of_cohort-4). The preservice teachers were taking courses concurrent with a full year of teaching in Birth–Pre-K classrooms and a full year teaching in K-3 placements. In addition, most of the student teacher supervisors had other roles on the project and thus had a better understanding of the CREATE principles. Through the Friday meetings, all supervisors were informed about the curriculum and the community engagements, because supervisors now participated in those meetings to discuss coursework, activities at teaching sites, and any concerns about preservice teachers' academic progress.

> Fridays are when the site faculty meet and so those are the conversations— the curriculum conversations that happen at those Friday meetings are more, 'How do these things dovetail. . . . Thinking about that and thinking about when certain opportunities and learning moments open up and how do we incorporate them in or not incorporate them . . . [into coursework].
>
> (Interview Response, 2013)

Progress with Understanding and Enacting CREATE Principles after Three Years

With many of the facets of the project in place, participants commented that it was now working like a "well-oiled machine." Because much of the work became operationalized, the enactment of the principles was more focused, and preservice teachers were better guided in using the principles as a framework for understanding their practice. In this section we report progress on teacher educators' reports of the understanding and enactment of each principle after working on the redesign for three years.

PRINCIPLE 1: VALUING THE FUNDS OF KNOWLEDGE WITHIN DIVERSE CULTURAL COMMUNITIES

The following statements illustrate the progress from the confusion and limited understanding documented in the first two years toward the recognition that the preservice teachers were making progress—that the CREATE principles were making an impact on their ability to enact the principles.

> I've noticed that there's a change like 'I'm here to help the kids, I'm here to save the kids', sort of thing, that there's a shift in that . . . I feel like [the family home visit] really changes their perspective on what teaching is as a profession and what it is that's going to be asked of them as teachers.
>
> (Interview Response, 2013)

> I was really impressed with their final presentations for the graduating cohort, cohort five, because of the language they were using, and the

fact that . . . they weren't saying key phrases and sort of making sure to hit certain markers, it was you could see that they were really thinking about diversity in a much more global sense.

(Interview Response, 2013)

PRINCIPLE 2: ENCOURAGING STORY AS A MEANING-MAKING PROCESS
TO UNDERSTAND SELF AND WORLD

In Year Three, teacher educators played a key role in making explicit connections to story within their classrooms, as illustrated by the following comments.

We talk about stories, written or oral. My purpose is to have them understand story as a cognitive thing, like a way of thinking and webbing your events in life. It's more conceptual. I think some of them would still like a very specific strategy or tool that you would use for something. I'm trying to help them understand the broad notion of story . . . Again, it's through reflections. We put a lot of emphasis on oral stories at the beginning of the semester. They go back to gather stories and events from their life. They reflect upon how those were significant and what they learn through those oral, written stories. We really try to help them understand story as a way of living and life.

(Interview Response, 2013)

So, this semester, I had implemented the cultural story boxes that they had put together . . . so that was a major project in the course was to think about how to create invitations and engagements around the cultural storybox, and the idea of story as a, not as a static thing, like we pick up this book and here's this story, but thinking about oral stories, thinking about stories that are passed down, and thinking about stories that we tell about ourselves. And, so . . . and then how that connects to the idea of print-bound literature based on story. So, I think they've done a lot of work as far as that. Like, we've talked a lot about read alouds, we've talked a lot about culturally relevant literature, we've talked a lot about how to use story to promote thinking and identity, and you know, interactions in the classroom, so hopefully, we've gone beyond just looking at literature for literature's sake, but thinking beyond story.

(Interview Response, 2013)

PRINCIPLE 3: CELEBRATING THE SIGNIFICANCE OF FAMILY LITERACIES
IN LITERACY LEARNING

The third principle involved developing a structure for bringing families into school- and community-based activities around stories, books, sharing sessions, etc. The first step involved establishing relationships with families and the community and developing and implementing the backpack project and organizing the family home visits. The following statements illustrate teacher educators' progress by the end of Year Three:

> In the backpacks, there was an audio recorder that the families were encouraged to use to record stories. When the participant was collecting the backpack, the teacher said, 'Can you please make a copy of this because the grandmother wants this.' But, I had not listened to it. So when I listened to it I had goose bumps because it was so emotive, and I burned the CD and gave it to the grandmother. I was building this relationship with the grandmother. I called her a few months later, and I did not remember her name, and I said, 'You are the grandmother—I gave you the CD' and just by those words she was totally committed to the project—to everything.
>
> (Interview Response, 2013)

> The home visits can give the preservice teachers, and even the researcher a very nice understanding of the family strength and really their hopes and needs . . . The home visits provide a rich perspective that you do not get in the classroom with young children . . . it's really getting the students to understand the dynamic of communities and families and children, and their roles as teachers in the future.
>
> (Interview Response, 2013)

PRINCIPLE 4: PROVIDING PROFESSIONAL LEARNING OPPORTUNITIES
FOR EDUCATORS ACROSS COMMUNITY, SCHOOL,
AND UNIVERSITY SETTINGS

For any of the first three principles to continue to guide and sustain CRE-ATE over time, this principle is key. Understanding the importance of the interconnected curriculum remained a priority for the participants, allowing each instructor to build on one another's work with the cohort of preservice teachers. The following quotes illustrate the considerable progress teacher educators had made by the end of Year Three:

> . . . So, we met regularly, and we were usually, my sense of those meetings was that we were trying to integrate the principles into the semester in a way that they were reinforced and scaffolded, not repeated.
>
> (Interview Response, 2013)

> . . . The cohesiveness and being able to say, all the mentor teachers, all the student teachers are going to get it, and this also crosses over into the instructor piece, that we're all going to get together, once a month, to me is a brilliant thing that we added, to make sure that we are all there together, and that you have, you're building, this community,

it's the relationship. The CREATE program, the way it's evolved, it's become very relationship based . . . I mean, that is so helpful, because then I'm not some disconnected faculty person who's asking the student to do something not knowing what on Earth is she talking about . . . I'm a real person, that now you can talk to, we can have a relationship . . . it builds those levels of trust with the community.

(Interview Response, 2013)

Although far from perfect, sustained attention to progress that was informed by ongoing data collection and analysis enabled CREATE participants to grow in their understanding of and in their (and their students') abilities to enact the CREATE principles.

Discussion

In some cases and in some universities, teacher preparation curricula can best be described as a loosely coupled set of courses and field experiences. Clift and Brady (2005) documented that much of the research on methods courses and field experiences centers on the impact of a course, seldom investigating how courses and field experiences are nested within intact programs. Several current calls for change in teacher preparation focus on preparing skilled teachers and the use of powerful teaching practices. Others call for more intensive grounding in clinical practice (NCATE, 2010). What both have in common is a sense that teacher educators cannot be isolated from one another, that there should be a certain degree of program coherence. For CREATE, developing program coherence around a set of guiding principles was the base that informed changes for courses, as well as clinical practice and the nature of partnerships.

Our research points to five important considerations when developing a coherent program that integrates curriculum and engagements across courses and clinical practice. The first point we learned in the first year: that structures must be developed that bring people together to examine program content and practice. In addition, teacher educators need time to report on their students' developing understanding of principles, content, and instructional practices and their students' responses. Just as teaching is about relationships, so is learning to teach teachers within a programmatic context. The second point is closely related: new and more experienced classroom-based teacher educators should expect to come together with university-based teacher educators and teacher candidates to negotiate a common understanding of the teacher preparation curriculum, the opportunities and challenges of assignments and practices expected of teacher candidates, and the school, district, and university constraints that impact curriculum and teaching.

The next two are not structural, but more philosophical. The first CREATE principle emphasizes valuing the funds of knowledge within diverse cultural communities. Within every teacher preparation program, all teacher educators (university and field based) and all students represent their own cultural heritage and have their own ways of viewing the world based on that heritage. What this means for us, in practice and in principle, is guarding against deficit thinking and revising our language and ways of thinking, as well as our curriculum, so that we are not advocating practices we do not exemplify. Students know when they are being held accountable to values and practices that teacher educators do not espouse.

Our fourth consideration is adapted from the field of educational leadership—the notion that in successful schools (we substitute programs), leadership is distributed among individuals, not concentrated in one or more titular leaders. In CREATE, each member of the leadership team made a different, but crucially important, set of contributions to establishing, developing, revising, and evaluating progress. In this chapter, we noted this idea specifically as a strength of CREATE, and while it did not occur as often in our second- and third-year interviews, it remained a strength. From those who taught, developed curriculum, or developed and maintained relationships with schools, to those who provided critiques, and established family and community events, it is clear that a program has and needs many leaders who possess complementary skill sets.

Our fifth and final consideration is that without the data reported in this chapter and throughout this volume, we would not have identified areas of success or concern quickly enough to address them. External funding enabled us to hire research assistants and to gather resources for collecting and analyzing data. And therefore, one challenge to sustainability is establishing ways to continue to gather this important information as we seek to sustain CREATE. There are examples of the importance of ongoing data collection and analysis throughout this volume—examples of data that prevent one opinion or one point of view from swamping all others. Perhaps the fact that we do have a base of data and that we do have incoming doctoral students will permit some of the research reported here to continue over time. Indeed, the work started here can serve as a springboard for important future research, such as following graduates into their first years of teaching, examining the challenges and the excitement of mentor teachers, or simply the forces that sustain CREATE.

We began this chapter referencing Doyle and Ponder's (1977) work on the practical nature of curriculum-making and curriculum change, and Fullan's (2001) work on including all stakeholders in the change process. We, the CREATE teacher educators, cannot claim that in the beginning we consciously did either; however, through our interviews, our meetings with the leadership team, our interactions with our colleagues and students, and our willingness to modify CREATE as our understanding of CREATE developed and changed over time, we reaffirmed Fullan and Doyle and Ponder. We attended to those stakeholders that directly affect our early childhood program. We realize, however, that there are remote stakeholders such as state-level and national-level policymakers who may affect CREATE without even knowing that CREATE exists—a perpetual challenge in all education arenas. Over time, therefore, we will likely need to develop leaders who can communicate with these remote stakeholders and to broaden our already distributed leadership capacities in order to prepare and sustain teachers who are skilled in working with diverse children, families, and communities and who are deeply committed to doing so.

Appendix A

CREATING CREATE: Third-Year Interview Protocol

1   What are your roles on the project?

- Principal Investigator
- Graduate Teaching Assistant
- Graduate Research Assistant
- Instructor
- Coordinator
- Supervisor

2   Administrator in school or district: Discuss the work you do in each of your roles. Who are the people you work with in each role?

3   Which cohort group do you work with primarily, OR have you worked with multiple cohorts OR none?

4   When you first became involved in CREATE, how did you conceptualize your work? How has this changed? OR if this is your first year, how were you oriented into the work of the program?

5   Do you feel that you are involved/invited to the right meetings or activities to participate in CREATE? Elaborate.

6   I'm going to ask you three questions about the CREATE principles, then I'll share each CREATE principle. The principles are on your handout for you to refer back to as I ask each question.

- First, give me a specific example of how you work with the principle.
- Second, how have you seen others using the principle?
- Third, how do you assess the understanding of the principle among the other people you work with?

  - Principle1: Promote early childhood educators' understanding of the cultural knowledge and competencies (funds of knowledge) within diverse cultural communities.
  - Principle 2: Use literature and story as a base for children's understandings of themselves and others.
  - Principle 3: Involve families in literacy education for children—and for teachers.
  - Principle 4: Provide prospective and practicing teachers and teacher educators with opportunities to work and reflect together in community and school settings.

7 Which CREATE principle do you feel most closely connected to? (How do you think your multiple roles affect your understanding of the principles?)

8 What data do you have to support the integration of the principles in your work for CREATE? We define data as qualitative or quantitative hard data that prove the integration of the principles.

9 What are the benefits of CREATE for you (as a *ROLE*)? (Ask for each role the participants mentioned above.)

10 What do you see as the potential benefits of CREATE for others?

11 At this point, what do you see as the challenges of CREATE? (Ask for each role the participants mentioned above.)

12 I'd like you to think about program sustainability and write down a few ideas before sharing your answer to this question: In your opinion, what do you think the project needs to do to continue without external funding?

13 Reflecting back upon this year, is there anything else you would like to add they I may not have asked?

Appendix B

Dedoose Codes Export for Project: CREATE Y3

curriculum

standards

assessment

specific activity/assignment/engagement

placements

alignment/coordination

suggestions for leadership

communication

most closely connected principle

specific activity/assignment

backpacks

panels—Description: Outside individuals from community invited into instructor's classrooms to serve on panels

final presentations—Description: Students conduct final presentations that represent all course benchmark assignments

summer institute

cultural story boxes

cafecito

home visit

sustainability

relationships with schools/mentor teachers

P1 FoK—Description: Principle1: Promote early childhood educators' understanding of the cultural knowledge and competencies (funds of knowledge) within diverse cultural communities.

P1a—Description: example of assessment of principle

P1 exp—Description: example of how interviewee works with principle

P1 exo—Description: example of how others work with principle

P2 Story—Description: Principle 2: Use literature and story as a base for children's understandings of themselves and others.

P2 exo—Description: example of how others work with principle

P2 exp—Description: example of how interviewee works with principle

P2 a—Description: example of assessment of principle

P3 Family literacy—Description: Principle 3: Involve families in literacy education for children—and for teachers

P3f exo—Description: example of how others work with principle

P3f a—Description: example of assessment of principle

P3f exp—Description: example of how interviewee works with principle

P3 Community—Description: involvement/interaction with communities

P3c exo—Description: example of how others work with principle

P3c a—Description: example of assessment of principle

P3c exp—Description: example of how interviewee works with principle

P4 PD—Description: Principle 4: Provide prospective and practicing teachers and teacher educators with opportunities to work and reflect together in community and school settings

P4 exo—Description: example of how others work with principle

P4 exp—Description: example of how interviewee works with principle

P4 a—Description: example of assessment of principle

ownership/lack of ownership

benefits

assessment

relationships with teacher candidates

data collection/use of data

certification

conversations

absence of conversations

challenge/concern

student teaching/co-teaching

success/accomplishment/joy

collaboration/working together

role defined by participant

conceptualization of role

Bibliography

Clift, R. T., & Brady, P. (2005). Research on methods courses and field experiences. In M. Cochran-Smith & K. Zeichner (Eds.), *Studying teacher education: The report of the AERA panel on research and teacher education* (pp. 309–424). Mahwah, NJ: Lawrence Erlbaum Associates.

Cobb, P., Confrey, J., diSessa, A., Lehrer, R., & Schauble, L. (2003). Design experiments in educational research. *Educational Researcher, 32*(1), 9–13.

daSilva Iddings, A. C., & Katz, L. (2007). Integrating home and school identities of recent-immigrant Hispanic English language learners through classroom practices. *Journal of Language, Identity, and Education*, 6(4), 299–314.

Dedoose. (2014). *Web application for managing, analyzing, and presenting qualitative and mixed method research data* [Version 5.0.11]. Los Angeles, CA: Socio-Cultural Research Consultants, LLC. Retrieved from www.dedoose.com

Doyle, W., & Ponder, G. A. (1977). The practicality ethic in teacher decision making. *Interchange*, 8(3), 1–12.

Fullan, M. G. (2001). *The new meaning of educational change* (3rd ed.). New York: Teachers College Press.

Guiding Principles of CREATE. (n.d.). *CREATE: Communities as resources in early childhood teacher education*. Retrieved from http://createarizona.org/about-create/principles

Kelly, A. E., Baek, J. Y., Lesh, R. A., & Bannan-Ritland, B. (2008). Enabling innovations in education and systematizing their impact. In A. E. Kelly, R. A. Lesh, & J. Y. Baek (Eds.), *Handbook of design research methods in education: Innovations in science, technology, engineering, and mathematics learning and teaching* (pp. 3–18). New York: Routledge.

NCATE. (2010). *Transforming teacher education through clinical practice: A national strategy to prepare effective teachers*. Retrieved from http://www.ncate.org/Public/Publications/TransformingTeacherEducation/tabid/737/Default.aspx

Short, K. G. (2012). Story as world making. *Language Arts*, 90(1), 9–17.

5 Prospective Teachers' Interactions with Families

Understanding Home Contexts

Norma Gonzalez and Rebecca Zapien

This volume takes as its central organizing principle the foundational understanding about community knowledge that challenges "narrow conceptions of language, literacy, personal stories, bounded or contained learning contexts (e.g., home, community, schools), hegemonic cultural and linguistic norms, quantitative and static views of 'resources,' and limited attention to the agency, identities, and strategic actions of diverse students and their families as they traverse contexts" (daSilva Iddings, this volume). The touchstone to this approach is "Funds of Knowledge" as it has been conceptualized for nearly twenty-five years. This chapter will briefly summarize the approach as it has evolved and will lay out the programmatic implementation as it unfolded within CREATE.

The foundational text for exploring Funds of Knowledge, *Funds of Knowledge: Theorizing practices in households, communities and schools* (Gonzalez, Moll, & Amanti, 2005) takes seriously the idea of "theorizing practices." While many teacher education programs have emphasized the practicing of theories, the Funds of Knowledge approach gives primacy to the social construction of community-based knowledge as community practices are "theorized" by teacher researchers, university-based researchers, and teacher candidates. As we emphasize social practices in language and literacy, we must come to know the contexts of these practices and how they are embedded in the everyday and ongoing lives of students and their communities.

The concept of "Funds of Knowledge" (hereafter F of K) emerged as a counterdiscourse to images and stereotypes of nondominant students and their households. Rooted in essentializations of deficit discourses, students and their families were and are framed as "lacking" not only material resources, but affordances for learning. From the strength-based perspective of F of K, the social and cultural capital of communities could be made visible as a base for asset-based pedagogies. Learning about, with, and from families, communities, and practices was seen as a source of richly layered pedagogical possibilities. A place-based excitement was accentuated by educators coming to know the local ecologies of place, literacies and learning, and the prospect and opportunity of constructing curriculum around local knowledge. F of K is a perspective that endows everyday labor and activities with academic legitimacy.

A critical component of the original work was recasting the role of teachers as producers of knowledge rather than consumers of knowledge. As teacher researchers approached households as "learners" rather than as educators or teachers, they were able to excavate deep layers of historically constituted knowledge in households. Teacher researchers saw themselves not as implementers of theories but constructing their own knowledge. Too often teachers are disempowered in the deskilling measures that derive from a narrowed curriculum and foreclosing of expansive learning opportunities. Teacher researchers in the original F of K were not consumers of the knowledge of others but producers of their own knowledge about communities and families. This production of knowledge was jointly negotiated within teacher study groups that invited dialogue and inquiry. Within these study groups, which took seriously a sociocultural perspective on the jointly mediated activities, teacher researchers were able to excavate their own insights, observations, and tensions around the household engagements. Study groups also provided affordances for leveraging their understandings into classroom practices. This last step was critical as classrooms were no longer "containers" (Leander, Phillips, Taylor, Nespor, & Lewis, 2010) but open spaces that transcended the walls of the classroom into community spaces and practices.

The original F of K work was carried out with in-service teachers who had their own classrooms and had accumulated years of their own teaching funds of knowledge. CREATE provided a new perspective on helping teacher candidates in their preservice experiences to center communities and families as integral to teaching and learning. While many teacher education programs pay lip service to engaging with communities, the foundational premises of CREATE were firmly planted on the unconditional and unreserved foregrounding of communities as providing pedagogical opportunities and spaces for learning. Rather than engaging in a binary of in-school/academic/decontextualized knowledge versus out-of-school, informal, contextualized knowledge, the flows of community knowledges across divergent domains and spaces is an important facet of asset-based pedagogies.

In addition, teacher researchers in the original studies were given opportunities to negotiate space and time for thinking together, reflecting a sociocultural perspective on jointly mediated activity. Through reflection and theorizing about community practices and embodying a role of researchers, the social representations of educators was interrogated and transformed.

Models of Home Visits

In considering how a Funds of Knowledge perspective would inform a Teacher Education program in Early Childhood Education, one point of entry was to consider how home visits have been a mainstay of Early

Childhood programs. It was important to differentiate that a Funds of Knowledge home visit was not about paperwork documentation, nor was it about teaching the family about particular Early Childhood programs. While other models of home visits are making connections with parents and families, a Funds of Knowledge home visit is predicated on learning FROM the household and community, engaging their processes of sense-making.

Creating Spaces for Inquiry into Funds of Knowledge

The first CREATE principle is "Valuing the funds of knowledge within diverse cultural communities." This of course begs the question: How do we access the funds of knowledge in the families and communities of young children? How do we know funds of knowledge when we see them? Creating a community of learners for teacher candidates involved several interlocking components that simultaneously scaffolded the learning of teacher candidates as observers and researchers of communities. These components include:

1   Building a basis for a shared perspective on equity, social justice and culturally sustaining pedagogies (Paris & Alim, 2014).

The building blocks for a shared perspective were laid out in the course content of a required course entitled "Cultural Pluralism in Early Childhood." It was within this setting that teacher candidates read broadly about issues in critical multiculturalism, linguistic diversity, Indigenous educational rights, race and other constructions of difference, immigration, social class and poverty, and critical teacher identities and transformative education, among other topics. Within this pedagogically expansive perspective, teacher candidates learned about the concept of Funds of Knowledge not as only a technique or a methodology to implement, but a critical epistemological stance rooted in theories of sociocultural and sociohistorical frameworks, anthropological ethnographic fieldwork, social and cultural capital, and critical teacher identities. Within the format of the course they engaged readings across disciplines and became familiar with concepts such as equity vs. equality, critical multiculturalism, theorizing social practices, and the geopolitics of our Arizona border region. Broader historical, political, and economic contexts framed discussion of educational equity and access for young children as students were reminded to take seriously the lives and struggles of parents and families. In addition to readings, students were asked to post a "Media-Watch" links to the course D2L site. These included postings by the instructors, including Chimamanda Ngozi Adichi's TED talk on "The danger of a single story" as well as films such as the Lemon Grove Incident and Fear and Learning at Hoover Elementary. However, it was also a course requirement that students themselves post some form of media link to topics that were relevant to the course topics. Students posted and commented on a range of topics that included a deconstruction of Columbus Day activities to circulating discourses surrounding immigration and immigrants and racial profiling and the use of police force. No topic was off limits, and students were invited to search broadly for their postings. The first part of class was spent in viewing the media postings and taking up the issues that they posed. Because the topics emerged from the students themselves, there was a possibility of more open discussions and engaged dialogue. Students were free to disagree with each other in respectful ways. Difficult topics were addressed, including their own racial and cultural identities. Because students were part of a cohort, they came to know each other quite well. These media postings allowed them to uncover aspects of their lives that were perhaps silenced or not talked about in other contexts. The class also became a space where they could explore different aspects of conveying difficult and complex thoughts and topics to young children. How do you talk to young children about race? How do teachers approach the issue of undocumented and refugee families? How do we value the backgrounds and households and families of all children, however they might be defined or constructed? By dialoguing frankly and openly about difficult topics, teacher candidates learned that these conversations have a place within educational discourses.

The essential elements of a Funds of Knowledge approach were part of ongoing reflections and discussions:

- Ethnographic/Qualitative analysis of households
- Teacher-Researcher Study Groups/ Dialogical Encounters
- Classroom Practices
- Parents/Community as intellectual resources

2   Preparing for the household engagements:

A second and critical component was the intellectual and theoretical preparation for engaging in household visits. Engaging with the teacher-authored chapters in the book *Funds of Knowledge: Theorizing practices in households, communities and schools* (Gonzalez et al., 2005) was an indispensable element in preparing teacher candidates for the household engagements. They were able to vicariously experience, through the words and experiences of the various chapters, both the apprehension and the exhilaration of approaching the households as learners. The teacher-researcher-authored chapters in the book are explicit in how teachers were willing to transcend the traditional boundaries between school and household and to approach their reciprocal roles as teachers/learners: a teacher who learns and a learner who teaches. The teacher-researcher-authored chapters also gave the students permission to validate their understandable apprehension about whether they would be able to respectfully approach the households and how to engage in rich conversations. The chapters authored by teacher researchers were minutely explicit in describing not only the sights and sounds of the neighborhoods and households, but the human face-to-face interaction that was integral to establishing relationships of trust and what we have called "confianza" (mutual trust). These chapters allowed teacher candidates to understand deeply the encounters with the everyday life situations of their students. Another reading that was meaningful for the students was an article in *Rethinking Schools* by Elizabeth Schlessman entitled "When are you coming to visit?" Although not in the Funds of Knowledge text, this chapter outlines the journey one teacher takes to a community that she thought she knew and understood. Three telling quotations from this chapter were useful for class discussions:

> Home visits invited me to ask and wonder instead of to label and assume.
> I sensed that on the other side of the bus ride home, students' lives were much richer and more varied than could be taken into account by classroom conversations, curriculum and conferences.
> Home visits taught me that, although students might live in the same apartment complex or neighborhood, and might share a demographic like Latina/o or working class or native English speaker, their individual lives are incredibly complex and nuanced. Home visits taught me humility. They taught me to wonder.

These three quotations opened up spaces for teacher candidates to approach their visits with a sense of wonder rather than apprehension or anxiety and to enthusiastically contemplate what repositories of knowledge might be contained within households.

Students met in groups to discuss how to approach families respectfully and how to present what they are doing with clarity and transparency. Teacher candidates also were given a range of topics for eliciting Funds of Knowledge. These topics are seen as conversation starters, not as prescribed questionnaire protocols. This is an important point since the engagements with the families are meant to be non-intrusive and conversational. Because teacher candidates were to conduct two interviews with the families, they had to prepare with their partner how they would approach the topics and how they might expand on them. The suggested questions included topics that ranged from household histories (asking to learn more about the household; how long family members have lived in the area; family's roots; household composition; relatives who live nearby) to labor histories (describing work experiences, duties and responsibilities of employment, where skills were learned, if children worked with adults, non-wage labor) to daily or regular activities (typical schedules and activities, faith communities, sports, distribution of household tasks, gardening or outside activities, etc.) to respectful queries about language and literacy and constructing their roles as parents. These topic areas have been distilled from a much larger array of possible questions in order to allow teacher candidates to explore possible avenues to funds of knowledge. For example, in conversing about household histories, parents often narrate their stories about how they or their parents came to be where they are. This often entails stories of struggle and adversity but also of resilience and fortitude. It also illustrates the embedding of each household in particular social networks in terms of with whom they associate with on a regular basis. Labor histories likewise are a rich resource for uncovering funds of knowledge. Frequently children learn from the work and skills of members of the household, and skills and knowledge that have traditionally been dismissed as non-academic are given pedagogical validity. Similarly the ongoing and regular activities of households are also repositories of funds of knowledge as children engage in an assortment of context-embedded activities that can imply linguistic, social, mathematical, or scientific sense-making skills. The language and literacy practices of households are important in that children may be read to in one language and older siblings may speak to them in another. It is not unusual to find literate activities embedded in multimodal venues, such as Bible reading and musical literacy within a faith community. Increasingly households converse about the fluid digital literacies that are present in households and how children interact with text at many levels, and perhaps in different languages as they make transnational connections. Parents are also asked about how they construct their roles as parents and how they themselves were raised as children. These questions typically elicit deep reflection on the part of the parents as they narrate their journey to parenthood.

As mentioned, these topics are meant to be starting points, not end points. Teacher candidates explore freely the conversational leads provided by household members. In order to prepare teacher candidates before the visits, role playing is modeled in class. Teacher candidates almost universally express a great deal of apprehension and hesitation prior to entering the households, and the role playing helps to alleviate some of their anxiety. Role playing allows them to practice making connections to their own life experiences that they can share with the families. It also allows them to scaffold their own learning by making intentional and overt connections with topics that are emerging in the conversations. Teacher candidates focused on uncovering the Funds of Knowledge in households through "following their nose" in the interviews to understand that deep engagements with the families implicated the theoretical frameworks that were conveyed during classroom conversations:

- Establishing relations of trust to learn from families ("confianza")
- Learning about "sense-making" in households.
- Understanding the movement of people as part of their social and economic history
- Studying the household economy through the analysis of social practices and productive activities.
- Understanding the formal and informal economy

- Documenting knowledge, practices, and lived experiences
- Documenting social networks and reciprocal exchanges

This theoretical context allowed teacher candidates to develop a lens and a vocabulary to think about households in new and expansive ways. Teacher candidates were also allowed to redefine their roles as mere implementers of teaching paradigms, and to construct teacher identities that could be transformative for themselves and their students.

In addition to the role playing, there are videos that model what funds of knowledge might be evident as we approach the households. Careful attention to detail even before the visit is emphasized in terms of where the home is located, the streets, neighborhood, parks, etc. Upon arrival, teacher candidates are asked to notice potential cues that might lead to funds of knowledge . . . Vintage cars? Gardens? Woodworking tools? Bicycle parts? Pictures on the wall? How do we come to know the family through their artifacts?

As part of their preparation we also emphasize how they will likely be seen as a valued guest. This is sometimes difficult for young teacher candidates to process, as they are not accustomed to being viewed as educational professionals. However in their role as representatives of a teacher education program, as teachers in training and future potential teachers of the children of the household, they are accommodated, fed, and welcomed.

3   Deconstructing the Culture Concept

One significant theoretical shift that teacher candidates come to understand is how the concept of Funds of Knowledge goes beyond the idea of "culture" and encompasses the multidimensionality and hybridity of households and communities.

Teacher candidates are presented with a thumbnail sketch of the fluorescence of what has come to be known as "culture" and its positioning as an antidote to the scientific racism of the time and how in some ways it has served to classify and essentialize students according to sedimented and sometimes simplistic and stereotypical classifications.

Culture as the antidote to scientific racism

The prevailing dominant paradigm of the early 20th century assumed that human groups could be classified within an evolutionary perspective, following the accepted biological trajectory of ranking the most "primitive" to the most complex or "civilized." Within this racialized hierarchy, it is not hard to imagine who and what groups occupied which rungs on this pseudoscientific ladder, as measurements of skull size and cranial capacity and other anthropometric measures were imputed as markers for intelligence. This pseudo-evolutionary ranking of racial hierarchies, with all that it implied, was not unequivocally accepted, and within the writings of early 20th-century anthropologists, most significantly, Franz Boas, the concept of culture became a powerful counterdiscourse for explanatory significance outside of biogenetic domains (González, 2005; forthcoming).

Boas argued that something extrinsic to the human organism (a.k.a., "culture) could account for human diversity in behavior and thought and thus sought to transform the biogenetic argument of human development and behavior. Through this powerful theoretical concept, an authoritatively compelling argument could be made for the relativism of human societies and hierarchical racial classifications could not be scientifically defensible. The idea of Culture, with a capital C, became the hallmark of what made us human, the capacity to transmit social knowledge from generation to generation, the adaptive mechanism that allowed us to evolve as a species through representing experience through symbols. Culture with a small c entered the public lexicon as it identified categorizations within groups, marked by a similar history, geography, and language, and the culture of peoples from sub-Saharan Africa to the Northwestern United States were categorized, described, and indexed through painstaking detail of the exotic otherness.

However, about thirty years ago, within the field of anthropology, the central paradigm was shifting, and the concept of culture did not hold up well in considerations of essentializing discourses as well as a postmodern and poststructural perspectives on contradictions, ambiguities, and contingent ways of positioning knowledge. More importantly, for our purposes in educational discourses, the tropes of bounded, internally homogeneous groups that uniformly shared a fixed and unchanging "culture" created the "other" through its regimenting lens. Culture in this way was reproduced across generations, implying static and fixed perspectives that sedimented groups of people in the public mind. Culture was bounded, fixed, equally shared, and homogeneous among groups, and a list of cultural "traits" could be enumerated.

Culture of Poverty

However, even within the acceptance and affirmation of the term, within education, and teacher education programs, "culture" took on the work of homogenizing groups of students based on race and ethnicity, and in many ways became a proxy term for race and poverty. What had in its intellectual and theoretical genesis been an emancipatory construct expunging scientific racism, began to be freighted with the political load of explaining educational disparities, to the detriment of the poor and marginalized. The "culture of poverty" took on unfortunate implications that continue to resonate to this day. In its simplest form, the anthropologist Oscar Lewis argued that membership in a group that has been poor for generations constituted a separate culture. The idea that poor students were shaped by a culture of poverty led to circulating discourses wherein poor and minoritized students were viewed through a lens of deficiencies, seen as substandard in their socialization practices, language practices, and orientation toward academic achievement. As Gloria Ladson-Billings (2006) argues, it is not the culture of poverty, but the poverty of culture.

A culture of domination was a hidden and invisible corollary to the culture of poverty, whose place on the nondominant end of the continua is pathologized. Because the culture concept could be appropriated and transformed to fit multiple political agendas, it became a two-edged sword. "Culture" became the roadblock that many students had to hurdle on their path to a quality education. Furthermore, since culture was assumed to be equally shared and equally distributed among particular populations, it was a small leap into the abyss of reification and reductionism. Culture X (often read as a racialized category) was said to share Y and Z traits. What had once been welcomed as an emancipatory concept to contest scientific racism had morphed into its more appealing, yet equally pernicious twin concept.

More recent formulations dismantle neatly integrated views of wholly integrated cultures in favor of a lens that allows for interculturality and constant fluidity and flux. However, for educators this poses a critical tension: How do we engage a diverse student population without falling into stereotypes of essentializing categorizations of our students? These theoretical shifts are important for educators because students are often viewed as bearers of particular discrete cultures rather than agents who fuse identities and subjectivities. The Funds of Knowledge perspective allows for viewing households through an appreciation and expectation of complexity and dynamic and fluid undulations and flows across communities. Understanding the complexity of communities, practices, identities, learning processes, knowledges, and contexts is necessary within a Funds of Knowledge approach. It allows a forum to acknowledge complexity without invoking deficit or culturological discourses. As a result, teacher researchers and teacher candidates can arrive at a deeper understanding of communities' cultural capital and its affordances for transforming pedagogy as well as relationships. Through respectful inquiry into the relationships that generate, distribute, and sustain community knowledge outside of school walls, relationships of power that render community knowledge invisible can be interrogated (González, Wyman, & O'Connor, 2011).

Teacher candidates were asked to consider notions of "practice" rather than culture, noticing what people do and what they say about what they do from the families themselves.

Relationships Matter

Perhaps the most important transformation that is engendered by a Funds of Knowledge approach is that relationships matter. Teacher researchers and teacher candidates who approach households as learners create relationships that transcend teacher-parent binaries. Through face-to-face interaction and respectful inquiry into how parents and communities engage in "sense-making," educators come to know through first-hand experience struggles and triumphs of their students. Teacher-student, teacher-teacher, teacher-family, and school-community relationships are nested within historically constituted dynamics of trust and/or mistrust that are shaped and can be reshaped over time. Historical narratives can be undone and transformed through social relationships of trust and reciprocity (González et al., 2011).

How the Participating Families Came to Participate

One question that is often asked about the process of engaging in face-to-face interaction with communities, households, and families is, "How do you find families who are willing to be visited by teacher candidates?" There is never a one-size-fits-all approach, but we will share our experiences and recommendations.

One key element has been the position that Rebecca Zapien has occupied as a family liaison. This is a pivotal positon for any implementation of an F of K framework as the logistical challenges can quickly overwhelm the best intentions.

Because Rebecca is deeply involved in the ongoing events of schools, she is a presence at a number of school events. She has built up a wide network of relationships through her continued interactions with families. As she attends events and special occasions, she takes the opportunity to reach out to families. She explains the approach, and if the families are interested, she obtains contact information. When she contacts the family at a later date, she is able to explain more fully what the goals and objectives of home engagements are and how their children and the teacher candidates might both mutually benefit. As she clarifies for the families what might be expected, she is able to answer questions and explain the F of K framework in a way that is accessible and comprehensible. She is careful to mention that the approach is about helping to prepare teachers to think about family practices that children and their families bring to the classroom for a more holistic learning experience. Families have been responsive to the idea of allowing the home to have a presence in the classroom as much as the classroom has a presence in the home. She emphasizes that home practices are not only about traditions, but about language, skills, and the varieties of knowledges that are present in households. Families have been open and enthusiastic about participating, especially since it is explained that the program encompasses the early education of children birth to age eight. Because early childhood programs tend to foster a sense of communication with families, doors are opened to further interactions. Since families have a presence in preschools, and preschool has a value in families, there is an openness to welcoming the visits. Families came from an assortment of backgrounds and experiences, from both public and private schools.

Families in general have been very open to receiving the teacher candidates in their home because they want to invest in supporting teachers, and they see a value in the teacher coming to their home.

Once families have agreed to participate, there is a match made with a pair of teacher candidates. Ideally the teacher candidates are matched with a family who has a child in their classroom community. This is the case in the overwhelming majority of cases. If possible, when teacher candidates are paired with each other, they will also be at the same school site. This allows a comprehensive and integrated context for moving between school and home. However, at times there is only one teacher candidate at a particular school site. Rebecca will accompany the teacher candidate on the first home visit and on subsequent visits as needed. Rebecca also served as a translator in case the teacher candidates were not bilingual. Although many of the families understood more English than they could speak, Rebecca made every attempt to serve only as a conduit of information between the family and the preservice teachers so that they had every opportunity to ask questions and decipher meanings. For example, holidays had vastly different meanings for families based on their cultural expectations and backgrounds. Rebecca would attempt to provide background information so that the conversation was more comprehensible to the teacher candidates.

As teacher candidates explained the reason for their visit, they asked the families to sign a permission form consenting to the visit. In addition, if the families were comfortable with an audio recording of the visit, a consent form was signed. This latter request was primarily for the teacher candidates to be able to reconstruct and recall the information for inclusion in their fieldnotes. Issues of confidentiality were stressed, and families were assured that their names would never be used.

The only criteria for recruiting families in the first year is their willingness to receive visits throughout the school year. There are three visits in the fall semester and three in the spring. It is explained that this is a learning process for students. The first semester interviews are more informal, while the second semester expands on what was learned in the first semester, and making linkages to emergent literacy practices. For example, in the second semester, when students are taking a course on early language development, they engage in community literacy walks and community events that further underscore the knowledge bases found in communities (see Reyes, this volume). By accentuating and emphasizing literacy as a social practice beyond concepts of print only, students grow into the idea that children can begin their literacy experiences by understanding and engaging with their surroundings and the world immediately around them. They begin to see how they, as educators, can make these connections. Further, the community events create opportunities to take what they have learned from families that reflects the populations in their neighborhoods and schools. One example is a community event that was co-sponsored with a University-based program, SEED, which is made up of Indigenous bilingual teachers from Mexico. These teachers bring a wealth of community knowledge from their home communities, or *saberes*, which they leverage in their own teaching practices. The SEED teachers engaged with CREATE students around an activity based on Dia de los Muertos, a traditional holiday that celebrates those who have passed on. Through traditional crafts, foods, and stories, children and teachers crossed borders to mutually learn not only about this traditional holiday, but the cosmological and metaphysical significance of how life and death can be viewed.

In various other chapters in this volume, we see the extension of building on funds of knowledge by creating cultural story boxes that take a multifaceted view on how ordinary practices, like play and school, can be experienced by children in different areas and locales.

The experience of visiting the homes has been overwhelmingly positive for the teacher candidates, as evidenced by their final evaluation of their experiences. They come away with a deeper understanding of and appreciation for the struggles as well as resources that are within households. Students come away deeply impressed with the lengths that families will go to make them feel comfortable, introducing them to traditional dishes and sharing vital information. Teacher candidates have been able to apprehend the layers of complexity inherent in the dislocations and migrations of many of the families and the tenacious efforts to obtain legal privileges. Interestingly, teacher candidates often find commonalities with the families, despite what might be viewed as a wide gap in their backgrounds and experiences. These commonalities allow them to build common ground around shared skills and family dynamics.

Parents also find the experience to be positive and enabling. Parents have developed deep and genuine respect and admiration for students going into the teaching profession. Some parents are inspired by their own children to further their own educational experiences, and share these aspirations with the teacher candidates. The mutually constructed nature of the household engagement impacts parents, teacher candidates, and children in productive and surprising ways.

Teacher candidates have deepened their perspectives on the thorny political and social issues that surround communities and households. For example, some teacher candidates have come away with a new understanding of and appreciation for the complexity of the immigration process. After conversing with families about the fraught issue of immigration, facile expectations and assumptions are replaced with nuanced complexities of how people are embedded in sociopolitical contexts not of their own making. As teacher candidates interact face-to-face with families, they personally encounter the struggles, hardships, triumphs, and successes of families as they endeavor to raise their children. They also come to more deeply understand systems of Early Childhood Education, such as PACE and Head Start, and the complexities of genuinely connecting with families within a matrix of mandates and requirements.

As successful as the home engagements have been, there have been challenges, and we offer our best advice for constructing a successful program based on similar principles:

1   **Be Flexible.** The funds of knowledge approach is grounded in ethnography, whose strength is the locally situatedness of practices within historical and cultural contexts. This means that local circumstances must be taken into account in order to be responsive to contextual factors that have arisen across generations and backgrounds. Adapting to local situations and conditions is necessary in order to fully integrate local community and school patterns into a more holistic and inclusive entity.

2   **Partner with mentor teachers in order to explain the strengths and assumptions of the framework.** Very often the teacher candidates were excited and enthusiastic about the home engagements, only to be discouraged by their mentor teacher about the validity and worth of such visits. Mentor teachers who are new to the concept may not find home engagements to be a worthwhile activity, and may even speak negatively about presumptive deficiencies of the community. It is important that teacher candidates not be deflated in their eagerness to engage in face-to-face interaction with community members, while at the same time maintaining a workable relationship with their mentor teachers. Mentor teachers should be given adequate information and supported in their expanding relationships with communities.

3   **A community liaison is critical.** As Rebecca's role unfolded, it became increasingly evident that her relationships with the community *and* with the teacher candidates was pivotal in ensuring successful outcomes. Since she served not only as a facilitator and contact person, but also as a translator/partner in many household engagements, her expertise was drawn upon at many levels. This is a key element of the sustainability of the framework.

4   **Value personal growth.** The idea that people who come from vastly different backgrounds can connect over similar experiences creates a unified idea about the value of relationships and how these can be mutually enriching and educative. Teachers and teacher candidates can grow in their ability to negotiate curriculum and how to still meet standards while introducing concepts that reflects the lives of children. Parents can grow in unexpected ways as they interact fully with educators, with concepts, and with their children. Growth as learning is invaluable as learning comes to be defined by connections and relationships.

5   **Provide consistency across the curriculum for teacher candidates.** The CREATE principles were the subject of many summer workshops in which faculty explicitly incorporated principles into class assignments and learning outcomes. In this way, students were able to connect the principles throughout their coursework and practicum experiences and to see the value of a unified paradigm. This required extra effort on the

part of the faculty, but it provided a clear framework for teacher candidates to observe the coherency and stability of the CREATE perspective.

6   **Be clear and explicit about the aims and assumptions about the program from the beginning with all participants.** In the first week of the fall semester, students were introduced to the core principles of CREATE, as well as the concept of Funds of Knowledge. They were asked to bring an artifact that represented some form of their own Funds of Knowledge and to share that as everyone was getting to know one another. This was an effective introduction to personalize the concepts of the program and to begin the journey of individually deepening their understanding of both the principles and the concepts that undergird the program. The internal consistency of the principles and the application of the principles across their learning experiences across semester was an essential element of formulating a shared vision of communities as resources. Teacher candidates must be made aware from the initial phases of the program that they are making a choice about their own education and that it may differ substantially from other teacher preparation programs. However, they can expect a richer and deeper set of learning environments that will ultimately benefit them and their future students. This is also critical when recruiting mentor teachers as to the expectations of the home engagements on the part of the students.

7   **Expect the logistics to be complicated.** It is not easy to negotiate and juggle the busy schedules of families and pairs of teacher candidates. Teacher candidates can get anxious as the semester slips by and they are unable to finalize their visits. This is where flexibility must be paramount and a rich experience for all is the ultimate goal.

These are guidelines drawn from our experience but speak to the logistical hurdles implicit in implementing a theoretical paradigm. It is important to trust the process and to allow the multiplicity of voices to be heard and appreciated.

This chapter has described how scaffolding the emergent understandings about communities of prospective teachers can be enriched through principled activities and an understanding of cultural and linguistic diversity as resources for teaching and learning. An ethnographic approach to households that is profoundly respectful of practices and processes of 'sensemaking' is at the core of the development of teacher candidates as producers of their own knowledge about communities, pedagogy, and families.

Bibliography

González, N. (2005). The hybridity of funds of knowledge. In N. González, L. Moll, & C. Amanti (Eds.), *Funds of knowledge: Theorizing practices in households, communities and classrooms* (pp. 29–46). Mahwah, NJ: Lawrence Erlbaum Associates.

González, N., Moll, L., & Amanti, C. (Eds.). (2005). *Funds of knowledge: Theorizing practices in households, communities and classrooms*. Mahwah, NJ: Lawrence Erlbaum Associates.

González, N., Wyman, L., & O'Connor, B. (2011). The past, present and future of "funds of knowledge." In M. Pollock & B. Levinson (Eds.), *A companion to the anthropology of education* (pp. 481–494). Malden, MA: Wiley-Blackwell.

Ladson-Billings, G. (2006). It's not the culture of poverty, it's the poverty of culture: The problem with teacher education. *Anthropology & Education Quarterly*, 37(2), 104–109.

Leander, K. M., Phillips, N. C., Taylor, K. H., Nespor, J., & Lewis, C. (2010). The changing social spaces of learning: Mapping new mobilities. *Review of Research in Education*, 34(1), 329–394.

Paris, D., & Alim, H. S. (2014). What are we seeking to sustain through culturally sustaining pedagogy? A loving critique forward. *Harvard Educational Review*, 84(1), 85–100.

6 Teacher Candidates Connecting to Community Resources and Children's Literacies

Iliana Reyes, Jesus Acosta, Ana Fierro, Yi-Ping Fu, and Rebecca Zapien

Introduction

In this chapter we share findings from a Community Literacy project where preservice teachers reflected on their experience getting to know the local community during their field placements. First, they took a literacy walk together with their case study child to observe and document the print environment—everything from street signs to product labels, bumper stickers to murals—found around a neighborhood and school community. Second, the preservice teachers then documented the community resources found within the neighborhood to examine the existing literacy resources available within the children's community. Some of the findings show that signs around the community were bilingual, found both in English and Spanish, which is relevant to the literacy practices of diverse families living within the Southwest area near the border. In addition, preservice teachers identified and mapped the local community resources to connect to their students' learning experiences. This research aims to broaden the current notion of literacy and potential resources available to support the learning of emergent bilinguals in their everyday contexts.

In this chapter we depart from the theoretical assumption that communities are equipped with resources for families as well as for teachers (González, Moll, & Amanti, 2005; Vélez-Ibáñez & Greenberg, 1992). In some communities there might be apparently more "limited" resources if only analyzed from a deficit perspective (Delpit, 1995). However, if these various resources could be identified by teachers and research educators as pedagogical tools, then these could serve as strategies to transform children's learning experiences. It is this phenomenon, identifying the cultural and linguistic funds of knowledge of children and their families, that we have been engaged in the last several years that we present here.

As daSilva Iddings and others described earlier in this volume, we center our work using the *Funds of Knowledge* perspective (Gonzalez et al., 2005; Vélez-Ibáñez & Greenberg, 1992) to guide preservice teachers in deconstructing their own potential biases and to give way to more context-situated learning experiences about language and literacy and social capital.

We place particular attention to community for our analyses—mainly how language and literacy development for diverse, in the majority bilingual students, is influenced by their families and communities. The preservice teachers' field placements are based on their own ability to identify and tap into those funds of knowledge that each of them, teachers and students, bring along to the classroom through their family and household experiences.

About Community Literacies and Resources

It is not surprising to us that with all the demands teachers face nowadays, they are not familiar with the communities that surround the schools in which they work. Because of the principles of CREATE, we make sure that our preservice teachers are more conscious of the benefits of working with and including families and other community members in their everyday practices. Ovando, Combs and Collier (2006) discuss the concept and the development of a *community portrait* by preservice teachers similar to what we want to accomplish with a community map, being a challenging task since the typical program does not equip preservice teachers to be sociolinguists or ethnographers within their classrooms or outside classroom walls. Along with these authors, we come to recognize that without a realistic understanding of the community based on the accumulation of cultural, socioeconomic, and linguistic detail, pedagogical innovations and family partnerships may not thrive.

Ovando et al. (2006) provide a framework for teachers who consider developing a profile of the community in which they work. According to them, community portraits should be organized around the following topics: (1) Characteristics of ethnicity in the community; (2) the socioeconomic structure of the community; (3) language use in the community; (4) the use of funds of knowledge and community-based research; and (5) ethnographies as resources. Throughout the program we work to shape our students' experiences to develop strategies and knowledge that help them understand the schools' communities in which they are placed.

Community and Print as Resource for Children's Literacies

Studies have shown that young children learn from everyday print found within their communities and neighborhoods, which plays a vital role in their early development and literacy experiences, particularly related to young children's print awareness (Owocki & Goodman, 2002). As part of our study, we share the observations and reflections from the *community literacy walk* project and *community mapping*. The project observations, through a literacy walk around the community with the preservice teachers and their students, aim to broaden the current notion of literacy supporting the learning of emergent bilinguals taking into account their everyday contexts and resources.

METHODOLOGY

Participants   The first year for this project consisted of a total of 37 students. As with most preservice teacher programs, there is little diversity in terms of demographics, where most of our own preservice teachers also identify as white and monolingual English speakers. The reconceptualized coursework of this program emphasizes the need to provide preservice teachers with the tools to work with linguistically and culturally diverse population of students and their families. Given that we focused on the first year data of preservice teachers' reflections and final assignments of each class, only the reflections and other assignments of those preservice teachers that were able to attend the community literacy walk along with their case study child were selected for this analysis. Not all preservice teachers were able to do a community literacy walk along with their case study child due to parents' conflicting work schedules. As a result, some preservice teachers took pictures of the literacy found within the community, then presented it with additional probing questions to have a better understanding of the family's own notions about language and literacy. Afterward, the selection was narrowed down to those students who included visual documentation of their community literacy and made clear connections to some of the theories presented throughout their coursework.

Our *community and family liaison* and outreach person in the program is key to making sure we coordinate these community literacy events. Because of her community connection, she brings a wealth of resources in finding families and children for our preservice teachers in the schools where they are placed. Most recruited families supporting the program are of different background and bring with them a great deal of experiences for our students. Criteria for participating families includes only two characteristics: a) a language other than English spoken at home; b) and families' willingness to work with preservice students in their child's classroom and at home.

Data Sources

Data was collected from different sources within two courses of the program project. For this chapter we focused on the first-year data of preservice teachers' reflections and final assignments for the Language Literacy class, and the Structured English Immersion (SEI) class. In the Language Literacy class preservice teachers focus on several theories of language development and early literacy to note how these theories inform practice in early childhood education. Using a funds of knowledge approach, the class studies the linguistic and literary resources found within the contexts of their case study's home, community and school. The class does have a special emphasis on the community literacy context to provide the preservice teachers in learning about how the community context impacts children's language and literacy development, but also to actively engage the preservice teachers in several community projects, workshops, or events taking place in the larger community. As for the SEI course, it also has a similar approach in focusing on the community context with a direct focus on the need to train high-quality teachers for English language learners (ELLs). The historical and political context of education for ELLs and their families is of the utmost importance in this class in order to engage prospective teachers in thoughtful ways of planning and implementing a variety of teaching strategies that promote the learning of academic content and the acquisition of English language and literacy of students.

As previously mentioned, the principles of CREATE along with the course requirements of these two classes permit preservice teachers to be more conscious of the benefits of working with and including the community contexts. Actively participating in the community literacy grants preservice teachers opportunities to better understand the relationship between language and literacy development. Through a series of projects, these two courses encouraged preservice teachers to reflect on their family and community interactions as a way to learn about children's literacies. The purpose of these activities is to broaden the understanding of language and literacy development beyond the home and beyond commonly accepted forms of language and literacy in the classroom because literacy can be found in various domains and through different expressive means.

Similarly, each class emphasized the importance of reflection as part of the process for preservice teachers to document their own learning processes about the many language and literacy practices already existing within the community context.

Reflections also allowed the preservice teachers to share their insights about the assignments and give us more in-depth perspectives as to how their own notions of language and literacy broadened due to the assignments we have analyzed for this chapter. Our analyses focuses on providing a closer look at these reflections made by the preservice teachers as part of their written assignments. As described by Reyes, daSilva Iddings, and Feller (2015), the new early childhood program involves a reconceptualized coursework. The preservice teachers were guided through a series of community literacy events and experiences that allowed them to get closer and understand the significance of community life and what is there for the children and families to experience. As part of the reconceptualized coursework, preservice teachers were provided with digital cameras to visually document the language and literacy practices existing within the context of community, and we include some of their own visual documentation in this paper. These field experiences have as an objective for the preservice teachers to pay close attention to the diversity of languages and literacies available to children but not always recognized by teachers (daSilva Iddings, 2009).

The analysis overall includes the preservice teachers' reflection on their interactions, observations, and their follow-up interview with the case study child and their family members to understand some of the community resources identified during the community literacy walk. We focused on what they learned from the child and family knowledge on environmental print around the community; then we analyzed the data for specific community resources around home and school that they recognized. All the sources were reread and analyzed by the researchers during the summer and fall semesters in 2014. Below, we describe the various sources we used to construct our analysis.

Family and Community Literacy Walk

Preservice teachers were asked to describe their participation at various community literacy events, and the research team guided and supported them in expanding their language and literacy knowledge and understanding of the local knowledge for their case study child and family. Specifically, the preservice teachers were provided with the following guidelines for their Community Literacy Walk project.

> As part of this project you will take a literacy walk around your site and community to explore the print environment that is part of the children's everyday routine. You will invite your case study child and family to go for a walk to document print awareness and resources that are part of their everyday literacy environments (make sure to refer to *Kidwatching* for review of concepts. Reflect on the following questions and documentation of your literacy walks as part of your midterm assignment:
>
> 1 (Literacy Walk-with Team Partner) What did you learn about the child's literacy environment and the family's neighborhood as part of the literacy walk with child and family?
> 2 How is community literacy influencing language and literacy development of the child?
> 3 Include documentation such images, flyers, and maps of your literacy walk as part of your assignment.
>
> As part of your final documentation, you are expected to reflect on the observations made throughout the semester by making connections of what you learned about the target child both within the home and out in the community literacy walk. As a result, relate your observations, reflections and findings with the assigned readings and previous discussions from the language and literacy class.

Community Resource Map

In the case of the SEI class, we assigned the "Community Mapping" project that connected to knowledge acquired as part of the community literacy walk. This activity was conducted a week or two after the literacy walk described above. For this assignment, preservice teachers explored resources around the community where they were doing their student teaching. Students were to follow the following guidelines:

Community Mapping—In pairs.

(by school placement)

The goal of this project is to understand the value of community as a resource for students. It also provides future teachers an opportunity to explore and make connections with the communities where their students live. You will investigate a total of 5 different community resources and/or community cultural wealth resources (making sure that others have not include them) available to your student and his/her family within two miles radius (or more depending on the geography of the neighborhood) from your student's home and school. Some resources you might include are local churches, non-profit organizations, activist groups, government based institutions, special programs provided in the community, translation services, mom & pop businesses, yard art, gardens, symbolic resources, etc.

As part of your project you and your partner must:

1   Describe each resource (you must gather this information by personally interviewing a person in this facility—have questions in mind before you go and include the interview/questions in your reflection paper). Complement the information you collected from this facility/organization with information by searching the webpage (these may have additional information)
2   Include a map. Here you will map out the location of the different community resources you identified.
3   State the contribution each resource makes to the community.
4   State how you might incorporate this resource into your teaching/curriculum or may help your students and/or families.

Findings and Sharing Reflections

Overall, the reflections described and explained what the preservice teachers noticed during these two activities. They were able to identify the *way* students were able to recognize print and familiar concepts as they went on for the literacy walk, and then as they researched and explored the community resources. We share their reflections first on children's observation about general print, and then their appreciation to take on the child's perspective, parents' perspective, and preservice teachers' challenges during these community experiences.

Community Literacy Walk

The teachers reflected and conveyed their learning on *what* they observed at home and their community—and although they were not sure on the *hows* of the process of literacy development, they did acknowledge that the environment and print around, and what children are or might be exposed to at home, also have an impact—even if indirect—on the child's learning. It seems that some of the preservice teachers had not realized that "anything" related to concepts of print could actually become knowledge on print and eventually competencies related to literacy (Owocki & Goodman, 2002).

> One of the major things is all the print that surrounds Miguel and his brother in their back yard. Miguel might not have been directly pointing these prints out to use but based on the sidewalk chalk writings in the back yard these bits of print are having some impact on these children.
>
> (P511)

> "We think that he recognizes that the *Food City* logo or print has meaning to him, which is why he grabbed it."
>
> (P510)

Parallel to preservice teachers' understanding of what the child might know more formally about print and letters was this other understanding of what in general a sign might mean for a child, and how a young child makes sense of that print according to her/his day-to-day experiences:

> Throughout the duration of our walk we were able to notice all the print that existed in this close-knit neighborhood community. There were house numbers on each of the mobile home units, houses with large signs advertising the things they sold within, such as '*nieve*' (ice cream) or 'soda', and vehicles that were adorned with pictures and words, as they were traveling food mobiles. We noticed two larger vans, that both had the same sign on the back of them, a large red stop sign that read "Stop for Children" across the back". This was familiar to the children, known as the "Banana Ice cream truck."
>
> (P512)

From the students we also learned how they went through the process of getting to know the families; as in previous analyses, we identified that these early childhood preservice teachers deepened their understanding of funds of knowledge and cultural resources throughout their time in the study and the ECE program (Reyes, daSilva Iddings & Feller, in press). We came to understand that the more extensive and guided experiences interacting with the families and in the community allowed for a new and space where preservice teachers could reflect on how their views and knowledge about young children and communities' resources and social capital had evolved. Specifically, some of them were able to connect emergent reading and writing concepts to activities and literacy practices they observed happening during home engagements. Moreover, there was a deeper reflection on what it means to integrate and get to know the family and community:

> As soon as we got out the door, I realized we were taking into account the families' funds of knowledge . . . We were constantly stop and go, asking the kids about what they noticed around them.
>
> (P511)

> I have come to realize the importance of developing a connection not only with the students in a class, but with the members of their families as well. Children are influenced by many diverse factors, including race, language, socioeconomic status, relationships with family members, and background experiences. Therefore, getting to know them merely as 'students' confined inside the four walls of a classroom is not substantial in understanding who they are and what experiences they need to help them receive the most from their schooling.
>
> (P515)

Moreover, as the students spent time with the family, they were able to identify other elements, like cultural characteristics that they shared among members of the community. For example, in the reflection below, the preservice teacher identifies food as a common cultural element, and she does this by identifying and utilizing the Spanish original print used in signs around the community to label Mexican food:

> Another important component of their close community's culture that we identified was food. Ana, Javier, and their mother pointed out many vans, carts, and homes that sell food in their neighborhood (See images 1, 2 & 3). While Ana and Javier were not able to read or interpret the words that were posted, such as *"tacos o burritos"*, *"birria, cabeza, y jugos"*, *or "hielitos*, sodas, *papitas, y dulces"*, they did recognize these vehicles and locations as places that sell food and drinks, implying a familiarity with their settings, and an understandings that signs, words, pictures, and things have meanings, whether illicit or implicit.
>
> (p.3)

Some more general reflections focused on teachers' own knowledge and inspiration to continue fostering learning in the young child:

> As my experiences become vaster, my knowledge expands to encompass the passion children have for life, and how I will foster each child's

imagination and capability of learning, through language, literacy, and beyond.

(P511)

Community Map Reflections

As the preservice teachers continued their course assignment to focus on getting to know the families and their particular communities, they began understanding not only the purpose of such an "academic assignment," but the meaningful aspects of engaging in such activity. The following quotes reflect a general analysis of the preservice teachers' process to understand such importance of getting to know the community in which their students live and interact with others in their community context. For all preservice teachers researching the community for resources was an eye-opening experience. They talked about the importance of the resources they found for families and students and the critical impact on themselves as teachers coming from outside the neighborhoods.

This assignment really helped me realize that there are so many resources available for students and families in the community. Even searching within such a small radius it was amazing how many places I was able

to find that offer support to my students. Many times families just do not know that these resources are available for them and teachers can help parents become aware of them.

Another preservice teacher described in more depth the complexity of the various reasons families often are not aware of some of these local and community resources:

> Overall I found this experience to be very useful. While it was challenging, once I found the resources I felt that I was better equipped with tools to help my students and their families. Although these resources would be particularly useful to my case study child, they are also resources that can be useful for any child. Many of them are all about spending time with the family and playing, two very important experiences that I feel children should experience all the time. I know that families are so busy, and have varying schedules, but with some of these, such as the park and the library, there are many different times and days for a family to work into their schedule. I really hope that I continue to learn about resources throughout the community during my time at Saguaro school. I am also really excited to find out what some of my fellow cohort members from Saguaro school put down as their resources. It will be really interesting to see the similarities and differences that we have in our maps.
>
> (P516)

In the quotes above the preservice teachers talked about this task *being challenging*; however, they also recognized that it has been very resourceful. They worked the community map around their case study child and her family, yet one of them stated that the resources she researched would be beneficial for *all* students. They also addressed the importance of family time with children and acknowledged that the families of their students have challenges, but having these resources available to them may help. Therefore, preservice teachers are recognizing that specific resources are available and that these could be put in use with the classroom community and the students.

In addition to identifying local resources, the preservice teachers reflect about the students and families facing a language barrier when they are new in the United States. Moreover, they related this challenge to not being familiar with the community and often what it has to offer them and their children. The preservice teacher in the example below identified language as a challenge and issue:

> It can be challenging for some of the families at my school to communicate because they do not know much English. Since several of our students' families have not been in the United States for very long, they

could be having a hard time learning what services are out there for them and their children. Teachers and schools have the opportunity to reach out to their families and provide them with the help they need in order to take advantage of the resources in the community.

(P520)

The preservice teacher below brings up the economic challenges and talks about resources having positive impact in all members of the community. For her it is important to let families know of resources that provide health services, in this case at a low cost for children and their families:

The process of creating this community map really opened my eyes to the different local resources available to students and their families. Each of the community resources that I picked out all has positive effects on all members of the community. I would ideally like to educate the parents of my students on the resources available within a close proximity to the school. I think that the most valuable resource that I picked was El Rio Community Health Center. I think that this resource is valuable because it provides health care at a low cost to children and their families. Having access to a doctor and proper medical care is essential to staying healthy.

(P518)

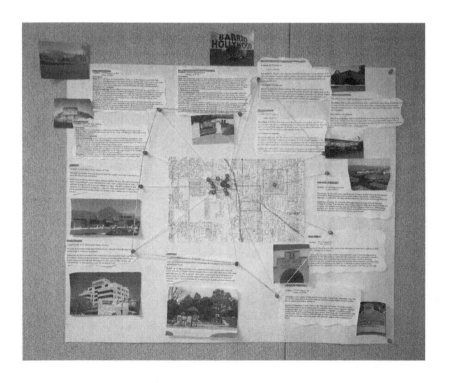

The assignment became an experience that immersed preservice teachers into the community, permitting them see it at a different level. This experience contrasts with the way the preservice teachers expressed they felt at the beginning of their placements. Specifically, several of the preservice teachers in this study expressed a concern and a feeling of not being completely comfortable in the community. For example, in the quote below the preservice teacher thought of herself as an outsider of the community of the school where she was placed; however, she found out that by looking at the resources from a teacher's perspective and thinking of the benefits for school and students as part of that community helped identified resources and dissipate concerns. In addition to physically exploring the resources, she found out that there is additional in the resources' websites:

> We enjoy doing working on the Community Mapping and feel it was a learning experience. Having an outsider's perspective from not living within the community, we began to understand how "resources" are defined in a particular community (school). *Some resources have more value than others, depending on the members of that given community,* visiting resources like the San Xavier Mission for example, with a teacher perspective gave us a different look on the resource, as we learned about its history and how that history has impacted the community. Before this project, neither of us knew the San Xavier Mission School existed, so that was interesting to learn about. We were able to get a lot of history and current topics about the school from the school's website, which was very helpful.
>
> (P218)

Conclusion

Overall, students connected this assignment and experience with other family literacy events, such as the home engagements (see chapters 5, 7, and 9 in this volume), and reflected on the benefits of creating relationships and establishing connections with the community of their students and families. In addition, they realized that by connecting to the curriculum the resources available to their students and families along with the stories and history that they learned would make their teaching more authentic and meaningful for their future students.

The reflections on these particular community and family literacy projects gave way to new encounters and experiences for the preservice teachers. A deeper reflection on what it means to integrate and get to know the family and community included the literacy walk where *local* print was analyzed as part of the young child's literacy knowledge. In particular, most of the preservice teachers identified and recognized bilingual print in English and Spanish, around the community. They talked how this diversity of print was relevant to the literacy practices of the families living within the area

(Reyes & Azuara, 2008). Without a literacy walk and a community resource project, they would have simply missed this print. Instead they identified it as knowledge that children bring to the classroom, and as teachers they now know that they can draw from this bilingual knowledge and ask parents—and children—to help them understand and translate the context of that print.

At the same time that the preservice teachers were faced with challenges, they were also confronted to view these challenges and turned them as opportunities to learn about their case study family and their communities. First, they learned to identify *what is there* as part of the community literacy print and potential resources for children and families. Second, they learned to problematize at a more thoughtful level *what is not there*, and challenge their own assumptions about why certain resources might not be part of these communities because of economic factors or funding opportunities. For our family and community research group, this has been an ongoing reflection not only as part of our research with preservice teachers, but also among our research team to redefine ways and strategies to continue guiding them to deconstruct and go beyond the "*lack of resources and limitations*" view to a funds of knowledge view. Last, from these curriculum experiences, preservice teachers were able to understand and shared that when working with diverse families, it is important to learn about the local community literacies and funds of knowledge in order to transform their own teaching and pedagogical strategies to include diversity as a resource and pedagogical tool for all.

Bibliography

daSilva Iddings, A. C. (2009). Bridging home and school literacy practices and empowering families of recent immigrant children: A sociocultural approach. *Theory into Practice*, 48(4), 304–312.

daSilva Iddings, A. C. (this volume). Introductory chapter. In A. C. daSilva Iddings (Ed.), *Re-designing teacher preparation for culturally and linguistically diverse young students: An ecological approach*. New York: Routledge.

Delpit, L. (1995). *Other people's children: Cultural conflict in the classroom*. New York: The New Press.

González, N., Moll, L., & Amanti, C. (2005). *Funds of knowledge: Theorizing practices in households, communities and classrooms*. Mahwah, NJ: Erlbaum.

Ovando, C. J., Combs, M. C., & Collier, V. P. (2006). *Bilingual and ESL classrooms: Teaching in multicultural contexts* (4th ed.). New York: McGraw Hill.

Owocki, G., & Goodman, Y. M. (2002). *Kidwatching: Documenting children's literacy development*. Portsmouth, NH: Heinemann.

Reyes, I., & Azuara, P. (2008). Emergent biliteracy in young Mexican immigrant children. *Reading Research Quarterly*, 43(4), 374–398.

Reyes, I., daSilva Iddings, C., & Feller, N. (2015). Promoting a funds of knowledge perspective: Preservice teachers' understanding about language and literacy development of preschool emergent bilinguals through family and community interactions. *Journal of Early Childhood Literacy*, 15(2), 1–26.

Reyes, I., daSilva Iddings, A.C., & Feller, N. (in press). Building relationships with diverse students and families: A funds of knowledge perspective. *Journal of Early Childhood Literacy.*

Vélez-Ibáñez, C., & Greenberg, J. (1992). Formation and transformation of funds of knowledge among U.S. Mexican households. *Anthropology and Education Quarterly*, 23(4), 313–335.

7 Thinking with Teacher Candidates

The Transformative Power of Story in Teacher Education

*María V. Acevedo, Dorea Kleker,
Lauren Pangle, and Kathy G. Short*

We eagerly walk into the professional development classroom to meet with teacher candidates for an end-of-the semester interview. As this is the first cohort to use the family story backpacks in their K-2 student teaching, we are impatient to find out what happened. We juggle our interview sheets, recorders, checklists for returning backpacks, and envelopes for collecting journal entries. We enter the room, chatting with each other, and run into a mountain of backpacks, haphazardly thrown one on top of another. Unsure of what this means, we ask for the entries from the family story journals that were in each backpack, only to be told that they are still in the backpacks and no one knows which backpacks came from which classroom.

Feeling dazed and uncertain, we go ahead with our plan and divide into three small groups for the interviews, quickly becoming aware of why the backpacks were so carelessly flung into a pile. Sophia tells us that the journal entries were just "a lot of pictures about whatever, not anything to learn about a family." Beth and Shawna complain, "Our teachers gave us no support and said it was our assignment, not theirs." Others nod, with Elise adding, "The backpacks were just too overwhelming to do on top of everything else we had for student teaching." "Yeah," comments Marisol, "it seemed like extra work in first grade because they already have reading activities and writing journals to take home every day." We finish the interviews, load the backpacks into our cars, and meet to debrief at a nearby restaurant, discouraged and confused.

Our interviews with teacher candidates were set up to document the ways in which they had used the family story backpacks to encourage families to share stories about their funds of knowledge with each other and with teachers. The stories that we hoped to hear from teacher candidates were *not* the stories that we were told. Despite the negative responses, we did not want to abandon the backpack engagement. The stories from teacher candidates instead compelled us to identify changes that needed to be made in the engagement and in our teaching and program. This experience convinced us that we need to create spaces as teacher educators to hear our students' stories about their experiences and to use those stories as the basis for transforming our teaching. Over time, what began as a research strategy became an important tool in growing our understandings as teacher educators. This chapter documents how the stories of teacher candidates informed our work with the family story backpacks over a three-year period.

Story as Meaning-Making in Teacher Education

Stories are much more than what we read in a book or hear on the news; stories are our means for making sense of the world. Short (2012) points out that stories are woven so tightly into the fabric of everyday life that it's easy to overlook their importance in framing how we think about ourselves and the world. We create stories to give meaning, order, and coherence to the happenings in our own lives and as an attempt to understand events in the real world. They help us move from the chaotic stuff of daily life into understanding while providing a way to structure and interpret our experiences as we work out their significance in the world (Rosen, 1986). Therefore, we live through a web of interconnected stories that captures the richness and complexities of our experiences and gives significance to those experiences.

Storying is a constructive process, unique to our own experiences, and thus has a multiplicity of meanings, which makes story an effective way to express knowledge arising from action. A story is a theory of something, so that what we tell and how we tell it reveals what we believe. Carter (1993) argues that it is the action feature of story that makes it so appropriate for studying teaching and teacher education. Since teaching is an intentional action based in belief, the stories that arise from that action provide unique access to teachers' knowledge, and so story has found a place in teacher education research.

The primary focus on story in teacher education has been on encouraging teachers and teacher candidates to compose stories as a means of reflecting on their practice and rethinking their experiences to reach deeper insights on self-identity, students, and practice. Huber, Li, Murphy, Nelson, and Young (2014) provide examples of this reflective process from their teacher education classrooms to show how narrative inquiry allows teacher candidates to negotiate and renegotiate their identities in order to better understand themselves and the children with whom they will work. Clandinin and Connelly (2000) believe that story creates a reflexive relationship between "living a life story, telling a life story, and reliving a life story" (p. 71). They advocate providing opportunities for novice teachers to reflect on practice at "moments of contradiction and discontinuity" so that they are able to recompose and relive their experiences through story.

Our interviews gave teacher candidates an opportunity to story about their experiences in classrooms with the backpacks, but more importantly their stories gave us a way to rethink our practice as educators and researchers. We were forced to retell *our* stories of these experiences. Story helped us transform our teacher education program to more effectively engage with teacher candidates in their work with teachers, children, families, and the broader community.

Family Story Backpacks as Story

Our understandings of story as a culturally based means of thinking and knowing led us to design an engagement using family story backpacks as a transportable curriculum to facilitate the sharing of stories within children's families. Ten different backpacks were created around themes significant to families, such as bedtime rituals, the origin of names, games and play, and birthday traditions. Each student teacher selects six of the ten backpacks to take to their K-2 student teaching classroom and sets up a schedule so that 4–6 backpacks rotate among the families on a weekly basis. The backpacks each contain three books (one informational global concept book and two picture book stories), a related artifact, and a family story journal. The purpose of the artifacts, such as Old Maid cards and the Mexican bingo game of Lotería in the play backpack, is to invite families to tell oral stories. Families are encouraged to draw and write entries in the family story journal to share their stories and experiences with a backpack. These journals stay with a backpack so that each family can read previous entries as the backpacks rotate home each week with a different child and household. Entries include family stories, descriptions of the use of the backpack, responses to books, and reflections on the experience. Children share with the teacher and/or class when a backpack is returned to school.

The backpacks are based on the CREATE principles and our belief that all children come to school with stories that reflect the culture of their families and communities. Our responsibility as educators is to encourage the telling of these stories as a way to know and value each family's funds of knowledge. We want to learn from and with families rather than only sending home materials that are school-like activities, thus engaging families with the question "*Who are we as a family?*" rather than with "*How can we do school at home?*" We hoped that the backpacks would build relationships with families through mutual respect and trust and through inquiry based in the family's knowledge and multiple literacies (Allen, 2008).

The backpacks also provide opportunities for co-learning among teacher candidates, mentor teachers, and university supervisors. The pressures of tests and standards have resulted in an increased focus on academic programs with prescriptive lessons and fewer opportunities for families to be invited into primary classrooms. The family story backpacks provide a potential space of tension by challenging a curriculum that limits the ways in which family and community inform the classroom. Since the teacher candidates have already interacted with the backpacks in previous university classes, the experience provides a more equal space for teacher candidates to learn alongside mentor teachers rather than only from mentor teachers (Bacharach & Heck, 2012).

Data Collection and Analysis

Our research was based in narrative inquiry as a methodology that allowed us to attend to and act on experiences by co-inquiring with teacher candidates in "living, telling, retelling, and reliving stories of experience" (Huber, Caine, Huber, & Steeves, 2013, p. 213). Narrative inquiry provides access to details, complexities, contexts, and stories of experiences with learning and teaching (Schaafsma & Vinz, 2011), and so was an effective methodology for examining the complexities of teacher candidates' experiences with the backpack engagement. We wanted to complicate, not simplify, our understandings of the events and their beliefs and to consider multiple perspectives on the ways in which they experienced the engagement.

In order to examine the perspectives of teacher candidates about implementing family story backpacks during student teaching, we needed to create a narrative inquiry space (Huber et al., 2013). We decided to conduct small group conversations with all of the teacher candidates around several broad questions to encourage them to story about their experiences. These small focus groups occurred at the end of the student teaching semester, and the conversations were transcribed for analysis. Teacher candidates also completed individual written reflections. Our analysis was organized around four major themes: their conceptual understandings about story and funds of knowledge, the strategies used in implementing and sharing in classrooms, their views of families, and the influence of this experience on their values and beliefs as educators.

Additional research questions focused on identifying the types of entries by families in the journals and the understandings explored by families as well as the insights gained by teachers from these entries. We also interviewed several mentor teachers to explore their perspectives. This chapter, however, will only focus on the teacher candidate interviews.

Transforming a Teacher Education Program through Story

We gathered stories from teacher candidates over a three-year period, each year meeting in small groups to have conversations around their experiences and then reflecting on and thinking with their stories to rethink our practice and program. Huber et al. (2013) remind us that to think with stories carries the responsibility of imagining future possibilities. The following narrative tells the story of this transformation through sharing the stories and the ways those stories informed us on a year-by-year basis.

Year One of Implementation: A Time of Blunders and Obstacles

The teacher candidates were introduced to the backpacks in their first semester through their children's literature course, which was reframed around a broad concept of story. At the same time, they explored an in-depth understanding of funds of knowledge through a course on cultural pluralism. The following semester, the backpacks were briefly introduced to teacher candidates and mentor teachers at the student teaching orientation meeting. Several weeks later, teacher candidates each selected six backpacks and received various forms to inform families about the backpacks and organize the backpack rotation within the classroom. Since they were also enrolled in a language arts methods course, they were asked to submit an organizational structure for the backpack rotation and use one backpack in a family home engagement to facilitate interaction with the family of a case study student. When we met with teacher candidates at the end of the semester and encountered the mountain of backpacks, their stories revealed our blunders and the obstacles they encountered around their understandings, beliefs, implementation strategies, and values.

Conceptual Understandings

Teacher candidates' stories reflected their struggle with the conceptual framework of family stories and funds of knowledge. They shared that they were unable to answer questions from mentor teachers about the backpacks and believed that the backpacks overlapped with book bags or other homework that mentor teachers were already sending home to build literacy skills. Additionally, many saw the backpacks as a university assignment rather than something of value for learning about family stories and funds of knowledge. As one teacher candidate asserted, "*I think there should be a backpack about dinosaurs—a lot of boys were really into dinosaurs. If I had that one, I'd feel secure in sending it out to all of my boys. Sometimes I'd feel bad saying, 'Here, have the grandparents' book. Here, have the rainy day book.' Whereas with dinosaurs, I'd be like, 'Yes, You will actually come back and talk to me about this.'*" Comments such as these communicated confusion over the purpose of the engagement and revealed that we had not created a deep understanding, resulting in teacher candidates not being committed to the conceptual framework.

Strategies for Classroom Implementation

Teacher candidates told stories about struggles with too many forms, confusing organizational systems, questions from families unsure about what to write in the journals, the lack of time for children to share after returning a backpack, families not returning backpacks, and little support from mentor teachers. When one teacher candidate shared how she first introduced only two backpacks and then increased the number to four (reserving the remaining two as backups), other teacher candidates turned to her in amazement. They assumed that they could not negotiate the way that the backpacks were used in classrooms, either with their mentor teacher or university instructor. We assumed that they would adjust as needed, but it had not occurred to us that they needed explicit permission to make those adjustments. In hindsight, we realized that they were used to meeting requirements in their undergraduate courses in order to get credit, so the negotiation that is a constant within teachers' lives was new to them. Some teacher candidates lacked strategies for negotiation, and others were not sure they were allowed to negotiate. They were also overwhelmed with the difficulty of student teaching; a big assignment on top of their courses and classroom teaching created more stress.

One teacher candidate expressed disappointment at not being given time in the classroom to find out what children and families were doing with the backpacks. She realized that this missing piece would have made that experience more meaningful for her and the children. Several also mentioned that their university course schedule meant that they were often not in the classroom when the backpacks went home and so the mentor teacher had to take over the responsibility. With many of the mentor teachers viewing the backpacks as a university "assignment," there was often a lack of consistency in getting the backpacks to families.

Views of Families and Their Responses

Instead of valuing the wealth and diversity of resources within families, teacher candidates often expressed deficit views of families. One teacher candidate stated that families in the school neighborhood were not involved with their children and so did nothing with the backpacks, saying, "*The kids are responsible for themselves*" and, "*No one checks in on them or does anything with them.*" Another comment was that the "*kids who do get literacy experiences in their families are the ones that do the backpacks and the kids who don't normally get these experiences did not do them.*" The purpose of the backpacks was often viewed as providing a literacy experience and so had value for "those" families who don't read aloud to their children. In contrast, one teacher candidate spoke positively about how parents came into the classroom when they dropped their children off and were positive about the backpack experience, but then added, "*I was shocked because everyone did the backpacks and seemed to like it.*" Clearly, she had expected otherwise.

Influence on Own Values and Beliefs

Teacher candidates expressed interest in thinking about this engagement for their future classrooms but had many qualifications for what they thought would need to be in place for the backpacks to be successful. These qualifications ranged from adjustment in the implementation and sharing once they became comfortable with their classroom schedule to using the backpacks only if there was "*good parent support and involvement.*" They believed that these parent relationships would already need to be in place in order to have a positive experience rather than seeing the backpacks as an avenue for establishing relationships. In contrast, one teacher candidate commented that "*getting an idea of family life for my students outside of school is a good way to begin understanding them at school.*" Several thought they might develop backpacks on topics studied in school or books of the child's choice, providing additional evidence that the purpose of the backpacks was not understood. In fact, no one mentioned story or funds of knowledge in their oral or written comments.

Our Learning from Teacher Candidates' Stories

After analyzing these stories, we better understood the mountain of back-packs that greeted us at the interviews and gained insights into the changes that needed to be implemented. We realized that we needed to work on a stronger integration of the concepts of story and funds of knowledge throughout university courses and student teaching experiences. We also needed to create explicit spaces and strategies for the teacher candidates to negotiate with instructors and mentor teachers, develop flexible guidelines for families to respond in the journals, and provide time and support for teacher candidates to analyze journal entries in order to challenge deficit views of families.

Year Two of Implementation: Spaces for Negotiation and Sharing

The stories of the teacher candidates in the first year of implementation led to small changes, such as reducing the number of forms and adding a cover sheet to the journals so families could see the kinds of possible entries. We also made major programmatic changes, including integrating the concepts of story and funds of knowledge more intentionally into the children's lit-erature course and meeting with other instructors and university supervisors to build their knowledge of these concepts. We realized that we needed to signal that this engagement was a negotiation between mentor teachers and candidates and so asked for an extended time at the student teaching orien-tation meeting, which both attended. Our introduction included a diagram of the negotiations and decisions that needed to be considered together, such as which backpacks to select, the rotation schedule, and a time for children to share upon returning a backpack. By providing space for decisions to be made *together*, we hoped to convey that this was a shared experience of co-learning.

Stronger support systems for teacher candidates were also integrated into their language arts course, where they were asked to submit a detailed plan for the introduction, rotation, and sharing of the backpacks based on decisions made with their mentor teachers. Periodically, they were given time in class to discuss concerns about the backpacks, and one class session was spent analyzing journal entries for insights on families. They also were asked to plan a unit of study based on their learning about family funds of knowledge. The stories told by teacher candidates after these changes reflected major shifts in their understandings, beliefs, values, and strategies.

Conceptual Understandings

In contrast to the first year, the majority of teacher candidates talked about how the backpacks helped them know students and families differently, providing deeper understandings about the lives of children. One teacher candidate commented, *"I got to learn so much about my students and their families. What goes on inside of the classroom, at home, was possible through the backpacks."* They gained insights into the stories of families through drawings, captions, and photos included in journal entries and learned about extended family members and significant family experiences. Because children had the opportunity to share their journals in class, teacher candidates gained insights into children's ways of thinking and the kinds of connections from school that children were incorporating into entries. The teacher candidates' conceptual understandings were also evident in comments about backpacks as a tool for creating *"a bridge between schools and home that allowed students to bring their experiences with culture from outside of the school, into the classroom."* Some noted that backpacks encouraged family-school connections, with one sharing, *"I love having a 'gift' for my class all semester. It brought families together, and I loved knowing they were grateful for the experience."*

Strategies for Classroom Implementation

Teacher candidates' descriptions of strategies indicated a major shift in their creation of a range of strategies and innovative approaches for implementing the backpacks, engaging children in sharing, and negotiating with mentor teachers and university instructors. Although some teacher candidates experienced *"scheduling as an obstacle"* or had difficulty deciding how to *"organize who got what when,"* all of them found ways to implement rotation schedules that fit their individual classroom structures. One connected the rotation to the Student of the Week schedule while others used the class roster. Several chose to start by *"selecting the most responsible students first,"* giving the first backpacks to *"reliable"* families who would provide a positive demonstration for other children and families. A few used backpacks as a reward system for good behavior or completed assignments.

Teacher candidates found ways to overcome daunting scheduling obstacles to ensure that all children had the opportunity to engage. Occasionally, some families, for a range of reasons, chose not to take home a backpack. One teacher candidate asked a tutor to use the backpack with a child during the after-school program, while others integrated the backpacks into class experiences such as projects, posters, or centers *"so that everyone got to use them even if they didn't take them home."* Developing strategies to ensure all children engaged with the backpacks was a significant change from the first year.

To introduce the backpacks, many teacher candidates sent letters home to explain the purpose and procedures and included information in class newsletters. Several students made an extra effort to make personal contacts and spark interest by introducing backpacks during Open House as *"a way to learn more about the child and family rather than telling them that it was an assignment."* One teacher candidate took the extra step of taking a backpack home, completing the journal herself, and bringing it back to school to share with children as a demonstration.

Some teacher candidates struggled with not speaking the same language as families and found it difficult to encourage families to engage with the backpacks. While the inclusion of a journal sheet on ways to respond alleviated confusion as to what families were expected to do with the journals, teacher candidates talked about difficulties in getting the backpacks returned, which they attributed to a *"lack of involvement or interest"* and *"unwillingness to participate."* However, one did comment, *"that not getting backpacks back was hard, but didn't outweigh the positives."* Teacher candidates also struggled with what they saw as *"meaningful responses."* Several mentioned that *"some parents wrote about the same thing regardless of the topic"* and that *"many of the entries were copied from the families before them."*

Similar to the first year, the level of support from mentor teachers varied. While a few teacher candidates stated that their mentor teachers *"liked the idea,"* the majority felt that their mentor teachers were *"not involved,"* *"didn't think it was interesting or purposeful,"* and thought it was *"too much work."* Teacher candidates especially felt that negotiating time for sharing was affected by their mentor teachers' lack of understanding and support: *"My teacher wasn't thrilled about the backpacks so I didn't get to let my kids share entries."* Difficulty in creating space for sharing time affected their valuing of the experience, with one commenting, *"I like the idea but it wasn't super powerful for me. The kids liked them but I didn't have much time to chat with the kids or learn things about them."*

Most teacher candidates were able to negotiate a time for children to share their families' experiences around the backpacks, a positive shift from the first year. They created space by having children share their journals individually, in small groups, or with the whole group during morning circle time. A few teacher candidates involved parents in the sharing: *"We shared first thing in the morning so parents came in to present with the child. They shared what they did with the backpack and then the parent read the entry and the child told about the book."*

Views of Families and Their Responses

The majority of comments about families centered around which family members were involved and the amount of perceived involvement.

Occasionally, these comments indicated assumptions about the lack of parent involvement, "*I don't know how much help the kids had. Apart from the grandparents backpack, most were pictures kids had drawn, no writing . . . not sure parents engaged with them.*" Interestingly, in one case, when a family did engage deeply with the journal, this was critiqued as too much involvement, with parents getting competitive and trying to outdo previous entries. Some teacher candidates assumed that the families could not or would not normally engage in these interactions on their own and thus viewed the backpacks as a way of increasing involvement: "*I think the most powerful part of this experience was getting to see some parent involvement, even though there wasn't much of it; I'm sure that those families appreciated it.*" Another common assumption was that families lacked the materials to have these types of engagements and thus the value of the backpacks was viewed as "*being able to send home books for the families to read because a lot of my families don't have books at home.*"

In a few cases, these assumptions were challenged when the journal entries revealed a large amount of family participation and valuing of the backpack engagement, "*I realized that a lot of my families took it serious, they included brothers and sisters, they sat down as a family, even grandparents would sit down with them, doing the whole family thing. That was surprising to me, especially knowing some of my kids, their moms work a lot, I thought they'd sit down and do it really quick but no, they actually set aside time—they read all the books, they played with the artifact, it was surprising, so I liked that.*"

Teacher candidates did become familiar with family practices through the journals and were able to speak about these: "*They have their own version of La Lotería at home. The children could actually read the cards in Spanish. Some parents used the backpacks to 'play school' at home.*" Although one mentioned that the backpacks were a great strategy for bringing "*their kinds of knowledge into the classroom,*" there were no deeper discussions about the types of knowledge or the extent to which these funds of knowledge were valued in the classroom.

Teacher candidates told stories about the backpacks as a way to learn about families, particularly who participated and in what ways. However, despite the bilingual materials in the backpacks, there was a common belief that a language "gap" or "barrier" was an obstacle to family participation: "*I feel like the parents are reluctant maybe . . . a lot of parents don't speak English.*"

Influence on Own Values and Beliefs

Teacher candidates thoughtfully considered possibilities for implementing backpacks in their future classrooms, while also expressing concerns about time and cost. Some saw the backpacks as a resource for getting to know students and families, saying, "*I would like this for my classroom because it can be a meaningful way to learn about family interactions at home and sharing is a great way to build community in the classroom."* Some had even thought about how they would incorporate the backpacks or how they might adapt this engagement to fit their classroom. Some wanted to use books from the classroom library in their backpacks, and others were considering ways to have children share their entries when they brought them back to the classroom. Although they were much more positive about the possibility of implementing the backpacks in their classrooms, a few were still concerned about the cost and time involved in organizing this engagement. *"This engagement was a lot of extra work so I don't know if I could take it on my first year, but it was a great project for engaging families."*

Our Learning from Teacher Candidates' Stories

When asked to reflect on the backpack experience, one teacher candidate replied, *"The most powerful thing about the experience was learning and reflecting on what I would have done to make the experience more meaningful."* The programmatic changes implemented at the end of the first year appeared to greatly enhance their experiences. They had stronger conceptual understandings, even though their mentor teachers did not, and understood the value of providing time for children to share entries. As a result, they were more excited about what they were learning about families, and children were more excited about taking the backpack home and being able to share their family with others.

The stories from this group of teacher candidates also revealed common struggles, most notably in their need for more university support across multiple contexts, including strategies for better communication with families regardless of home language, ways to bridge the gap between the university and schools in order to better engage mentor teachers, and ongoing opportunities to analyze the journal entries and connect these stories to instruction. We celebrated the success in their stories in contrast to the first year but also identified areas where we needed to spend additional time.

Year Three of Implementation: Time for Reflection and Analysis

One of our major realizations was that we had excluded a key group of people from our collaboration—the university supervisors. The university supervisors were the ones who spent time with the teacher candidates and mentor teachers in classrooms and could most easily facilitate negotiations by offering suggestions for organizing, implementing and sharing within the specific schedules and routines of each classroom.

The supervisors had no background with the backpacks, however, and did not understand their conceptual or procedural basis and so felt no responsibility for checking on their use when they were in classrooms. Therefore, in the third year, we met with the university supervisors in a professional development session at the beginning of student teaching and worked with them to make monitoring the backpacks part of their assigned duties. The supervisors asked teacher candidates to develop a plan for implementing and sharing the backpacks in their classroom and worked with them to analyze the entries in the journals.

We focused on encouraging negotiation between mentor teachers and teacher candidates throughout the year. During the initial orientation with mentor teachers and teacher candidates, we provided examples from previous years of strategies teacher candidates had used to organize the backpack engagement and to create space for children to share in the classroom. Later in the semester, we met with the mentor teachers, teacher candidates, and supervisors to look at journal entries they had gathered from families. Through a guided analysis of the journal entries, teacher candidates and mentor teachers worked together to explore what they could learn about families. We hoped that this time to closely examine and think collaboratively about the entries from families would challenge deficit views and encourage mentor teachers to value time for sharing journal entries in classrooms.

In addition, teacher candidates were given time to familiarize themselves with the books in the backpacks in the children's literature course in the semester prior to student teaching. Strategies for responding to parent questions about books and artifacts were also explored, using examples of issues previously raised by parents, such as concerns about the appropriateness of young children talking about skin color in *You Be Me, I'll Be You* (Mandelbaum, 1990).

One change in the third year that we did not anticipate was a major increase in pressure from school districts on K-2 classrooms due to the Common Core State Standards and the fear of the national testing that would occur the following year. Many K-2 teachers were given scripted programs and required to follow schedules where every minute was monitored by district personnel, with no flexible time available during the school day. Because these programs and schedules were new to mentor teachers, they had not had time to figure out where they might be able to build in flexibility and so tended to rigidly follow the regulations.

Conceptual Understandings

Despite these challenges, teacher candidates continued to show deeper conceptual understandings of family stories and funds of knowledge. The majority saw the role of the backpacks as a tool for learning about children and families, saying, "*I was able to learn so much from families that I know I wouldn't have learned without the backpacks.*" They also commented on using the backpacks to encourage family interactions and learning about children's lives outside of school in order to inform curriculum.

The depth of conceptual understandings was particularly evident as teacher candidates reflected on the dynamics in their classrooms and the misunderstandings of mentor teachers. They noticed that the backpacks created space in the classroom for children's voices, observing how children *"made it their own thing"* and responded freely to the backpack themes. One teacher candidate stated, *"I thought the backpacks were really awesome in my classroom, specifically because the kids don't really have ownership of anything that happens in the class."* This stronger conceptual understanding also allowed them to notice instances in which their mentor teachers had misunderstandings about the purpose of the backpacks as literacy skills rather than story. As one shared about her mentor teacher, *"She didn't see it having a purpose when it's really powerful for the kids, and it develops that community that our classroom doesn't have and she didn't see that you could use it for anything. If I wasn't using it as a literacy backpack then she believed that the purpose wasn't there."* Another noted, *"My mentor teacher was okay about the backpacks, but did not see the backpacks as a resource for her. She never looked at them or saw them as an asset to understand the families. She saw them as what I needed to do for the university."*

Strategies for Classroom Implementation

Similar to the second year, teacher candidates shared many strategies for implementing the backpacks and negotiating with mentor teachers, as well as struggles with implementation. They continued to introduce the backpacks by sending letters home describing the purpose and procedures but found new ways to interest families in the backpacks. One teacher candidate personally called families when a backpack was going home and found that *"the journal entries were a lot richer than the ones who didn't get that phone call."* Another talked with families who were getting a backpack as they picked their children up from school, greeting them with the backpack to get parents and children *"interested and excited about it."* A few continued to have difficulty encouraging families to participate and found ways to engage children with the backpacks at school.

To get children excited, several teacher candidates told children that the backpacks had *"things that they were going to be able to take home and talk about with their families."* Many showed children the contents of the backpacks and others first took a backpack home to write in the journal and share their own stories. Some children were excited about the books and artifacts, while others *"loved the idea of the backpacks."* All of the teacher candidates commented on the children's positive responses, saying, *"They were always excited to take one,"* so much so that the children *"wanted to keep backpacks."* The teacher candidates spoke noticeably more about the children's positive responses and provided more specific examples than they had previously.

When children take the backpacks home, they are encouraged to write in the journals about their family stories and experiences. Teacher candidates shared stories about what they had learned about families and children from these journals, but a few continued to struggle. One teacher candidate felt that "*it was hard to get back meaningful information and entries from the students,*" and several commented that the majority of entries were children's drawings that sometimes were "*not related to the backpacks.*" One teacher candidate realized that the parents' participation in journals was affected by the mentor teacher's expectations around language use, commenting that the parents would have written in Spanish, but "*the teacher told the kids that they could only speak in English and so parents were afraid to write in their own language and so many did not write in the journals.*"

Teacher candidates recognized the importance of creating space for children to share their families' stories and often had to communicate that importance to their mentor teachers and negotiate a time for sharing. Some mentor teachers were "*supportive and open*" and thought "*that it's really nice that they share.*" One said that her mentor teacher "*worked with her the whole time*" including analyzing journal entries with her and another thought the backpacks were "*something that would be really awesome to do in class.*" However, similar to previous years, other mentor teachers viewed the backpack experience as the teacher candidates' responsibility and a "*project to do for the university.*" Mentor teachers with this perspective were often less engaged and put more restrictions on the amount of time available for sharing.

As in previous years, teacher candidates made comments such as "*my teacher wasn't thrilled about the backpacks so I didn't get to let my kids share entries*" and "*if the teacher wanted to do it, then it became part of the classroom,*" indicating that the views of mentor teachers impeded interactions with children. The negotiation between teacher candidates and mentor teachers increased in the third year—especially when the university supervisor actively checked with teachers. Regardless of the mentor teachers' perspectives or support, teacher candidates were able to negotiate 5 to 20 minutes during the day for children to share in whole group, a small group, or individually.

The excited responses of children to sharing their families' stories and experiences with the backpacks supported teacher candidates in valuing space for sharing. While one teacher candidate viewed sharing as difficult because some children "*said they hadn't read the books, they hadn't played with the things in it, they didn't show it to their family and so they had just drawn some pictures not related to the books,*" most told stories about positive experiences, making statement such as, "*they love getting up there and talking and sharing about their journal entry. They would get very personal talking about their families, what they like to do and the other kids would get really excited because they knew they would be able to take home a backpack.*" Children shared favorite books as well as journal entries from the backpacks. The comments from teacher candidates about children's excitement in sharing stories made for another noticeable difference from the previous two years and further established the importance of supporting negotiations between teacher candidates and mentor teachers.

Overall, teacher candidates were very positive about their experiences with backpacks, but they did acknowledge some struggles with implementation, as in previous years. Some considered it a struggle to work around their university course schedule, which required them to be out of the classroom for two days every other week. Other common challenges included difficulty getting backpacks and items returned to school. A new challenge was their struggle *"to implement the theme of the backpack into the classroom"* curriculum, which was mainly due to nonnegotiable structures. And while having books in English and Spanish was considered a positive, the need for books in other languages was raised because of the increase in languages within certain schools. This increase in awareness and valuing of linguistic diversity contrasted with previous years in which teacher candidates identified language differences as barriers.

Views of Families and their Responses

Overall, teacher candidates reflected a range of perspectives on whether families were viewed as being involved with children and the backpacks. Many spoke positively about the involvement of families, saying, *"All of my entries, except for one, involved parent involvement, whether they talk about how they played La Lotería or it was the parent's handwriting and the kid's words. There were a lot of those where the parent wrote it out but it was obviously what the kid wanted to say, or like kid's art and parent's handwriting, so everything that I have was both parent and child."* Others had definite ideas about what constituted "involvement" and were quick to make assumptions. One teacher candidate noted that all the words were spelled correctly in a child's entry and so she assumed that *"her parents told her how to spell every word but they didn't sit and interact, they were just giving her how to spell the words. So there was very little family involvement and not in a way that helped them do things with the backpacks."*

Occasionally, teacher candidates were surprised by parents who did not interact with the backpacks to the extent that they expected: *"I assumed that they would have parent involvement because the parents are really involved in our classroom and they, the parents, didn't do anything with them and they didn't read any of the books so I was kind of surprised by that."* More often, there was surprise that families actually did engage, suggesting that assumptions were held that families would not do so, as evidenced in this comment: *"a lot of birthday traditions came out and that was where I really saw parents participating but also, the kids including their younger siblings and letting them draw, draw about their birthdays—I wasn't really expecting that."* While one teacher candidate recognized the diversity within a single class, saying, *"Our parents are all really different types of families,"* another held strong assumptions about the lack of English proficiency and resources in the home, commenting, "*I think that my kids liked the journal the most because most of them can't read English and their parents don't either so just having the crayons I think was exciting for them because I don't think many of them have those things at home.*"

In addition to direct comments about children and families, the ways in which teacher candidates talked about journal entries provided additional insights. They gave detailed accounts of journal entries and what students shared in the classroom, making statements such as "*seeing which parents participated in the backpacks and learning about the routines of the families was powerful.*" Teacher candidates learned about their immigrant families' journeys, as in this story: "*We had one entry from a family from Iraq, who wrote in English and drew and wrote 4 pages about their journey from Iraq to the U.S. and how they stay in contact with their family back in Iraq through Skype. Malik could explain what was happening in all of the pictures that the mother drew.*" They also learned about the diverse cultures within families through children's comments about the different skin colors in a family and different family structures. One noted, "*There's a lot of families in my class that are different dads, different moms, different cultures in one family. It was very interesting for me to be aware of that in my classroom and know which families have which family members.*" They also learned about home language practices, as parents often commented that they loved the bilingual books in the backpacks and wrote in various languages in the journals. The teacher candidates felt that the journals provided them with insights and understandings of families that they would not have had access to, saying "*I learned a lot about my students. If I hadn't have done that, I wouldn't have known a lot of that information.*" Another teacher candidate shared a story: "*This one boy took it home—he's just this budding author—he wrote this big long thing about his name, where he got his name and his parents added to it and it started this big classroom conversation and all the kids were talking about, 'well, I actually like to be called this' and it's a name that nobody calls them. I thought it was so interesting that we don't know any of these things about our kids.*"

Influence on Own Values and Beliefs

Most teacher candidates expressed a strong desire to implement family story backpacks in their future classrooms. Some comments indicated a general interest in the backpacks such as, "*I would love to integrate this into my classroom.*" Others focused on the backpacks as a means of family involvement stating, "*I really want to have family involvement and sharing.*" The majority went beyond these general comments to specifically talk about implementing backpacks to gain knowledge about families and to create cultural connections between home and school. Their comments indicated that they valued the backpacks as a means of exploring family funds of knowledge, saying "*I want to create engagements that allow students to share funds of knowledge.*" Several talked about using what they learned from backpacks to plan instruction and to be aware of students' experiences within families in order to build from that knowledge in the classroom. They also saw the backpacks as a means of getting to know what family members are living in the home, recognizing that many children are part of large extended families, and to understand family structures and activities. Teacher candidates noted that the backpacks could play multiple roles, making statements such as, "*I hope to use this engagement to have parent involvement and so parents feel comfortable sharing stories about their cultures. It is also a great community builder for the children to share.*"

Our Learning from Teacher Candidates' Stories

The stories from teacher candidates reflected the pressures faced by mentor teachers facing new scripted programs and extremely tight schedules. Finding time for any kind of additional experiences—no matter how valuable—was difficult, and so some mentor teachers viewed the backpacks as an assignment for student teaching. For the first time, the stories showed that the majority of teacher candidates had strong conceptual understandings of the backpacks; they valued families' stories and were advocates for creating space and time for children to share—even when mentor teachers weren't fully on board. Their stories also revealed their willingness to disrupt the dominant narrative of the programs shaping school and an understanding of the multiple curricula that can be shaped by the lives of children, families, and teachers coming together in a classroom (Clandinin & Connelly, 2000).

The teacher candidates benefitted from the support of university supervisors to find these spaces, but regardless, they searched for time because they valued the engagement, not because it was an assignment. They continued to develop strategies for implementation and inclusion, but still struggled with strategies for talking, listening, and learning with families (Klassen-Endrizzi, 2004). They also shifted from making assumptive statements as facts about families and children to making statements that were qualified as an opinion or possibility.

As we reflected on their stories, we recognized that we needed to plan ways to work with mentor teachers in developing deeper understandings through multiple opportunities to interact with the backpacks and to analyze the journal entries. We planned professional learning experiences with mentor teachers and several opportunities for mentor teachers and teacher candidates to work together in analyzing entries from the journals. We also decided to start with a partial implementation of two backpacks during the fall practicum before spring student teaching in order to provide more time for conversation and negotiation. In addition, we noted ways that the university supervisors could support teacher candidates from our data and the types of support needed in order to more effectively consider their role.

Final Reflections

The shift in the stories told by teacher candidates is especially evident when viewed across the three years through Wordles created from the small group conversations. In the first year, the Wordle highlights the complaints of teacher candidates about backpacks taking a *lot* of *time* and their struggles to get the backpacks *back* from *parents* and *homes*. Their stories reflect their misunderstandings about the purpose for the backpack engagement and their struggles with all aspects of implementation and negotiation in the classroom and with the mentor *teacher*.

During the second year, their stories indicate a shift to descriptions of effective strategies for implementing backpacks. The Wordle highlights *families, parents, students,* and *kids,* reflecting a move from complaining about backpacks to considering ways to engage *children* and *parents* and many discussions of ways to *share entries* from the journals.

The third year of stories reflect a shift from strategies to understandings teacher candidates were developing through analysis and reflection on the entries in the journals and children's sharing. The move from *students* to *kids* is significant in indicating a more holistic view of children along with a strong focus on *home, family,* and *parents. Lot* came from their comments about learning a *lot* about families rather than complaints and time referred to the value of finding *time* to share. They talked about specific *books* and *entries* that families *wrote* in journals.

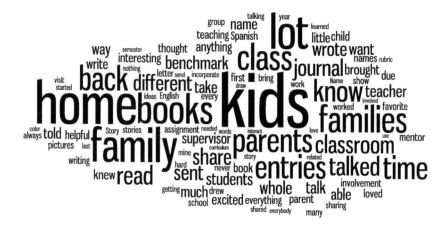

Our work with teacher candidates initially revolved around gathering data for research to document their perceptions and understandings. Once we recovered from the initial shock of our first interview, we realized that their stories offered a much greater potential in our work as teacher educators. Conducting the interviews as conversations in small groups created a narrative inquiry space that facilitated the sharing of stories, which in turn challenged us to reframe our stories about our practice and to make important changes in our program. We became action researchers and storytellers in the same way that many teacher educators promote the use of action research and story for teacher candidates.

Narrative inquiry gave us a strategy for disrupting our dominant narratives as teacher educators and engaging in a process of learning and transformation. We were challenged to think *with* teacher candidates through their stories, not just think *about* their experiences. The stories that we tell and retell, live and relive, in teacher education have tremendous potential for shaping programmatic changes and for engaging with complexities in order to move to action.

Bibliography

Allen, J. (2008). Family partnerships. *Educational Leadership*, 66(1), 22–27.
Bacharach, N., & Heck, T. (2012). Voices from the field: Multiple perspectives on a co-teaching in a student teaching model. *The Renaissance Group*, 1(1), 49–61.

Carter, K. (1993). The place of story in the study of teaching and teacher education. *Educational Researcher, 22*(1), 5–12.

Clandinin, D. J., & Connelly, F. M. (2000). *Narrative inquiry: Experience and story in qualitative research*. San Francisco: Jossey-Bass.

Huber, J., Caine, V., Huber, M., & Steeves, P. (2013). Narrative inquiry as pedagogy in education. *Review of Research in Education, 37,* 212–242.

Huber, J., Li, Y., Murphy, S., Nelson, C., & Young, M. (2014). Shifting stories to live by: Teacher education as a curriculum of narrative inquiry identity explorations. *Reflective Practice: International and Multidisciplinary Perspectives,* 15(2), 176–189.

Klassen-Endrizzi, C. (2004). We've got to talk: Redefining our work with families. *Language Arts,* 81(4), 323–333.

Mandelbaum, P. (1990). *You be me, I'll be you*. LaJolla, CA: Kane/Miller.

Rosen, H. (1986). *Stories and meanings*. London: NATE.

Schaafsam, D., & Vinz, R. (2011). *Narrative inquiry: Approaches to language and literacy research*. New York: Teachers College Press.

Short, K. (2012). Story as world making. *Language Arts,* 90(1), 9–17.

A list of the backpacks and their contents along with related forms can be found online at http://www.createarizona.org/curricular-experiences/story-interactions/family-story-backpacks-1

8 Understanding Children's Funds of Knowledge through Observations of Play

Haeny S. Yoon

There is so much pressure on children from parents and society to be the best at so many things. Children are not given a chance to really explore their own interests and talents . . . children are so individually unique and should be given opportunities to express themselves as individuals, not molded into the perfect modern day child. I find it sad how success of children is so defined by academics and testing, but that is how our society is. There are so many standards set in place for living the right life, attending the best colleges, that there is no time left to just enjoy, play, and live.

(Kristi, written response)

Kristi was a preservice teacher in the teacher education program who obviously believed in the power of play. While many early childhood educators agree with Kristi, there are numerous pressures (also identified by Kristi) that marginalize play in schools. In the current educational climate, the push for academics dominates the discourse on "readiness" (Graue, 2006), privileging basic skills related to reading, writing, and numeracy over social, cultural, and emotional work. Academics related to language mechanics often replace the intellectually rich work that children engage in through play episodes, especially in kindergarten classrooms. Fueling this idea are neoliberal policies that advocate for competition (both nationally and globally) and standardization. Consequently, children, schools, parents, and society are involved in figuring out what is best for children and how to enable them to succeed in a global world. But what about children? What voice do they have in advocating for their own learning and growth?

With these questions in mind, I describe a semester-long project conducted by preservice teachers (PSTs) as they engaged in classroom-based research around children's play. In a series of observations in early childhood centers, they analyzed major themes related to children's interests, knowledge, and resources. Supplemented with multiple forms of data (interviews, home visits, artifacts, informal/formal assessment data), PSTs learned to create an in-depth case study of one child. From their analysis, PSTs created play centers that emerged from their data with the purpose of extending children's existing play. This chapter highlights the importance of positioning teachers as researchers who co-construct curriculum with children rather than simply handing it to them. Attempts at standardizing a teacher's work (in addition to standardizing children's learning) are part of neoliberal agendas working to create a set of homogenous practices and knowledge that deprofessionalize teaching (Sleeter, 2008). Instead, this project aimed to position teachers as "transformative intellectuals" (Giroux, 2010) who systematically uncover children's social, emotional, and cognitive growth through play. Thus, teachers can empower children by designing play opportunities that purposefully give children voice in guiding and directing their own learning experiences. As Kristi reminded us at the beginning, schools need to be places where children learn to "enjoy, play, and live."

Play as Critical Early Childhood Curriculum

Play, according to Chudacoff (2008), is spontaneous, inventive, and pleasurable, "easing a child's adjustment to the present and [making] life meaningful" (p.1). Childhood, therefore, is not just a matter of preparing children for their future selves, but an enactment of present identities. Thus, play has functional and intellectual qualities, allowing children to navigate space, relationships, emotions, and the larger culture. Children learn through free, unstructured play; implicit in this learning is the role of peers as socializing agents in constructing, revising, and challenging beliefs. Teachers, then, have the important role of capitalizing on children's existing resources or "funds of knowledge" as they interact with the diversity of realities and resources experienced by other children in classroom settings.

Gonzales, Moll, and Amanti (2005) engaged teachers in qualitative research to uncover the familial practices, the cultural traditions, the generational stories, and household knowledge that shape children's unique experiences and resourceful practices (funds of knowledge). Furthermore, children draw upon their funds of knowledge to make meaning in the classroom, to negotiate with their peers, and to understand curricular content. As Gonzales et al. (2005) assert, discovering and utilizing a child's existing knowledge is vital to engagement in school. Play is one place (in addition to the home) where teachers can discover how children use cultural tools to show *what they know* and *how they interpret the world*. Thus, children are not deposited with only new knowledge, but they build upon prior knowledge and ideas within social situations.

Dyson (1997) extended this notion of funds of knowledge to include both cultural practices inherent in children's homes and communities as well as popular culture knowledge that many children use a resource in their play. Bringing in popular culture in the classroom is unavoidable, but at times, the enactments can also be problematic. She discussed how children took up stereotypical images of superheroes as strong and male while female characters were helpless, beautiful, and white. When the black girls vied for coveted female roles, they were denied entry due to underlying issues of race

and class. Children (with the help of popular culture and media) perpetuated traditional images of male and female, black and white. Within these
tensions, children worked to preserve these roles, but also used play and
writing to change these roles and redefine heroes and heroines. Thus, while
dominant hegemonies persisted in play, they were also resisted through alternate images of strong, beautiful black females. Similarly, Corsaro (2003)
looked across multiple contexts across the U.S. and Italy to show that children enacted cultural norms within their play, expressing ideas learned from
their families, communities, popular culture, and the larger sociocultural
landscape. At times, children enacted troubling notions of race and gender
that were often stereotypical and reproductive.

Play is a space where subjectivities are both realized and actualized, making children's play a highly contentious act of competing discourses and
ideologies. For example, Paley (2004) worked hard to illuminate the ways
young children interpreted the social, cultural, and political context; they
often explored issues of death, war, terrorism, and poverty in complex ways.
Paley (2007) showed educators the potential of listening to children's play in
order to inform curriculum. At the heart of her work was the close observation and analysis of children's play that is only possible when there is space,
flexibility, and time for children to engage in their own cultural activity.
Paley saw her role as that of a curious inquirer who was genuinely interested
in how children viewed the world around them. Through children's voice
and commitments, she was able to shed light on alternative perspectives to
social realities. Thus, the teacher critically examines inequities and social
issues *with* children from their constructed realities. This kind of research is
crucial in viewing classrooms and situating the role of teachers.

Teachers as Researchers: The "Critical" Role of Early Childhood Educators

At the heart of the teacher's role is asking questions and finding answers.
Embedded in this process of inquiry is that questions, at times, lead to more
questions than answers. It is never neatly tied up, but messy. Therefore,
I contend that an early childhood educator is not simply someone who man-
ages the stage, organizes materials, mediates conflict, or assesses learning.
Instead, they should be engaged in critically examining children's play by
analyzing the content, interactions, and ideologies that play out in every
classroom. Templeton (2013) in her discussion of preschool children in the
aftermath of Hurricane Sandy in New York City demonstrated the power
of careful notes and transcriptions in uncovering inequities and disrupting
the authoritative stance of teachers. She showed that children were social
actors whose comments about race, ethnicity, gender, and ability were not
just "background noise or just another funny story to tell" (p.187) but a
window into how they were processing the world. Underlying this description is that investigation and inquiry are necessary in order to look back

on events and discussions that are often dismissed or overlooked. Thus, classrooms should act as democratic spaces where children and teachers are working together to understand and construct the social scene (Langford, 2010). "Everyone within this democratic centre acts, reacts and responds in relations with each other in complex and entangled ways, with growing knowledge, skill, power, judgment and agency" (Langford, 2010, p. 121). In this social enterprise, field research can act as a social tool to design curriculum that intellectualizes the place of play. Therefore, early childhood educators should be mobilizers of play as they theorize and take seriously the students' social interactions (Dahlberg, Pence, & Moss, 2007; Langford, 2010; Templeton, 2013).

Teachers are responsible for deconstructing the classroom, "reading social life as though it were a text, for what is both said as well as not said" (Ryan & Grieshaber, 2005, p. 38). Teachers, according to many teacher educators, need to be repositioned as curricular leaders who are not simply transmitting curricular texts, but transforming them through systematic research and analysis (Ayers, 1989; Giroux & Simon, 1988; Gore & Zeichner, 1991; Kilderry, 2004; Moll, Gonzales, Amanti, & Neff, 1992). Thus, the intellectual work of teachers must be foremost in the preparation of teachers. Most important to a teacher's work is "critical questioning and reflection" (Kilderry, 2004, p. 37). Shifting the role of the teacher from "learning to teach" to "learning to inquire" follows the idea that to "learn deliberately is to conduct research; every lesson can be an inquiry for the teacher" (Fueyo & Koorland, 1997, p. 337). This chapter contributes one way for teachers to position themselves as serious researchers who design curriculum and theorize learning from observing and analyzing children at play.

Background of Study

Drawing from a year-long case study on preservice teachers' development as literacy teachers, I accumulated documents over the course of the semester and conducted interviews (after the course was completed) in order to understand teacher beliefs and practices. Part of the project required PSTs to implement play centers into their classroom sites, which allowed me to see the design and enactment of curriculum. Using data from the semester, I followed three PSTs placed in kindergarten classrooms to observe throughout the following school year. The second part of this research was designed to see how coursework carried over into their fieldwork, identifying the challenges of negotiating different philosophies toward children's language development. Additionally, it allowed me to consider the difficult transition that PSTs undertook as they moved from play-based early childhood centers to pressure-filled elementary schools. This chapter will focus on one semester where PSTs engaged in developing a case study of one child using ethnographic methods. The case study was used to design curriculum that extended children's play around major themes. I used the following research questions to guide this chapter:

1   How do PSTs theorize play within sociocultural and sociopolitical contexts?
2   How do they begin to understand and negotiate the tensions between schools and children's cultural backgrounds?
3   How do preservice teachers draw on children's "funds of knowledge" to design curriculum?

Site and Participants

The project was designed using CREATE principles with the belief that children possess unique "funds of knowledge" (Gonzales et al., 2005) that should guide curricular design. Given the narrow measures that children are evaluated by, a "funds of knowledge" approach encourages teachers to see children as resourceful in their own cultural practices rather than deficient in predetermined categories. Therefore, teachers should explore children's existing language repertoires, learned familial practices, and unique cultural knowledge that all children possess before coming into the space of school. This is especially important for minoritized children whose competence is overlooked by dominant ideologies and practices.

The project was conducted by PSTs in the CREATE program, most of whom were white, middle class; all students were female. In this data set, all students were white and female (see Table 8.1); however, most of their field-work took place in centers where the majority of the children spoke English as a second language. Throughout the semester, PSTs gathered data in the

Table 8.1 Participants.

Name	Race
Annabel	White
Renee	White
Lisa	White
Christine	White
Lana	White
Kate	White
Bella	White
Raven	White
Megan	White
Elizabeth	White
Bridget	White
Liv	White
Heather	White
Hillary	White
Kristi	White

form of observations and fieldnotes, audio recordings and transcriptions, interviews, and artifact collection. I was the instructor of the course; the language and literacy course was designed around notions of play, especially designed with children from birth to 4 years old in mind. The students were also concurrently placed in early childhood centers, working with children from infancy to preschool aged.

Data Collection and Analysis

This chapter looks at how preservice teachers built their ideologies about play over the course of one semester through experiences in their coursework as well as their fieldwork in early childhood centers. Using a case study methodology (Genishi & Dyson, 2005), I gathered data in multiple spaces with the assumption that learning occurs in multiple worlds as students learn to negotiate, implement, and grow ideas through involvement and participation (Holland, Lachiotte, Skinner, & Cain, 2003; Lave & Wenger, 1991). Data from 15/21 students was collected from the cohort of students beginning in the spring of 2013. During this period, students conducted observations (3–5) and created fieldnotes for one child in a classroom during unstructured, free play as their own case study. Additionally, they collected artifacts and photographs as well as engaged in 3 home visits throughout the semester in order to support their observational data. From the data collected, the students created a play center that drew on children's interests and engagements uncovered through data collection. All parts of the project were collected (description of the play center, fieldnotes, and play center reflections) in order to answer the research question: How do PSTs draw on funds of knowledge to design curriculum?

Additionally 4 response papers were collected where PSTs responded to controversial issues in the educational context surrounding young children's development and learning. Topics were accompanied by media clips and focused on the following: the multiple literacies in children's lives, the development of children's language at infancy in various sociocultural contexts, the place of play in childhood, and the nature of schooling in a neoliberal world. These responses helped to answer the questions: How do PSTs theorize play within sociocultural and sociopolitical contexts? How do they begin to understand and negotiate the tensions between schools and children's cultural backgrounds?

The data was analyzed using the research questions as a guide. Analysis around the response papers revealed themes related to language ideologies, political perspectives, and teacher agency or lack thereof. The projects were analyzed with a specific intent of understanding how students made theory practical in designing curriculum. Thus, the projects were analyzed on different stages: first, observation data were analyzed to see how teachers examined and analyzed data, specifically in terms of social, cultural factors. Next, the projects were analyzed to see how PSTs connected data and applied it to designing curriculum. This paper focuses on how theory and practice come together in curricular spaces, specifically through designing play opportunities.

Using a Funds of Knowledge Approach as Teacher Researchers

Emergent curriculum involves the co-construction of knowledge between teachers, students, communities, and families. In the common space of school, children arrive with valuable and varied cultural practices that act as resources for their participation in school. This "funds of knowledge" approach positions children as curricular informants while teachers work actively to discover cultural resources as the basis for accessing academic, social, and cultural knowledge necessary for success in school (Gonzales et al., 2005). Liv described her interpretation of a co-constructed curriculum:

> The way that my classes talked about this idea was in the term, "funds of knowledge." This is a new idea that goes along with family and home visits. Teachers will go to as many children in their class's houses as possible and learn from that visit with the child and in the child's home to later bring that information, or funds of knowledge, into the classroom. This is said to help the children relate to what is happening in the classroom on a personal level. It also allows for the children to learn from each other and learn about a culture, tradition, or customs that they may not be familiar with. Having the children be the basis of curriculum is such a great idea for so many reasons. It takes less pressure off of the teacher to think of and plan a lesson that is perfect for everyone. The ideas are going to be part of the children! The children are going to feel like they matter and that their family matters, and that they are important enough to be something that the class is learning about. Also the best thing about funds of knowledge and making a curriculum based off the children is that, we need to learn from our children and use the knowledge that we learn from them to continue to teach them and also to teach ourselves so that we can learn to teach in a better way.

In the above excerpt, Liv discusses several aspects of funds of knowledge that are both superficial and beneficial. For instance, simply incorporating culture and limiting this to traditions and customs is often a surface-level way of becoming a multicultural teacher. At times, exoticizing other people's cultures does more harm than good (see Sleeter, 2001). This was a common struggle for many of the PSTs engaged in the research—making superficial connections. For instance, two teachers might ask a parent to come in to make tortillas—one teacher might look at it as a nice cultural activity that highlights Mexican culture. Another teacher might frame it as a familial practice in one student's home that is an activity passed down for generations. One teacher might plan the activity with very surface-level knowledge about a child's culture using ethnicity as a determining factor; another teacher might look deeper into the cultural practices of a student through repeated observations, rich dialogue, and ongoing conversations. For the sake of being "cultural," teachers are in danger of essentializing culture rather than celebrating cultural diversity (Omi & Winant, 2008; Pollock, 2004). It was difficult to communicate that an activity can have multiple intentions, both positive and negative. Thus, cultural practices can perpetuate stereotypes if not framed with deep understandings about children's unique home culture. However, Liv also understood that ultimately, children and their families needed to feel genuinely valued in classrooms in words and practice. Curriculum, as she stated, based on children's interests, experiences, and resources provides teachers with a better way to teach to children's strengths, but also to teach content that represents the communities in their classrooms. While the process of understanding funds of knowledge was far from perfect, it was imperative for PSTs (especially white teachers) to start exploring taken-for-granted notions of normal and standard. As Megan mentioned, "When entering the program, I immediately noticed a change in everything I knew to be 'school'—both in my childhood and adult life."

Given this perspective, many of the PSTs struggled with the nature of interactions in their classroom environments. Bella, a PST, talked about how her cooperating teacher directed children toward predetermined tasks rather than co-constructed knowledge in collaborative ways. The idea that children and teachers are both knowledgeable and co-contributors is not a new idea but an idea that proved to be a point of tension in PSTs' field experiences. Freire (1970) asserted that classrooms should be dialogic spaces where all members of the community created knowledge through shared experiences and dialogue. For many of the PSTs, they encountered a reality where school was a difficult space for children and their families. Many of the students (like Megan) saw their schooling as filled with positive memories and fluid connections between home life and school life. They learned from her fieldwork that many families (especially from diverse cultural backgrounds) did not share in that same experience. More often than not, these families felt like outsiders in the school, and their cultural practices did not easily cohere with school values and practices. Furthermore, Megan learned from readings that literacy, broadly defined, moved beyond print-based texts. Instead, literacy in its multiple forms was about how people used language to communicate with each other rather than as a decodable skill (which will be discussed in more depth at a later section). Thus, by entering children's out-of-school spaces as well as their unofficial practice within play, the PSTs saw children's resourcefulness and capacities.

Kristi described her case study child as having a photographic memory based on her observations as well as well as interviews with his family.

From really focusing and observing his play and social communications, I have been able to make many connections about Harry's world.

I understand much more about where his ideas and inquiries have been coming from and how they inspire his choice of activities. It is truly interesting to see how many influences some together and help build on knowledge and extend his learning.

(play center reflection)

Harry (the case study child) referred to events and ideas as existing in "my world." Kristi found that entering Harry's world was essential in designing curricular opportunities that made sense to Harry's sense of identity and his place in the world. Arguably, Kristi used funds of knowledge as a qualitative tool that helped her teach into Harry's strengths. Therefore, the curriculum emerged from close observation, careful analysis, and productive interactions between school and home.

Play as Cultural Expression

Embedded in children's play are cultural values. In play, children begin to theorize about social limitations, structures, and constructs. While grappling with these notions, children use conversations with each other to explain uncertainties, reproduce cultural norms, as well as produce variations to common practices. The following excerpt collected by Kristi features Harry and Tiffany, who share about their personal experiences as well as their conceptions of age as an identity marker.

> Harry and Tiffany are sitting at a table eating snacks from their lunch boxes. Harry tells Tiffany that he wanted to be bigger and be thirteen. Tiffany asks him, "Why do you want to be thirteen?" Harry answers, "Because it's so much fun to be thirteen and to be a grown up." "Why?" Tiffany asks him again. Harry says, "Because it's fun to be thirteen because you can do magic tricks. One time I put a money under my closet and it disappeared when I woke up in the morning. I woke up in the morning and it was all gone." Tiffany asks him where it went, and he tells her, "It went, I think it went to California. California is in my world and it's where my grandma lives. I have two grandmas, maybe three, I can't remember." Tiffany looks up smiling and says, "My grandma lives in Canada."

(Kristi, field note)

Kristi noted the presumptions that age carried in a person's social life and opportunities. For Harry, the age thirteen marked being "grown up," which allowed one to do magic tricks. The magic trick conversation led Tiffany and Harry to discuss disappearances. Although the conversation seemed to move from one thing to another, Kristi connected the series of events in her play project. In her discussion of the event, she pointed to several aspects of Harry's "world" that were worthy of exploration: magic, age connotations, his relationship with his grandmother, and his visits to California. Kristi learned to ask more informed questions that emerged from Harry's ongoing conversations.

The "age" issue was an ongoing discussion between many children in Kristi's classroom—some used age to assert their authority over others while others used it as a reference point that allowed them certain privileges. In addition, geography and maps were discussed in her classroom, especially since many children had traveled during the break to see their families in different parts of the country. Because of this, the class had numerous discussions about where families lived, marking on a classroom map where these places were. In that sense, the topics for these conversations aligned with the content of conversations and learning inside the classroom. Harry and Tiffany used these concepts to theorize about life as adults, abilities that (according to their worldview) were not within their grasp yet.

Megan described an interaction between her case study child, Andrew, and his friend Jasmine. The conversation took place right after Valentine's Day.

> When asked whose baby was sleeping on the table, Jasmine said, "This is our baby Butterscotch. We're her mom and dad." She goes on to say they got married and asks Andrew, "When did we get married?"
>
>> "We got married 24 years ago," Andrew stated.
>> Jasmine turns to Andrew and asks, "When did we fall in love in April?"
>> "We fell in love in April . . . 24th."
>> Jasmine proceeds to say, "He got lost . . ." She turns to Andrew and whispers, "Where did you get lost?"
>> "In the forest. We got married there."

Megan described the exchange as that of a married couple. The two were enacting a typical male/female relationship—marriage, anniversaries, wedding ceremonies (in this case, the forest). The children also demonstrated sophisticated dialogue patterns associated with the cultural enterprise of marriage—they were able to improvise their play and sustain the conversational exchange.

Liv also described a wedding ceremony that took place in her classroom as well. Liv had created a "flower shop" because of her case study child's vast experience with gardening. Shari (the child) took a group of pink flowers from a vase and began the following exchange taken from Liv's fieldnotes.

Shari: I'm gonna hold these.
Me: Okay.
Shari: We can take these to our wedding. It's our wedding, Liv!
Me: It is! (Shari is nodding yes.)
Me: So who's getting married?

Shari: Um, you and me. (Shari points her bunch of flowers to herself and then to me.)

Me: We are!

Shari: Yeah.

Me: Who's going to come to our wedding?

Shari: Um nobody. We're just gonna dance.

Me: Really, we're gonna dance? Okay!

Shari: Come on, you need to come dance with me. (Shari is taking my hand and directing me over to an open area. Shari puts the bunch of flowers in the air.)

Me: Are those for me?

Shari: No I'm gonna hold them and you need to put your phone down. (I was videotaping all of this.)

Me: Haha, okay. (I place the phone on a surface so it can continue to record us while we dance.)

Me: Can I twirl you?

Shari: Yeah.

Similarly to Megan's example, Shari was able to carry the conversation and used materials and resources around her to enact the play. She demonstrated sophisticated ideas related to marriage and knew common traditions—dancing, carrying a bouquet, and partnering up with another person. In fact, several of the PSTs documented play scenes that centered around marriages, household chores, husbands/wives, and taking care of children. Thus, children were using play as a way of expression. More specifically, they interpreted common social practices using materials, dialogue, role-taking, and scene arrangements. Children used play as a way to express their beliefs and understandings about the world around them. They created their own world, drawing from the larger cultural landscape. As children play out these scenes, they take up scenes from their own lives but they also take up scenes from popular culture as well. Therefore, in the space of play, children are making sense of multiple worlds.

Noticeably absent from the preservice teachers' analysis is a discussion on gendered roles. Megan presented the marriage scene with fondness and intrigue, as is always the case when adults witness young children acting out romantic love in innocent ways. The cross-gender friendship between Jasmine and Andrew ultimately turns into a love affair and marriage—a traditional gender marker for heterosexual males and females. But is this always the case in cross-gendered friendships? Do they all end in romantic love, and do children (especially these two children) see boy/girl friendships as such? While the level of sophistication in conversation and content was visible, there were underlying social norms related to gender that fell under the radar within Megan's observation and analysis. As Templeton (2013) reminds us, ". . . an unexamined child-centered philosophy can actually serve to perpetuate the status quo" (p.186). Similarly, Liv does not mention

Shari's willingness to play outside of the gender box in her wedding ceremony. Both PSTs (although extremely committed to respecting children's voice) failed to question or counter the normalized social constructs children played out, specifically in terms of gender.

Play as Language Expression

At times, child-guided activity is reserved for preschool settings where children's play is deemed acceptable, often seen as a "childish" exercise with no explicit, intellectual value. The highly structured environment of Christine's kindergarten classroom left little room for the interactions that she witnessed and participated in as a preschool teacher. Comparing the two experiences, Christine underscored the intellectual potential of children at her preschool placement where, she argued, children seemed to be "more advanced academically" than her kindergartners while "making more growth." She illustrated this notion further through her fieldnotes:

> Lulu was playing with the cash register. She asked the teacher which menu item the teacher would like. The teacher pointed to the hot dog on the menu. Lulu then pointed to each coin on the menu next to the hot dog and counted that it was worth three coins. She told the teacher, "Okay, that will be three." Lulu opened the cash register, counted three coins, and handed them to the teacher. She then asked the teacher to pay her for the food and yelled to another girl in the kitchen near the oven to start making a hot dog. The other girl began to cook while Lulu took the money and put it back in the cash register. She then took the notepad, scribbled on it, and gave the teacher the piece of paper. Lulu told the teacher what it said what she had ordered. The food was ready soon after and the two girls gave the teacher the hot dog, saying the restaurant was now closed.
>
> (Christine, field note)

As Christine analyzed her data, she mentioned that children constantly reappropriated the setting and materials at this center. They had different ideas regarding the type of restaurant, such as a diner or an ice cream shop. Children took on different roles and managed the materials differently depending on these roles. Christine also valued the emergent literacy behaviors of children scribbling on the notepad and taking orders. She noted, "literacy props (notepad and pencil) were easily incorporated and did not seem out of place in the center." As a result, she saw potential in placing literacy props at centers for children to use at their own discretion. In her reflection, she thought bringing in menus from popular restaurants across town would further literacy opportunities as children would recognize logos and print. Christine understood that literacy was not gained by drills, but understood through embedded practices within authentic contexts. The idea of bringing in "menus" was a teacher-initiated idea that worked to extend children's existing literacy practices and offer them another literacy concept— environmental print. Annabel also saw reappropriation of materials, roles, and emergent literacy behaviors.

> This is also an idea that was reinforced from my field notes that students can have very different interactions with the materials but still have a meaningful experience at the center. James and Jane worked together to be the architect and draw out their plans and then they also created their structure from their plans. Wendell, Javan, and Hanson took on more defined roles in the center and Wendell was the architect and drew a plan and Javan and Hanson were his construction workers and were in charge of making his plan in blocks.
>
> (play center reflection)

Liv created a flower shop center, based on her case study's interest in gardening. Similar to Christine, she saw their pre-writing behaviors as an important language milestone. Furthermore, she did not dismiss the writing as "scribbles" but a language opportunity rooted in purpose.

> The children were clearly using language that they have heard, reenacting situations that they have seen, and creating new memories while also developing during the play in this center. The children were "writing" on the order forms and while the children are still young and cannot write, they were practicing with a piece of paper and a pen. This is all practice for when they actually do formal writing.
>
> (Liv, play project reflection)

The excerpts above reveal several important connections between play and children's learning of academic skills. First, the children naturally incorporated academic skills within their play when it was appropriate for that situation. Lulu operated the cash register, set a price for the food, counted out the exact number of coins, and handed them to her teacher. In the natural course of play, children drew on their language, literacy, and numeracy skills in order to accomplish social ends. Second, the children displayed communicative competence across multiple settings. Lulu knew how to be a cashier at a diner, appropriating the relationship between a cashier and a short-order cook using language as a tool. Instead of speaking to her friend as if in a fancy restaurant, she yelled at her friend to "start making a hot dog." Lulu demonstrated a clear conception of conversational patterns/discourse, voice inflections and registers, and social cues necessary to sustain her play. Third, the children started to experiment with pre-writing behaviors. Lulu scribbled on the notepad (mimicking writing) and articulated to the teacher what the piece of paper said. She understood that the "words" on a page needed to stand for something, and those words were written for the customer. Similarly, Annabel's students drew architectural plans to communicate to construction workers how to build structures as envisioned by the designer. In both cases, messages were written and delivered for mutual understanding, a concept that sets an authentic purpose for writing. Therefore, play served as a natural space for emergent literacy.

The Role of the Teacher

> After setting up the area, I thought about what might happen. Will Andrew engage with others or play solo? Will he make connections between the words and the drawings on the map? How might he surprise me when interacting with the materials?
>
> (Megan, field note)

This chapter highlighted PSTs' use of inquiry to understand children's practices. More importantly, the observations place importance on teachers as inquirers who start with meaningful questions, watch children closely to come up with answers, and ask new questions based on what they see. Questions like the ones Megan used to approach her observations help teachers design curricular opportunities, and more importantly, revise their approaches based on children's needs. Consequently, I argue that curriculum does not emerge from happenstance, but through systematic efforts to enter children's worlds. Additionally, "field notes and anecdotal notes are proof of the immense amount of learning that this [play] helped to facilitate" (Lana, play reflection). Lana went on to voice her enthusiasm over her new learning: "I was ecstatic to observe all of the developmental growth that was happening at this center. It was reassuring to witness all of this growth because many people view play centers as just that—'play'." While taking on a new role as a teacher (mostly a participant observer) was different from how they initially perceived a teacher's role, many of the PSTs recognized the value of being a witness to children's growth and development during play.

However, the teacher has a responsibility to work toward social justice and equity, even with young children who (as demonstrated by the excerpts) have already developed ideologies and stances toward dominant ways of thinking. While PSTs engaged in thorough, observation-based research, only one of them took on an inquiry about social issues regarding stereotypical gender roles. Furthermore, while several of the PSTs recorded play events where children positioned for power, or marginalized others based on race/ethnicity, or created gender binaries, none of the PSTs chose to broach this as a possible exploration with children during play. Several of the teachers intervened in order to mediate conflicts, but none of the PSTs documented intervening to discuss with children social justice issues. Therefore, while it may be agreed upon that children can think critically and deeply about the world, the PSTs in this study failed to actively take on a social justice stance in their observations, analysis, and enactment of play opportunities. Without a specific attention to the socially reproductive ways that children "innocently" play out stereotypical behavior (e.g., gender, race, class, disability), it is likely that these important social issues are pushed to the margins.

Reframing the ways that PSTs view data, then, is a clear step toward refining the definition of teacher researchers. While true inquiry requires sophisticated questions and detailed methods, the most important part of analyzing fieldnotes (arguably) is the theoretical frame and lens with which teachers approach their data. As Megan noted earlier, many PSTs come to sociocultural teacher education programs with a set of privileged experiences rooted in status—racial identities, class status, and/or their gendered behavior. Thus, the issues faced by marginalized populations appear invisible to a mostly white, middle class, female population. Part of the work, then, involves uncovering PSTs' own ideologies and offering a different narrative on the experiences of others. Additionally, social constructs (e.g., gender, race, ethnicity, class, difference) should be the focal point in analyzing children's play. Thus, teachers can create curriculum that not only exposes children to meaningful content, but equips them with dispositions toward social justice. For our youngest children, my hope is that we foster learning opportunities that are about "encouraging empathy, thinking outside the box, coming up with creative solutions, and taking action in the school and community" (Wade, 2007, p. 2).

Bibliography

Ayers, W. (1989). *The good preschool teacher: Six teachers reflect on their lives.* New York: Teachers College Press.

Chudacoff, H. (2008). *Children at play: An American history.* New York: NYU Press.

Corsaro, W. (2003). *We're friends, right? Inside kids' culture.* Washington, DC: Joseph Henry Press.

Dahlberg, G., Moss, P., & Pence, A. (2007). *Beyond quality in early childhood education and care: Languages of evaluation.* New York: Routledge.

Dyson, A. H. (1997). *Writing superheroes: Contemporary childhood, popular culture, and classroom literacy.* New York: Teachers College Press.

Feuyo, V., & Koorland, M. A. (1997). Teacher as researcher: A synonym for professionalism. *Journal of Teacher Education, 48*(5), 336–344.

Freire, P. (1970). *Pedagogy of the oppressed.* New York: Continuum International Publishing Group.

Genishi, C., & Dyson, A. H. (2005). *On the case: Approaches to language and literacy research.* New York: Teachers College Record.

Giroux, H. (2010). Teachers as transformative intellectuals. In K. Cooper & J. M. Ryan (Eds.), *Kaleidoscope: Contemporary and classic readings in education* (12th ed., pp. 35–40). Belmont, CA: Wadsworth.

Giroux, H., & Simon, R. (1988). Schooling, popular culture, and a pedagogy of possibility. *Journal of Education, 170*(1), 9–26.

Gonazales, N., Moll, L., & Amanti, C. (2005). *Funds of knowledge: Theorizing practices in households, communities, and classrooms.* New York: Routledge.

Gore, J. M., & Zeichner, K. M. (1991). Action research and reflective teaching in preservice teacher education: A case study from the United States. *Teaching and Teacher Education,* 7(2), 119–136.

Graue, E. (2006). The answer is readiness—now what is the question? *Early Education and Development,* 17(1), 43–56.

Holland, D., Lachiotte, W., Skinner, D., & Cain, C. (2003). *Identity and agency in cultural worlds.* Cambridge, MA: Harvard University Press.

Kilderry, A. (2004). Critical pedagogy: A useful framework for thinking about early childhood curriculum. *Australian Journal of Early Childhood,* 29(4), 33–37.

Langford, R. (2010). Critiquing child-centred pedagogy to bring children and early childhood educators into the centre of a democratic pedagogy. *Contemporary Issues in Early Childhood,* 11(1), 113–127.

Lave, J., & Wenger, E. (1991). *Situated learning: Legitimate peripheral participation.* New York: Cambridge University Press.

Moll, L., Amanti, C., Neff, D., & Gonzales, N. (1992). Funds of knowledge for teaching: Using a qualitative approach to connect homes and classrooms. *Theory into Practice,* 31(2), 132–141.

Omi, M., & Winant, H. (2008). Once more, with feeling: Reflections on racial formation. *PMLA,* 123(5), 1565–1572.

Paley, V. (2004). *A child's work: The importance of fantasy play.* Chicago, IL: The University of Chicago Press.

Paley, V. (2007). HER classic: On listening to what children say. *Harvard Educational Review,* 77(2), 152–163.

Pollock, M. (2004). Race wrestling: Struggling strategically with race in educational practice and research. *American Journal of Education,* 111(1), 25–67.

Ryan, S., & Grieshaber, S. (2005). Shifting from developmental to postmodern practices in early childhood teacher education. *Journal of Teacher Education,* 56(1), 34–45.

Sleeter, C. (2001). Preparing teachers for culturally diverse schools: Research and the overwhelming presence of whiteness. *Journal of Teacher Education,* 52(2), 94–106.

Sleeter, C. (2008). Equity, democracy, and neoliberal assaults on teacher education. *Teaching and Teacher Education,* 24, 1947–1956.

Templeton, T. (2013). Young children as forces of nature: Critical perspectives in a preschool classroom. *Childhood Education,* 89(3), 185–187.

Wade, R. C. (2007). *Social studies for social justice: Teaching strategies for the elementary classroom.* New York: Teachers College Press.

9   Stories that Travel: Preservice Teachers Using Photography to Understand Children's Funds of Knowledge in Literacy Learning

Eliza Desirée Butler, Nayalin Pinho Feller, and Ana Christina daSilva Iddings

"In predominant school practices, the knowledge that is constructed outside of the school walls is often viewed as irrelevant, and therefore, may be ignored as teachers proceed to teach passive students" (Macedo, 2006). Within the current push for prescribed curricula in the U.S. schools, the child's voice is lessened. This push denies the recognition of children's agency and of their abilities as social actors in and out of school. As Giroux (1988) projected:

> Traditional curriculum represents a firm commitment to a view of rationality that is ahistorical, consensus-oriented, and politically conservative. It supports a passive view of students and appears incapable of examining the ideological presuppositions that tie it to a narrow operational mode of reasoning.
>
> (p. 15)

This restrictive type of curriculum fails to acknowledge diversity by marginalizing the knowledge and experiences of children and their families in relation to academic content (Freire, 1970). In contrast to the passive positioning of students, this study focuses on an approach to early childhood teacher education that places the child's familial experience in the home at the center of curriculum and instruction. This approach is inspired by Vygotsky's sociocultural theory (1978), by Freirian critical pedagogical approaches (1970; 1987), and by the concept of funds of knowledge (González, Moll, & Amanti, 2005), which are articulated throughout the design of the two-year Early Childhood Teacher Education program. Through the program coursework, preservice teachers are continuously introduced to opportunities in which building relationships with children, families, and communities is prioritized. Simultaneously, they are encouraged to think critically about their personal pedagogical positionalities (Lave & Wenger, 2002) as well as their own ideologies and actions toward the education of linguistically and culturally diverse students (Souto-Manning, 2013).

As our focus was to observe how the preservice teachers bridged in and out of school knowledge for children, we used photography as a mediational tool (Vygotsky, 1978) between preservice teachers and their students in the process of teaching and learning about emergent and multimodal literacy practices (Kenner, 2004). Six preservice teachers were observed for one academic semester while enrolled in a course titled *Literacy for Young Children*. An integral part of the course design emphasized collaboration with families. Each preservice teacher was matched with a voluntary case-study family with whom they conducted their home engagements throughout the 2-year program. Pivotal characteristics of the course design included a personal literacy memoir, 3 home engagements, guided reflections, and the construction of a co-authored guided reading book inspired by classroom observations, photographs taken by the case study child, and informal interviews with the child and their family. Through this process, preservice teachers engaged in praxis (Freire, 1970), as they applied the theory they learned in the university courses to their practice with the children at home/school, and last as they reflected on the teaching strategies/pedagogies they employed. These were our research questions:

> How do preservice teachers can gain insights into ways to provide a bridge between in and out of school learning by observing how children make sense of, think about, and speak back to their worlds?
>
> In what ways do preservice teachers explore and interrogate their assumptions about cultural and linguistic diversity and attempt to create a space for children's agency and identity within the classroom curriculum?

The use of children's photography and the co-construction of stories as a base for teaching emergent readers (Rowe, 2010) allows for families and children to record their experiences in textual form. In militarized border states, (e.g., Arizona) in which language is policed and testing is directly correlated to funding, much of the culminating stress can fall on families. Thus, the nurturing of trusting relationships can be a potential source of inspiration and hope (Freire, 1994) in identifying schooling as a community resource. Schools can be spaces in which children of migrant families have access to educational rights paralleling children born within the U.S. (*Plyler vs. Doe, 1982*).

Our goal is for preservice teachers to become aware of the importance of families' lived experiences and knowledge of community and daily practices (Reyes, daSilva Iddings, & Feller, 2015), as well as the power teachers hold to contribute to positive associations between schooling and the meaningful development of children's creative energy and literacy practices. This gradual transformation requires preservice teachers to consider their personal privilege, their own schooling experiences, and their assumptions of teaching (Souto-Manning, 2013). The process of self-reflection and continuous engagement with their school placement, community, and case-study family provides a space for continuous feedback from and through family members, peers, and course assignments and in-class workshops. This approach positions literacy as a social practice (Freire, 1970; Rowe, 1994; Vygotsky, 1978), which will be further elaborated through the overview of our conceptual framework. In this chapter, we first describe our conceptual framework, then walk the reader through the process we went through as we analyzed the data and the stories we heard from the preservice teachers, weaving in our discussion on the preservice teachers' perceptions of emergent literacies.

Conceptual Framework

In order to gain a broader understanding of the underpinnings of this study, we must first examine the extant literature involving central topics in this research design. Theoretically, this study emphasizes a Vygotskian (1978) perspective of teaching and learning as well as critical literacy practices (Freire, 1970; 1987), funds of knowledge (González et al., 2005), and the role of literacy in transformational pedagogy (Souto-Manning, 2013), as demonstrated in Figure 9.1.

Through the cohort model, the preservice teachers enrolled in the Early Childhood Education program were able to be in continuous dialogue with their peers, and future colleagues, instilling a sense of community within the university setting. This structure supported relationship building and group reflection, especially during their student teaching placements in which there was a physical distancing from the university campus as they began to engage in the larger school communities and the navigation of the complex dynamics and systems of public schools. Therefore, the type of engagement reinforced in this structural model hinges on the preservice teacher's participation and relationships based on trust over time.

The importance of emergent literacy practices has been long explored by authors in the field (daSilva-Iddings, 2009; Freire, 1970; González et al., 2005; Kenner, 2004; Reyes, 2006; Vygotsky, 1978). The sociocultural context in which these practices happen in Arizona are critical to this study as well as the overall relevance to the children and families with whom our preservice teachers work. Curricular choices and English-only language policies have a tremendous social and emotional impact on children who do not see themselves as belonging to the dominant narrative of whiteness (Lipsitz, 1995).

The Arizona Context

Arizona's anti-immigrant policies have perpetuated racial and linguistic profiling, which contributes to a constant state of insecurity for migrant families. This political rhetoric does not stop when children come to school.

Phase 1: Observations and Sharing of
Personal Literacy Memoire, Intro to Child's
Camera

Phase 2: Analysis of Child's Photos
with Child at Home during 2nd home
engagement

Phase 3: Share Child-Authored Photo
book during 3rd Home Engagement

Phase 4: Self Assessment and
Reflection of Emergent Literacy
Instruction

Approaches to the teaching of English include the subtractive model of bilingualism (Garcia, 2009), in which young children's home language and cultural symbols are replaced with English and "American" cultural symbols.
Through these models of curricula, children of immigrant descent encounter few opportunities to use their funds of knowledge in the classrooms as
the English-only policy Proposition 203 and the SB1070 law continuously
deprive them from sharing their rich linguistic and cultural knowledge in

regard to their academic development (Wright, 2005). These policies and the larger national context of racialized geographies and policing of language attribute to the silencing of children and families who do not speak the state-mandated language, English, as Proposition 203 denies migrant families their right to bilingual education and SB1070 constantly pushes these families into places of fear.

This type of rhetoric also affects the preservice teachers with whom we work, many who are not of Hispanic descent and who have expressed fear of visiting family homes, considering them "dangerous." Education is political (Giroux, 1988), as well as literacy, and in order for this work to be understood comprehensively, we must acknowledge the volatile environments that immigrants face within the American Southwest. Even though immigrant children have access to free public education (*Plyer v. Doe*, 1982), families must navigate safety and access as part of their daily experiences. Thus, the development of *confianza*/trust is a crucial part of our instructional design as preservice teachers learn about the "teaching" of literacy.

In turn, it is important that preservice teachers think critically about literacy practices (Reyes et al., 2015; Souto-Manning, 2013), and that they examine deeply rooted emotional perceptions of the role of the teacher as well as their own ideologies related to language and nationality.

In providing opportunities in our coursework for preservice teachers to think critically about their own positionalities with respect to issues of language, literacy, race, and culture, we aim to disrupt the dominant narrative influenced by "the culture of poverty" discourse (Crenshaw, 1988; Ladson-Billings, 2006; Lewis, 1966). Importantly, among these opportunities were the family home engagements, where preservice teachers visited the homes of volunteering families on a consistent basis at least 3 times during the semester. As a result, the relationship between family members, students, and their classroom teachers strengthened and the preservice teachers were ever more able to create meaningful experiences within the classroom that were connected to the child's lived experiences, or funds of knowledge.

Notably, the family engagement was not meant as a form of intervention. Instead it was designed as an invitation to participate in a dialogue with families outside of school. The aim of family home interactions was to shift preservice teachers away from crippling deficit-oriented perspectives of migrant children and families, to one of reciprocity as well as a resource for curriculum development. Home engagements became the center of curriculum development through our Early Literacy course as preservice teachers utilized photography to mediate their understanding of literacy identified as children's funds of knowledge.

Using Photography as a Pedagogical Tool

We, the instructors of *Literacy for the Young Child's* course, incorporated the use of photography as a pedagogical tool for preservice teachers to participate in ethnographic-like case studies with children and families (see also Barker & Smith, 2012; Pyle, 2012; Schiller & Tillett, 2004). A core tenant of this assignment was for each preservice teacher to support the children in communicating their meaning-making process as they used photography to tell their stories. "Successful use of photography requires mediation and interpretation (Myers, 2010; Newman, Woodcock, & Dunham, 2006) and the photographers' initial intent and meanings must be recovered and communicated" (as cited in Barker & Smith, 2012, p. 97). Through conversation with the child, the preservice teacher took fieldnotes on what the child described about the subject of the photo and the photo-taking process. This dialogue served as the base for the creation of a guided reading book in which 20 of the child's photos were used as the illustrations of the book content and the text was composed by the child. In those ways, the book connected the child's lived experiences with the written word (Macedo & Freire, 1987), which reflected the "voice" of the child.

Children's stories and photographs were interpreted as sources of literacy and embraced as multimodal representation of knowledge during the study of emergent literacy. Rowe (2003; 2008; 2009; 2010) has explored in depth what emergent literacy means for young children. She continues to question *what literacy means as a social practice* (Rowe, 2010). She uses examples from her studies of preschoolers' early writing interactions to illustrate her expanding perspective of early literacy learning as well as her use of photography within classrooms and the authoring of books by young children. As Rowe, in our instructional design we require students to rethink literacy from a traditional perspective to more than just reading and writing, as their lived experiences and that of their case-study children directly influence what literacy might look like. Using this ample perspective in turn acknowledges the funds of knowledge that children and their families already possess, and facilitates the learning process for the children with whom they work.

Methodology

The following sources were used as data for this research. We observed a total of 6 preservice teachers in their final year of their undergraduate degree, who were purposefully chosen based on their background and their willingness to participate. We analyzed the following data sources: the personal literacy memoirs, the child-authored guided reading book, the 3 home engagement reflections, and the end-of-year interviews with the preservice teachers from year 1 and 2. Figure 9.2 highlights the instructional design we employed during our study:

For our analysis we were particularly interested in the ways in which preservice teachers were able to articulate the significance and take action to bridge literacy practices happening at the home and at school through their use of the children's co-authored guided reading books. Simultaneously, we focused on the ways in which preservice teachers did or did not interrogate

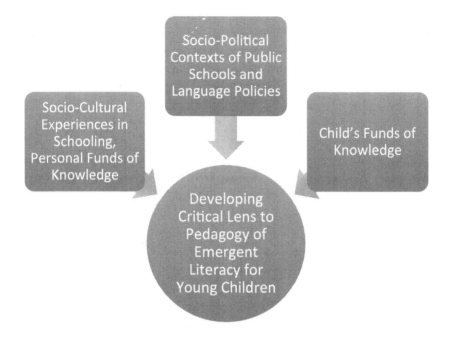

their assumptions of culturally and linguistically diverse populations with whom they were working.

In order to analyze the data, we employed a cross-comparative analysis. Once each student's data was outlined and coded according to each research question (first phase of analysis), we continued the second phase of our analysis by looking across each preservice teacher's cumulative data (personal literacy memoir, 3 home engagements and reflections, guided reading book, and end-of-year 1 and 2 interviews). Through this multiphase analysis, we were able to look at the overall behaviors and perspectives of preservice teachers within our program instead of only mapping each preservice teacher's learning process over the course of the semester. The next section will explain in more detail how we understood larger narratives through the analysis of the cumulative comparisons.

Findings

The first phase of analysis informed our understanding of the preservice teacher's processes and developing relationships to curriculum, their case-study child, and application of theory. The second phase of analysis is a cross comparison of the analysis of each preservice teacher's cumulative data, which in turn guided our research findings away from the individual to their shared experiences within our program in order to gain insight into the role of the photobook as an instructional tool on their developing teaching pedagogies. It is important to acknowledge the role of the first phase of analysis in informing our second phase of analysis. What is critical about this is that we were able to identify that each preservice teacher is unique in their learning stories, but for the purpose of this research, we are informed by the intersections of those stories. The following section describes in detail the major findings from our data categorized by emergent themes. These themes became clearer as we analyzed the preservice teachers' stories and perceptions of emergent literacy. The next section explores in depth each one of the emergent themes.

Preservice Teacher's Literacy Memoirs

The analysis of the personal literacy memoir assignment was used as a base for gaining an understanding of developing perceptions of literacy and the comprehension of the concept of funds of knowledge. Although this is a core phase of the instructional design, this assignment stood out as being significant because of the richness of data gathered about the preservice teachers' personal stories. Before asking preservice teachers to identify the funds of knowledge and the literacy practices of their case-study child, they were asked to focus on their own perceptions and values regarding language, literacy, and culture in particular. The practice of personalizing literacy is a key element to the instructional design in which preservice teachers engage in their own histories before the "teaching" of their students. This practice is supported by multiple ongoing opportunities to engage with theoretical understandings of funds of knowledge through several of their required college courses, which acted as scaffolding of the development of critical literacy practices for emergent literacy teachers.

The content of each literacy memoir was chosen by each preservice teacher. They understood that they were creating a book about themselves for the case-study child with whom they were working. Overarching common themes found throughout the memoirs included description of family structure, family labor histories, travel experiences, and the inclusion of the motivation for becoming teachers. Sometimes the books also included questions to the reader as a way to provoke conversation with the case-study child. Through this assignment, students actively engaged in identifying their personal uses of literacy. They shared their perceptions of traditional literacy within their lives, often connecting to their emotional attachment to American popular culture, including Disney stories and movies.

Not only did they stress the role of traditional texts in their lives, but they also included broader definitions of literacy within their memories—for example, the role of dance or nature as modes of literacy. One preservice teacher, Jennifer, positioned dance juxtaposed to reading, while another preservice teacher, Sarah, asked what nature can teach coupled with photos from hiking. Many of the preservice teachers included their travel for vacations with their families, which indicates access to mobility and a certain amount of privilege socioeconomically. Another preservice teacher reflected on how traveling acts as a source of literacy. Kylie wrote, "When I traveled I was forced to communicate with people who spoke a different language than me. I learned new languages and new ways to communicate with others" (Personal Literacy Memoir). This is an example of how the preservice teachers acquire and think of language. Angelica, who grew up in Mexico and had moved to the U.S. as a young adult, intentionally choose to create a bilingual book in an attempt to nurture a connection with her case-study child. She included photos from her childhood in which she would play "fieldworker" with her sister. She identified dramatic play as a demonstration of literacy. The analysis of the personal literacy memoirs indicated a strong connection to childhood experiences as influential in defining literacy as well as a deeply rooted emotional connection to literacy events. However, overall, the interpretation of the concept of funds of knowledge within their own lives was superficial in that they included photos of their families, what they read when they were children, and leisure activities such as traveling without an in-depth explanation of what it meant to them. As for broadening the definition of literacy, several of the students included other modes (i.e., dance, nature) as part of their meaning-making processes.

Preservice Teacher and Child: Co-Construction of Curriculum Rooted in Children's Fund of Knowledge

Once completing the personal literacy memoir and sharing their stories in the homes of their case-study children, preservice teachers then continued with the next step of the instructional design, sharing cameras with children and asking the children about what they value within their homes and relationships. The cameras were child friendly and left with the child for more than a week. Preservice teachers were able to prepare for family engagements through course workshops in which early literacy theory and methods were explained and discussed as well as the use of role play in preparation for family visits. They developed a critical lens to the observations they were making within their course placements and adjusted their own teaching philosophies as they actively engaged in the process of co-constructing the guided reading book with children's photography. Jessica discussed her understanding of how to apply funds of knowledge in the classroom within her instructional design reflection. She wrote,

> The books used for her reading lessons in class usually are pretty generic that really have nothing to do with anything she has done before, i.e. they are out of context. But by putting the reading into context I was seeing her use much more strategies to read the pages than she had before. Our reading lessons in school are really geared toward letter sounds and sounding out words, but when reading our book I saw her

repeating sentences for repeated meaning, and using the pictures to understand the text.

(Jessica, Reflection Home Engagement 3)

In this reflection, Jessica identified the curricular potential for the application of funds of knowledge in the teaching of reading. She described how the teaching approach observed within her placement classroom is less effective due to the lack of connection between the child's spontaneous knowledge and scientific knowledge (Vygotsky, 1978), or knowledge taught in schools. The emphasis on the decoding of the alphabet in a decontextualized framework is not an uncommon form of literacy instruction for ELs enrolled in public schools in Arizona, as language ideologies greatly influence the learning environments, pressuring these students to perform in English.

Not only did preservice teachers develop their critical lens of curriculum practices employed within their school placements (where subtractive bilingualism is often practiced as part of the state regulations of language use within public schooling), but they were also able to articulate the significance of applying funds of knowledge within the creation of child-authored guided reading books as a pedagogical support to their students. Kylie explained,

The photobook was [*supportive for reading development*] because at the time when I designed it, the teaching points in the book were appropriate for Pedro because they were the constant stretches that I saw him combat as he read to me every single time. It was also a good support with the use of the pictures that he took with the camera. In the reading program that my placement uses, it uses a lot of shared stories that have characters that I know Pedro can't relate to, therefore there is no way that any interest can be generated towards reading.

(Kylie, Self-Assessment of Emergent Literacy Instruction)

Kylie was able to apply her in-class observations about language and literacy development specifically to the case study child's classroom experiences. She also highlighted the importance of connecting children's experiences with the texts they are learning to read, grounding the child's emergent reading and writing in contexts that place value on the child's life experiences.

Reflections and Perceptions of Teaching: Co-authored Guided Reading Book

Another emergent theme highlighted through the data was the ongoing reflection of the perception of the role of the teacher in teaching students from linguistically and culturally diverse backgrounds. Ana examined her personal language ideologies and attempted to develop a relationship with her case study child's family through employing her own emergent bilingualism developed throughout her schooling experiences. In her second home engagement reflection, she explained her attempt to relate to the feelings that emergent bilinguals may experience as they communicate in more than one language. She explained,

> I was able to connect to this right away taking Spanish courses in college. As you move up in courses, you can only respond in Spanish and I would have so many ideas but was unable to voice them the way I wanted to. So, I wanted to let her know that she can always talk to me in Spanish and in English. This phase let me see that mom preferred reading her the book that was in Spanish, and just showed me that they are most comfortable in using this language.
>
> (Ana, Self-Assessment of Emergent Literacy Instruction)

Ana continued by describing how she engaged with her case study child's family in discussing the child's use of the camera to document her interests and home life experiences. Ana discovered through multiple visits to the home that the mother of the child had little formal education and ability to read in English or Spanish, as she stressed that,

> I learned that the mom is unable to read in Spanish or English; this reiterated the fact that I knew this family has some really wonderful oral stories to be told. While she may not be able to read, she takes her daughter to church and she hears and sees language being used there in addition to the skills she is learning in the classroom.
>
> (Ana, Self-Assessment of Emergent Literacy Instruction)

Initially Ana believed that the use of Spanish within the home was a constraint that impeded the family from communicating with school, but with her home engagements she learned that the constraint was not language use (L1 or L2) but instead the lack of communication between the school and the family due to the text-based communication used by the school coupled with the lack of access to formal literacy instruction by the mother. Ultimately, this was a pivotal phase in the realization of Ana's agency as a new teacher. In her last reflection, she moved onto validating the family's literacy practices existing within the home through the process of sharing the guided reading book. She stressed that,

> This is why she really values her children learning how to read and write in both languages. She told me how happy she was when Sarai brought home the guided reading book we created and read the entire book to her. I thought about what an impact this must have had on her, to see her daughter reading and knowing that she's helped create this wonderful learning environment for her daughter.
>
> (Ana, Reflection Home Engagement 3)

She adjusted her teaching approach to one of advocacy in which she repositioned literacy being expressed through multiple modes. She explained how the use of the camera became a bridge for communication and relationship building as well as a foundation for creating a book designed on the child's developing literacy practices. In her second home engagement reflection Ana wrote,

> I was not surprised that Sarai enjoyed using the camera the most, because I knew from my prior home visit that personal stories are the most dominant form of literacy for this family. I think this is a great medium for her to share her life with me and with others in general because she does not often strike up conversations without prompting, and the pictures allowed her to remember things she had done in the prior weeks and share those with me.
>
> (Ana, Reflection Home Engagement 2)

She continued by identifying the role of the case-study child in the data collection process, in which the preservice teacher took on the role of advocate as the child shared her perceptions and lived experiences. Once Ana was able to build a trusting relationship with the mother of her case study child, she then began to adjust her teaching approaches in which she began to think critically about the methods of communication between school and the home as well as the ways in which traditional literacy is valued. She expressed her hopes for co-authoring a guided reading book utilizing the child's multiple literacy modes.

After initial skepticism about family home engagements, Ana expressed the value they gave to connecting in and out of school knowledge. She moved away from her original idea in developing the guided reading book focusing on sight words and decoding to one that included the child's experiences and words as an attempt create an emotional bond demonstrating an acknowledgment of the child's funds of knowledge and life experiences while focusing on extending the child's emergent literacy awareness (whole language, the complementing role of illustrations and text).

Personal History Intersections with Pedagogy: Angelica's Story

Angelica grew up in Mexico and moved to the U.S. as a young adult. Throughout her coursework she expressed the connections she was making through the course content to her lived experiences of having a transnational identity. Within the university classroom, she often took on the role of a leader in which she placed her bilingualism as an asset in relation to her developing teaching pedagogy. In Figure 9.3, she describes her developing teaching pedagogy in relationship to her childhood and her cultural value system.

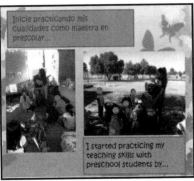

reading to them and telling them stories about my culture. Like my birthday parties.

Inicie practicando mis cualidades como maestra en preescolar...

leyéndoles y contándoles acerca de mi cultura, así como mis fiestas de cumpleaños.

I started practicing my teaching skills with preschool students by...

In addition, she leveraged her personal history to employ her own agency in the construction of a child-authored guided reading book with the use of photography by intentional inclusion of text in both Spanish and English as well as the inclusion of cultural symbols, such as significant traditions expressed through birthday parties. She was the only student who included text in more than one language, even though all case-study children were identified as emergent bilinguals. She explained, "I guess that, me being bilingual, it's actually a plus, because I'm able to reach more to the families because of that second language" (End of Year Interview 2).

In Figure 9.4, Angelica began to enact her own language practices as a tool for the biliteracy development for her case study child. She emphasized the significance of including Spanish text in response to the acknowledgment of the child's home language and valued the child's voice and expressive modes of early literacy by including the child's photographs of drawings, as well as text representing the child's words in both their L1 (Spanish) and L2 (English).

Mom, dad, myself, baby brother and big brother.

This is a drawing of my family. I did it in the journal Ms. Vanessa gave to me. We live all together in my house.

Este es un dibujo de mi familia. Lo dibuje en la libreta que Ms. Vanessa me dio. Todos vivimos en mi casa.

I cannot wait for my baby brother to grow up. This is a drawing of him as a grown up which I did by myself.

No puedo esperar a que mi hermanito crezca. Este es un dibujo de mi hermanito de grande, el cual hice yo misma.

She was also able to identify that the child engaged in multiple modes through which she developed her diverse literacy practices. This is an example of the deepening of the application and recognition of the concept of funds of knowledge. Angelica took on the role of an ethnographic participant observer as she reflected on her observations of funds of knowledge through the home engagements as she wrote,

> A source of funds of knowledge of my case-study child is about Mexican music, some Mexico cities and beaches, baseball because her brother used to play baseball, and about her religion. She had good knowledge about her family in Mexico in Altar and Hermosillo. Lastly she has 4 clay figures of Virgin de Guadalupe in her room; she knows some things about her religion (Catholic).
>
> (Angelica, Reflection Home Engagement 1)

Clearly, Angelica applied her own bilingual knowledge in her relationship with the family, and as she reported, mainly speaking with the parents in Spanish. In her interview she described her thinking as the following when reflecting on the guiding reading process,

> We talked about the cover of the book. And I asked her if she had taken the photograph from the cover. She said yes and giggled. My standard for the guided reading was relating to retelling a story. I also incorporated a translation in Spanish with the purpose of honoring her home language.
>
> (Angelica, Reflection Home Engagement 3)

She also made mention to the child's bilingual proficiency in her second reflection and how her inclusion and support of emergent bilingualism had an impact of the case study child's emergent literacy practices through the modeling of biliteracy practices in her teaching. She explained,

> The parents told me that Karen has recently been speaking more Spanish than usual. I wonder if I was an influence for her decision of language, since we talked to her during the last visit about the importance of knowing Spanish (or another language). I told her about my experience as a bilingual adult.
>
> (Angelica, Reflection Home Engagement 2)

In this reflection, Angelica communicated the ways in which she began to perceive her own experiences as being resources in her teaching of literacy because she recognized the direct effect of her actions as a preservice teacher in relation to the family with whom she was working. Angelica began to integrate her own funds of knowledge within her teaching identity as she worked alongside her case-study child. Angelica was an exception in our participant pool as she was the only fully bilingual preservice teacher we observed within our program.

Preservice Teacher's Perceptions of Voice and Language Use

Not only did preservice teachers actively begin to reclaim the role of the teacher, we also found from our data that preservice teachers started to identify their own biliteracy skills as tools for advocating and supporting the emergent biliteracy practices of their students, as seen in Ana and Angelica's stories. As the semester progressed, preservice teachers engaged in subversive teaching methodologies by including the child's home language within the child-authored guided reading books. This action is directly related to their own critical literacy development in which they respond to the oppressive language ideologies supported by the state policies and the methods they identify as being the most efficient in teaching young emergent bilinguals. This is particularly significant in relation to the larger sociopolitical context of ethnic studies within Arizona public schools and the anti-immigration rhetoric that supports English monolingualism as a norm as well as a characteristic of national identities. Kylie reflected on her understanding of the child's process saying,

> She is five years old, and learning about two cultures, two languages, and learning all of this challenging curricula, and she's really just amazing. I have watched her come out of her shell more and more each week, as she becomes more comfortable using English. She's learning how to read and sound out letters: it's remarkable, and I am enjoying sharing her accomplishments with her.
> (Kylie, Reflection Home Engagement 3)

Through this exploration of using child-authored books in relation to home engagements, young teachers could think critically about their roles within institutions to engage in teaching pedagogies that nurture all children and their families, and to respect their processes as they develop their voices as well as discover spaces for professional agency. Their relationship is not defined by the classroom walls and the actions of their mentor teacher. Instead they are asked to engage in intimate relationships with children and their families in which the use of photography mediates dialogue between the preservice teacher and the child within the child's home space. "Home engagements have the power to give students a voice that they may not have been aware they possessed, and they tell our students indirectly that we value them and we want to know them on the most personal level possible" (Ana, Reflection Home Engagement 3). A broader definition of literacy was also identified through preservice teachers' reflective practices. Literacy was valued as an integral practice within family homes connecting in and out of school learning. As Jessica wrote,

> She comes from a diverse background and a home full of literacy. One the first home visit I looked at the pictures she took of her family, and in

this home visit I had more of an opportunity to talk to her father about their linguistic and cultural backgrounds.

(Jessica, Reflection Home Engagement 2)

The reciprocity experienced by both students and preservice teachers through dialogue surrounding the use of child photography is an intentional shift away from the banking model (Freire, 1970) and the historically ethnocentric deficit perspective of culturally and linguistically diverse children and families. Jennifer explained,

[I have become] more reflective and responsive. I don't want to say that I was disrespectful before but now I have an even better understanding of what respect really is. How to value what they [families and children] have and know that it is no better or worse than what I have or what I'm doing.

(Jennifer, End of Year Interview 2)

The co-construction of child-guided reading books became a catalyst for preservice teachers to deconstruct their sociopolitical privileges and emotionally rooted language ideologies within the course workshops/ class meetings. The child-guided reading books acted as a tool for reciprocal information sharing in which barriers of class, race, and language use were crossed through the action of creating dialogical tools for relationship building that were ultimately used to support children and preservice teacher's literacy development.

Self-Assessment and Reflective Practices

This process would not have been as effective without the inclusion of ongoing reflective assignments as part of the instructional design. Preservice teachers were asked to write their reflections after each home engagement. These reflective essays became spaces that supported reflective teaching practices. As early childhood teacher educators, we understand that the action of writing is one in which higher order thinking may be realized through connecting inner thought to the material world (Vygotsky, 1978). This process of connecting the inner narratives with the written world parallels what we were asking the preservice teachers to explore through their teaching of emergent literacy. Through these reflections, preservice teachers were able to see themselves in the children with whom they are working while demonstrating a greater sense of equity in and dignity in teaching.

I think the most significant part would be learning how to interact with people that are different from you. You grow up in a certain area and you think you know how to work with people. You meet someone who is from a completely different country, who doesn't speak your language

and it's a whole new experience. Yet, learning how to develop that relationship, because you both have the common goal of working for their
child.

(Sarah, End of Year Interview 2)

Many of the preservice teachers faced challenges throughout the semester
as they grappled with issues related to social inequities as related to the
education of ELs within their local school communities and also with the
overwhelming realization of their own privilege. They initially emphasized
a resistance to the concept of funds of knowledge, often engaging in larger
narratives of discriminatory and racialized teaching methodologies positioning children from linguistically and culturally diverse background as
being a minority or exception within the classroom with whom they could
choose not to teach by looking for schools in different neighborhoods. As
the semester progressed, students were faced with understanding that the
demographics of the United States is forever shifting and that in order to
teach emergent literacy they must engage in a pedagogical approach that
identifies how their own funds of knowledge and sociopolitical positioning
directly influences their teaching and relationships with children and families. Jennifer exclaimed,

Home engagements have the power to influence families' beliefs on
school, we have to remember that not everybody has had positive experiences with the school system and we need to constantly work to show
that our classroom is a safe and learning environment: where the child
is allowed to be a thinker, tinker, an actor, a playmate, a creative individual, and a teacher.

(Jennifer, Reflection Home Engagement 3)

Discussion

The emergent themes from the analysis of preservice teachers' learning processes gives us great insight into the importance of including concepts such as
funds of knowledge (Gonzalez et al., 2005) and emergent literacy (daSilva-
Iddings, 2009; Freire, 1970; González et al., 2005; Kenner, 2004; Reyes,
2006; Vygotsky, 1978) into the curriculum of early childhood teacher education programs. (See Figure 9.5.) The reflective process experienced by preservice teachers throughout the semester-long instructional design provided
access into the sociocultural contexts that preservice teachers navigate daily.
This theme also correlates to preservice teachers' ability to internalize critical literacy practices concerning issues of privilege, race, and socioeconom-
ics (daSilva Iddings, 2009; Gonzalez et al., 2005; Ladson-Billings, 2006).

Furthermore, there was a shift from enduring school into actively seeing oneself in the curriculum (self-preservice teachers and children/families).
Many teachers approach schooling in a way that "tolerates" and "includes"

Intersection of Emergent Themes from the Analysis of Preservice Teachers' Learning Processes

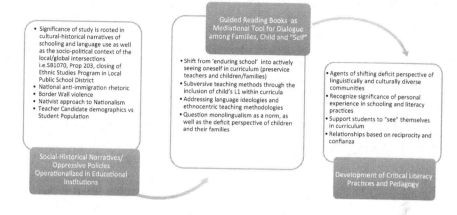

the concept of "diversity," which sadly has ultimately become a synonym for the children who are not of Anglo-American descent or who do not speak English as their first language. This adjustment of curriculum in order to "include" children is not sufficient. It denies the complexities of the history of the United States and the role of the institution of education has played in perpetuating a Nativist stance to nationality, one in which whiteness as normalized. Souto-Manning (2013) presents a "critical and situated" (p. 8) sampling of approaches, each of which "problematize dominant views of learning" (p. 8). Thus, we supported the preservice teachers in developing a critical literacies lens, which sustains the critical examination of emergent literacy practices.

As in Gonzalez et al. (2005), preservice teachers started to shift their view of culture "as loaded with expectations of group norms and often-static ideas of how the people see the world and behave in it" (p. 10) into focusing on practice "what households actually do and how they think about what they do" (p. 10). In this study, Ana, Angelica, Jessica, Jennifer, Sarah, and Kylie start to envision the role of teachers as one of advocacy for children and families in which they bridge in and out of school learning and knowledge, which ultimately contributes to their personal development of critical literacy practices. This is understood as a reflexive process. "Teacher preparation should go beyond the technical preparation of teachers and be rooted in the ethical formation both of selves and of history" (Freire, 1994, p. 23). Through the creation of child-authored guided reading books, preservice teachers were faced with examining their perceptions of literacy, language use, and their role as a teacher based on their previous schooling experiences and their own experiences with privilege. "Literacy spaces are ideologically loaded in ways that both reflect and shape local literacy practices"

(Rowe, 2010, p.140). In these spaces where children are the experts of their own literacy practices, preservice teachers were challenged to move away from a deficit perspective, from the discourse of culture of poverty (Crenshaw, 1988; Ladson-Billings, 2006; Lewis, 1966), into reshaping their views of emergent literacy and language development.

The preservice teachers developed and internalized their ongoing understanding of they own agency as teachers (Freire, 1970; 1994; Macedo & Freire, 1987) through the process of self-reflection and continuous engagement with their school placements, home engagements, and case-study family relationships through ongoing and continuous feedback from the course instructors and school-based mentors. They also explored the intricacies of relationship "confianza" building (Gonzalez et al., 2005) as fundamental to the teaching of early literacy practices they continue to develop their future teaching identities. This approach positioned literacy as a social practice (Freire, 1970; Rowe, 1994; Vygotsky, 1978). Last, preservice teachers engaged in critical literacy practices as they considered the larger sociopolitical contexts of their school communities as well as the significance of spontaneous and scientific knowledge for emergent bilinguals through the mediation of children's photography (Barker & Smith, 2012; Pyle, 2012; Rowe, 2010; Schiller & Tillett, 2004) and stories coupled with family home engagements and course content.

We have learned from this study that although preservice teachers within our courses parallel the national demographics of early childhood students enrolled in teacher education programs (i.e., white, female, middle class, in their early 20s), photography coupled with supporting theoretical and methodological coursework can act as a bridge for preservice teachers to evaluate their personal language ideologies, language use, schooling stories, and socioeconomic affordances and how these variables affect the development of their personal teaching philosophies ultimately influencing their teaching pedagogies. Instead of engaging in curricular and teaching decisions that bank (Freire, 1970) on the children's resiliency as a means for surviving schooling, this approach engages preservice teachers in pedagogical practices that emphasize the family and community as resources and the child's experiences as knowledge (González et al., 2005; Reyes et al., 2015). The relationship between the teacher and the child, in turn, exemplifies the pedagogy of hope (Freire, 1994). The preservice teachers' intersecting stories are a demonstration of literacy as social practice.

A major implication of this study is the reflexive teaching made possible through children's photography, and their authored text served to inform the creation of emergent literacy curricula. Children's photography and the co-authoring of guided reading books mediate dialogue between teachers and students as they transgress sociopolitical barriers through creating humanizing teaching methods. This research implies that teachers can develop critical literacy/ awareness of constraints and privilege within their geopolitical spaces and local communities through multimodal tools for the teaching of emergent literacy. As preservice teachers' learning processes are not static, they are able to transition into active agents as social actors.

Bibliography

Barker, J., & Smith, F. (2012). What's in focus? A critical discussion of photography, children and young people. *International Journal of Social Research Methodology*, 15(2), 92–103.

Crenshaw, K. (1988). Race, reform, and retrenchment: Transformation and legitimation in antidiscrimination law. *Harvard Law Review*, 101(7), 1331–1387.

daSilva Iddings, A. C. (2009). Bridging home and school literacy practices and empowering families of recent immigrant children: A sociocultural approach. *Theory into Practice*, 48(4), 304–312.

Freire, P. (1970). *Pedagogy of the oppressed*. New York: Continuum.

Freire, P., & Macedo, D. (1987). *Literacy: Reading the word and the world*. Westport, CT: Bergin & Garvey.

Freire, P. (1994). *Pedagogy of hope: Reliving pedagogy of the oppressed*. New York: Continuum.

Gabhainn, S., & Sixsmith, J. (2006). Children photographing well-being: Facilitating participation in research. *Children and Society*, 20, 249–259.

García, O. (2009). *Bilingual education in the 21st century*. Oxford: Wiley-Blackwell.

Giroux, H. A. (1988). *Teachers as intellectuals: Toward a critical pedagogy of learning*. Granby, MA: Bergin & Garvey.

González, N., Moll, L., & Amanti, C. (Eds.). (2005). *Funds of knowledge: Theorizing practices in households, communities and classrooms*. Mahwah, NJ: Lawrence Erlbaum Associates.

Kenner, C. (2004). *Becoming biliterate, young children learning different writing systems*. Trentham: Stoke on Trent.

Ladson-Billings, G. (2006). It's not the culture of poverty, it's the poverty of culture: The problem with teacher education. *Anthropology & Education Quarterly*, 37(2), 104–109.

Lave, J., & Wenger, E. (2002). Legitimate peripheral participation in communities of practice. *Supporting Lifelong Learning*, 1, 111–126.

Lewis, O. (1966). The culture of poverty. *American*, 215(4), 19–25.

Lipsitz, G. (1995). The possessive investment in whiteness: Racialized social democracy and the "White" problem in American studies. *American Quarterly*, 7(3), 369–387.

Macedo, D. P. (2006). *Literacies of power: What Americans are not allowed to know*. Boulder, CO: Westview Press.

Macedo, D. P., & Freire, P. (1987). *Literacy: Reading the word and the world*. Westport, CT: Bergin & Garvey.

Myers, J. (2010). Moving methods: Constructing emotionally poignant geographies of HIV in Auckland, New Zealand. *Area*, 42, 328–338.

Newman, M., Woodcock, A., & Dunham, P. (2006). "Playtime in the Borderlands": Children's representations of school, gender and bullying through photographs and interviews. *Children's Geographies*, 4, 289–302.

Plyer v. Doe, 457, U.S. 202 (1982).

Pyle, A. (2012). Engaging young children in research through photo elicitation. *Early Child Development and Care*, 183(11), 1544–1558.

Reyes, I. (2006). Exploring connections between emergent biliteracy and bilingualism. *Journal of Early Childhood Literacy*, 6(3), 267–292.

Reyes, I., daSilva-Iddings, A. C., & Feller, N. P. (2015). Building relationships with diverse students and families: A funds of knowledge perspective. *Journal of Early Childhood Literacy*, 16(1), 8–33.

Rowe, D. W. (1994). *Preschoolers as authors: Literacy learning in the social world of the classroom*. New York: Hampton Press.

Rowe, D. W. (2003). The nature of young children's authoring. In N. Hall, J. Larson, & J. Marsh (Eds.), *Handbook of early childhood literacy* (pp. 258–270). London: Sage.

Rowe, D. W. (2008). Development of writing abilities in childhood. In C. Bazerman (Ed.), *Handbook of research on writing* (pp. 401–419). New York: Lawrence Erlbaum.

Rowe, D. W. (2009). Early written communication. In R. Beard, D. Myhill, J. Riley, & M. Nystrand (Eds.), *Sage handbook of writing development* (pp. 213–231). Los Angeles: Sage.

Rowe, D. W. (2010). Directions for studying social literacy as a social practice. *Language Arts*, 88(2), 134–143.

Schiller, J., & Tillett, B. (2004). Using digital images with young children: Challenges of integration. *Early Child Development and Care*, 174(4), 401–414.

Sharples, M., Davison, L., Thomas, G., & Rudman, P. (2003, October). Children as photographers: An analysis of children's photographic behaviour and intentions at three age levels. *Visual Communication*, 2, 303–330.

Souto-Manning, M. (2013). *Multicultural teaching in the early childhood classroom: Approaches, strategies, and tools, preschool-2nd grade*. New York: Teachers College Press.

Vygotsky, L. S. (1978). *Mind in society: The development of higher psychological processes*. Cambridge, MA: Harvard University Press.

Wright, W. E. (2005). The political spectacle of Arizona's proposition 203. *Educational Policy*, 19(5), 662–700.

Zentella, A. C. (Ed.). (2005). *Building on strength: Language and literacy in Latino families and communities*. New York: Teachers College Press.

10 Making Race and Racism Visible

Respecting and Valuing the Voices of Educators of Color in Teacher Preparation Programs

Kelli Gray

Understanding who we are and how that influences what we do can be a powerful and empowering process. Like many, I never gave much thought to segregated schooling. I just accepted the bleak picture of the inadequate schooling of African Americans before the landmark decision of *Brown v. the Board of Education* (hitherto *Brown*) in 1954. I had accepted, uncritically of course, the picture that had been painted of segregated schooling as truth. This all changed in 2010.

In June of 2010, I entered a Master's-Certification (MCERT) program at the University of Maryland in College Park. My focus was teaching English as a second language. During my student teaching, I was confronted with the reality of the treatment of English learners (EL) in today's schools. This reality was especially hard during my student teaching in high school. I saw firsthand how schools systematically worked to oppress and push out ELs, especially Latino males. I saw the frustration of ESL teachers worn down by the constant struggle to obtain equitable opportunities for their students. Although years earlier I had been introduced to the idea of liberatory education (Freire, 1970; hooks, 1994), my student teaching posts triggered serious and critical thinking about issues of social justice for emergent bilinguals. After receiving my acceptance letter to start a PhD program at a large, public university in the Southwest, I remember a colleague in the MCERT program questioning my decision to go to Arizona as it had an infamous reputation for oppressive laws and practices against bilingual education and toward emergent bilinguals. I remember telling my classmate that although the state had some clearly racist and oppressive laws, I did not believe I would face these same macro and microaggressions at the university. I was wrong.

In order to fund my PhD program, I was given undergraduate courses to teach in both the CREATE program and the elementary education program. Unfortunately after teaching for two and half years in these programs, I left that teaching post due to the micro and macroaggressions I experienced as a result of my attempt to teach from a critical lens. This expository essay, told through an autoethnographic inquiry lens, chronicles my process in coming to understand how who I am impacted in powerful ways who I became as an educator, and how my dissertation research on segregated schooling deepened these understandings. I conclude the chapter by turning my attention to teacher education programs and the importance of including the voices of educators of color as preservice students learn culturally relevant and sustaining ways to meet students' linguistic, cultural, and educational needs. Including the voices of faculty of color can help move students to a place of critical compassionate intellectualism (Cammarota & Romero, 2006), through which students will be able to form emerging/transforming stories as critical educators, countering the stock stories they were told. My hope is that by creating new stories, transforming stories, they can foster the same critical compassionate intellectualism in their own classrooms.

The conceptual and theoretical framework for this article is grounded in critical theories. My personal story, reconstructed from a collection of narrative-type papers I wrote throughout my doctoral program I call my "Goin' for Broke" series, were based on critical race theory (CRT), specifically the tenet "the centrality of experiential knowledge" (Solórzano, 1997, p. 7) and framed using Bell's (2010) framework of storytelling for social justice. Within this narrative I briefly reflect on and analyze how my experience teaching mostly white, female preservice teachers helped me rethink my role and responsibility as a Black educator preparing teachers to teach students of color.

Two concepts were important in this analysis: King's (1991) idea of dysconscious racism and hooks's (1989) description of revolutionary feminist pedagogy. I suggest that preservice teachers must grapple with, understand, and ultimately come to terms with their dysconscious racism (King, 1991). What I advocate for in this article is that the voices of educators of color within these teacher preparation programs can be an important asset to white students as they reflect on their own dysconsciousness and white privilege.

Goin' for Broke

From 2011 to 2013 I wrote a series of papers I titled my "Goin' for Broke" series. These papers documented my journey and reflections about being a Black, Spanish-English bilingual educator teaching in a teacher preparation program that prepared mostly white, female, monolingual preservice teachers. I wrote these papers because I was convinced that as educators we have a moral and ethical responsibility to ensure that all students succeed, and that in light of the miseducation of many Black, Latino, and Latina students it was time for teachers everywhere to "go for broke"; that is, to "[do] whatever it takes to shine the brightest lights on educational inequities experienced by poor children, African American and other children of color, children identified with disabilities, and children affected by the intersection of all these issues" (Blanchett, 2009, p. 385).

In the fall of 2011, my first semester in the PhD program, I taught my first class, a literacy course for preservice teachers who were getting their endorsement in either bilingual education or English as a Second Language (ESL). I taught a curriculum course to a similar group the next semester and then moved into teaching social studies. All of these courses were either for students in the early childhood or elementary education programs. As I learned and read more about social justice and critical pedagogy and began to understand the failures of our current education system for black and Latino communities—the communities I generally focused on in my own reading and research—I felt an obligation to take a more critical approach to the way I taught. As most of the preservice teachers in the program where white, female, monolingual, and middle class, I felt a responsibility to these teachers' future students to bring a critical lens to my work in the classroom. Initially, I was unsure about how to do this and struggled to find a balance between what students expected to see in a social studies methods course and my commitment to teaching from a social justice perspective. What also made this marriage of ideas difficult to balance was that I often felt alone in this quest, especially with how to deal with student resistance. Even though there were young assistant professors working in the teacher preparation program who were committed to issues of social justice, most were not folks of color, and they were not part of my immediate cohort instructional team. Within my cohort instructional team, there were colleagues who claimed to work from a critical lens and who claimed to be concerned with issues of social justice and multiculturalism; however, they adhered to a more liberal form of multiculturalism instead of working from the theoretical lens of critical multiculturalism (May & Sleeter, 2010). I later found an ally in the university community—the community liaison for CREATE, a Mexican American woman who had a deep understanding of social justice and who worked from a critical lens. During my last semester working in the program she often accompanied me in the classroom and was someone with whom I could discuss student resistance. She was a wonderful support. I also found allies in a few other educators in the department, but unfortunately there was never a critical mass outspoken enough to effect the kind of change I thought the program needed.

Microaggressions and My Presumed Incompetence

In 1969, Pierce described what it meant to be black and living in the United States at that time. He stated, "[t]o be black in the United States today means to be *psychologically terrorized, politically tyrannized, socially minimized,* and *economically ignored*" (p. 303). In 1970 he coined the term "microaggressions." These "offensive mechanisms" (Pierce, 1969) or "racial microaggressions" (Pierce, 1970) are "brief and commonplace daily verbal, behavioral, or environmental indignities, whether intentional of unintentional, that communicate hostile, derogatory, or negative racial slights and insults toward people of color" (Sue, Capodilupo, Torino, Bucceri, Holder, Nadal, & Esquilin, 2007). Furthermore as Pierce suggested in 1969 and other scholars since then (see for example Franklin, Smith, & hung, 2014; Smith, Allen, & Danley, 2007) dealing with these seemingly innocuous comments or behaviors in fact cause psychological and physical harm to people of color; what some scholars call racial battle fatigue. Racial battle fatigue describes the "social-psychological stress responses (e.g., frustration; anger; exhaustion; physical avoidance; resistance; verbally, nonverbally, or physically fighting back; and coping strategies)" and is "the result of constant physiological, psychological, cultural, and emotional coping with racial microaggressions in less-than-ideal and racially hostile or unsupportive environments (campus or otherwise)" (Smith et al., 2007, pp. 552 & 555 respectively).

Forty-five years later since Pierce's description of what it meant to be Black and live in the United States, I would suggest that this is still what it means today to be Black living, working, and being schooled in the United States. Likewise, for many Black educators teaching in universities today social minimization—being considered "insignificant" and "irrelevant"—is a daily occurrence.

The title of the book edited by Gutiérrez y Muhs, Niemann, González, and Harris (2012), *Presumed Incompetent*, expresses exactly how I regularly felt during my two and half years teaching in the teacher preparation program at my university. The fact that I taught from a critical len, made several of my undergraduate students uncomfortable, and they complained about the content of the course and the way that I presented it, as well as questioned my competence around such issues. For example, one day students were sharing some of their experiences in their cooperating teachers' classrooms, and one student commented on an incident with an "oriental student." When I mentioned that that term should no longer be used to talk about people, the student responded stating that her cooperating teacher used the same term, and then asked if the use of the term was something I considered to be inappropriate or something others as well considered inappropriate. It seemed that my explanation was unconvincing, and so I consulted with a new assistant professor I was getting to know, who worked from a critical lens, and who happened to be Korean and asked if she would come to class and give a presentation on some of the issues on how the Asian and Asian American communities are labeled in the United States.

Although situations like the one described above were frustrating and disheartening, they were tempered at times by the comments and support of students of color in the program who often had just the opposite reaction. They identified with the social justice topics discussed and were glad that I was willing to discuss them; although a couple of students specifically told me that they would not speak up in class because they did not want problems from their white classmates.

After my advisor, a Mexican American man committed to issues of social justice and a long-time professor in the department, explained to me that he had been summoned to meetings convened by university administrators to talk about student complaints, I decided to discontinue my graduate teaching assistantship in the program. The meetings about how I organized and conducted my classes were convened without my knowledge and input, and when my advisor asked if they had talked with me about these complaints, the response he received was about how difficult it was to talk to me. Not only was I presumed incompetent by students, staff, and faculty; in addition, I was perceived to be an angry Black woman with whom it was difficult to talk. My decision to stop working in the program was influenced more by the micro and macroaggressions experienced at the hands of faculty than by those from students. I remember my advisor telling me, "They don't understand what you are trying to do." I knew he was right, but I did not understand at that time why he was right.

Eventually the department came to a realization that microaggressions were pervasive in the teacher preparation programs and concerned not only me, but all the other educators of color as well. From this realization, the department chair convened what would later be known as the Equity and Social Justice Committee (ESJC) to help guide explorations of adequate and compassionate responses to the everyday aggressions experienced by students, faculty, and staff of color in the department. However, by the time I graduated in 2015 there still had not been sustained change in the department. The reason I believe there was not the kind of change I had hoped for was because although at our program and department meetings and in the ESJC committee meetings many faculty and staff spoke about the ideals of social justice and multiculturalism, they adhered, nonetheless, to liberal multiculturalism while I sought critical multiculturalism.

May and Sleeter (2010) state that the focus of liberal multiculturalism is "on getting along better, primarily via a greater recognition of, and respect for, ethnic, cultural, and/or linguistic differences." They go on to say that "[l]beral multicultural education may be easy to implement but this is only so because it abdicates any corresponding recognition of unequal, and often untidy, power relations that underpin inequality and limit cultural interaction, however well meaning" (p. 4). On the other hand May and Sleeter (2010) explain that critical multiculturalism "gives priority to structural analysis of unequal power relationships, analyzing the role of institutionalized inequities, including but not necessarily limited to racism" (p. 10, emphasis in original). "Central to critical multiculturalism is naming and actively challenging racism and other forms of injustice, not simply recognizing and celebrating differences and reducing prejudice" (Berlak & Movenda, 2001, p. 92 as cite in May & Sleeter, 2010, p. 10). I assert that some faculty and staff held a more liberal view of social justice and multiculturalism, and most likely one of our major differences was in the "naming and actively challenging racism and other forms of injustice."

Although I was no longer teaching in the teacher preparation program, I continued to reflect on my own practice as I was interested in continuing to provide future students with a space where they could begin to reflect upon some of their taken-for-granted concepts of society and education. I desired a pedagogy that had "political power" and that was "radical" (hooks, 1989). I wanted a space where students could be transformed and experience "education as the practice of freedom" (Freire, 1970/1993).

One notion that resonated with me was hooks' (1989) idea of a feminist classroom as a place:

> where there is a sense of struggle, where there is visible acknowledge-ment of the union of theory and practice, where we work together as teachers and students to overcome the estrangement and alienation that have become so much the norm in the contemporary university. Most importantly, feminist pedagogy should engage students in a learning process that makes the world "more rather than less."
>
> (p. 51)

Although I did not necessarily see myself as a feminist, hooks's characteriza-tion of a revolutionary feminist pedagogy was representative of the work I desired to do with students.

She describes revolutionary feminist pedagogy as having the following characteristics:

- A pedagogy that relinquishes ties to traditional ways of teaching that reinforce domination,
- A pedagogy that focuses on the teacher-student relationship and the issue of power,
- A pedagogy whose standard of valuation differs from the norm,
- A pedagogy that defines the terms of engagement,
- A pedagogy that constantly tries new methods, new approaches, and
- A pedagogy taught by revolutionary feminist. (hooks, 1989, pp. 52–54).

Guided by these characteristics, I began to rethink the teacher-student role in the classroom, desiring to give students more of a voice in the con-struction of the class. This was challenging due to university constraints; however, this approach allowed me to reflect on how schools, and in this case a university, are simultaneously "sites of both domination and libera-tion" (McLaren, 2009, p. 62). I began to wonder what my role would be in negotiating spaces of liberation for my students as these ideas intrigued me.

In my last semester in the program, I was offered to teach a course that specifically addressed issues of race, language, and culture in education. Stu-dents in the course came from a variety of disciplines across the university. Most of the students were white, but I also had two female students who identified as Black, one male student who identified as Black, and several students who identified as Latino/Mexican/Mexican American/Chicano. As students had elected to take the course, I did not get the push-back from stu-dents I had experienced in the teacher preparation program, and I was able to see firsthand how the school can be "a cultural terrain that promotes student empowerment and self-transformation" (McLaren, 2009, p. 62); not just for my students, but for me as well.

The Role of Race and Racism in Teacher Education

Racism is "the major stumbling block in preparing teachers for success with African American students" (Ladson-Billings, 2009, p. 465). Furthermore, when considering how racist ideologies can have a negative impact on students, one essential component of any teacher preparation program must be to get students to examine race and racism and its impact and influence on the lives of students of color both inside and outside of school (see Milner IV, 2015).

Cammarota and Romero (2006) describe the silencing that happens in schools by the enactment of power through the curriculum, racist ideologies, and pedagogy. This silencing has a detrimental effect on students of color and may lead to their dropping out of school or their checking out of school mentally. To counter the silencing imposed by such institutional power, they put forth a pedagogical trilogy Cammarota and Romero (2006) call "critically compassionate intellectualism" (p. 18). This pedagogical approach brings together the essential elements of critical pedagogy, authentic caring, and social justice curriculum. They suggest that implementing these components simultaneously in the classroom will better prepare students of color to be active participants in developing a truly democratic society, and one in which the students thrive academically.

Likewise, Solórzano and Yosso (2001) working within a critical race theory in education framework suggest that racial stereotyping can cause teachers to have low expectations of students of color, segregate students of color to separate schools or separate classrooms within schools, "dumb down" the curriculum for students of color, and have the expectation that students of color will occupy lower-level jobs.

Understanding these possible consequences when future teachers are not encouraged to confront issues of race, racism, and white privilege led me to address these topics in my classes. This entailed significant changes in the curriculum. These changes, as mentioned, were met with resistance from students and from faculty and staff in the program. Many students insisted on a more color blind approach to working with students of color, than reflecting on the role race or social class plays in education.

Although experiencing resistance is not uncommon for educators working within an antiracist framework (Ladson-Billings, 2009), getting students to think critically about what King (1991) describes as dysconscious racism is challenging, but necessary if students of color are to ever receive an equitable education.

King (1991) describes dysconscious racism as "the limited and distorted understanding [some] students have about inequity and cultural diversity—understandings that make it difficult for them to act in favor of truly equitable education" (p. 132–133). She goes on to say that it is "a form of racism that tacitly accepts dominant white norms and privileges. It is not the absence of consciousness (that is, not unconsciousness) but an impaired consciousness or distorted way of thinking about race as compared to, for example, critical consciousness" (p.135). She asserts that dysconsciousness is "an uncritical habit of mind (including perceptions, attitudes, assumptions, and beliefs) that justifies inequity and exploitation by accepting the existing order of things as given" (p. 135). What these definitions highlight is that this type of thinking is limited, distorted, and uncritical that allows students to readily accept what they know to be true. Furthermore when confronted about their dysconsciousness students feel attacked; their identity challenged; common reactions expressed by students in my classes. King (1991) affirms that "[a]ny serious challenge to the status quo that calls this racial privilege into question inevitably challenges the self-identity of White people who have internalized these ideological justifications" (p. 135). So, what is to be done?

King (1991) asserts that students need the opportunity to not only analyze racism from a structural, cultural, or individual level, but classes also need to "address the cognitive distortions of dysconscious racism" (p. 140), for example understanding that there are multiple ways of reading and making sense of the world. If teaching programs do not tackle both these issues, she believes students will not be able to "distinguish between racist justification of the status quo (which limit their thought, self-identity, and responsibility to take action) and socially unacceptable individual prejudice or bigotry (which students often disavow)" (p. 140). If we want students to truly consider the changes needed in society and education then such ideologies must be challenged. King (1991) maintains that if we want what she calls "liberatory, social-reconstructionist educators" (p.142) then teaching preparation programs have to provide students with the tools to "adequate[ly] understand how society works as well as the "opportunities to think about the need for fundamental social change" (p. 142).

To address the issue of dysconscious racism and move her students to a more liberatory social-reconstructionist perspective King (1991) uses a pedagogy that is transformative, critical, and liberatory in nature. She attempts to provide her preservice students a context where they can "consider alternative conceptions of themselves and society" (p. 134). Although pedagogies such as King's or Cammarota and Romero's are not new, many teacher preparation programs continue to do an inadequate job in preparing teachers to work with linguistically and culturally diverse students (Darling-Hammond, 2010; Howard, 2006; Ladson-Billings, 2009; Milner IV, 2015; Nieto, 2009). In fact, I would contend that when teacher preparation programs choose not to teach their students to examine their own dysconscious racism, these programs become accomplices in the violation of Black and Brown children already perpetrated on them by the educational system.

Respecting and Valuing the Voice of Educators of Color

One of the tenets of Critical Race Theory (CRT) is "the centrality of experiential knowledge" (Solórzano, 1997, p. 7); specifically the lived experiences of people of color as told through methods such as storytelling, family histories, narratives, testimonies, or biographies (Solórzano & Yosso, 2002). Their knowledge and experiences are seen as critical, legitimate, and valuable. Although CRT was originally used to examine issues of race and racism in legal studies, it and its tenets can be a crucial tool in analyzing, understanding, and teaching issues of race and racism in education (Dixson & Rousseau, 2005, Ladson-Billings & Tate, 1995; Solórzano & Yosso, 2002).

The voices of educators of color are essential in education because they often provide counterstories to what Bell (2010) has called the stock stories, or the normative stories students have been told throughout their educational studies. Solórzano and Yosso (2002) posit that counterstories are "tool[s] for exposing, analyzing, and challenging the majoritarian stories of racial privilege" (p. 32).

My voice as a Black educator and mother was in many ways silenced in teacher preparation courses, and with my voice, my counterstories and those of my community were also silenced—counterstories of resilience, resistance, and liberation; counterstories that could speak truth to the relationship between racial oppression and white privilege; and counterstories that disrupt the presumed universality of the dominant stock stories. When Black educators and other educators of color are not included in teacher preparation programs, an important voice in understanding privilege and oppression goes unheard.

As for me, my experience as a Black teacher educator in a predominately white department has pushed me to think deeper about my role and place in teacher preparation programs. My commitment and resolve to teach for social justice is unwavering and even firmer thanks to my doctoral studies, my dissertation research on the important role Black teachers played in the lives of students in segregated schools, and my teaching experiences. The journey has not been easy. Educating for equity is not easy. It takes a great deal of time and effort on the part of teachers; however, the building blocks for how to do this well have been thoroughly researched (see Darling-Hammond, 2006; Darling-Hammond & Bransford, 2005; Ladson-Billings, 2009, among others). Thus there is no excuse for why every teacher completing a teacher preparation program should not have the knowledge, skills, and strategies to meet the diverse needs of all students. Teacher education programs and the colleges of education that house them must become the change they want to see in their students. There is variety in how programs model the culturally responsive and activist approaches they hope to see in the nation's P-12 classrooms, but programs must become more proactive in how they train teachers for classrooms that are becoming more Black and Brown.

Teacher preparation programs must recruit and retain educators of color as their lived experiences and the experiences of their communities will help white students on their journey to understanding their own dysconscious racism and becoming more critically compassionate in their intellectualism. These are the steps programs must take to pay more than just mere lip service to educating for equity and begin to put into place the elements of "powerful teacher education" grounded in the ideals and principles of teacher education for critical social justice. Our students' lives depend on it.

Bibliography

Bell, L. A. (2010). *Storytelling for social justice: Connecting narrative and the arts in antiracist teaching.* New York: Routledge.

Blanchett, W. J. (2009). Disproportionate representation of African American students in special education: Acknowledging the role of white privilege and racism. *Educational Researcher, 35*(6), 24–28.

Cammarota, J., & Romero, A. (2006). Critically compassionate intellectualism for Latina/o students: Raising voices about the silencing in our schools. *Multicultural Education, 14*(2), 16–23.

Darling-Hammond, L. (2006). *Powerful teacher education: Lessons from exemplary programs.* San Francisco, CA: Jossey-Bass.

Darling-Hammond, L. (2010). *The flat world and education: How American's commitment to equity will determine our future.* New York: Teachers College Press.

Darling-Hammond, L., & Bransford, J. (Eds.). (2005). *Preparing teachers for a changing world: What teachers should learn and be able to do.* San Francisco, CA: Jossey-Bass.

Dixson, A., & Rousseau, C. (2005). And we are still not saved: Critical race theory in education ten years later. *Race Ethnicity and Education, 8*(1), 7–27.

Franklin, J. D., Smith, W. A., & Hung, M. (2014). Racial battle fatigue for Latina/o students: A quantitative perspective. *Journal of Hispanic Higher Education, 13*(4), 303–322.

Freire, P. (1970/1993). *Pedagogy of the oppressed.* New York: Continuum.

Gutiérrez y Muhs, G., Flores Niemann, Y., González, C. G., & Harris, A. P. (Eds.). (2012). *Presumed incompetent: The intersections of race and class for women in academia.* Boulder, CO: Utah State University Press.

hooks, b. (1989). *Talking back: Thinking feminist, thinking black.* Boston, MA: South End Press.

hooks, b. (1994). *Teaching to transgress: Education as the practice of freedom.* New York: Routledge.

Howard, G. R. (2006). *We can't teach what we don't know: White teachers, multiracial schools.* New York: Teachers College Press.

King, J. E. (1991). Dysconscious racism: Ideology, identity, and the miseducation of teachers. *The Journal of Negro Education, 60*(2), 133–146.

Ladson-Billings, G. (2009). *The dream-keepers: Successful teachers of African American children* (2nd ed.). San Francisco, CA: Jossey-Bass.

Ladson-Billings, G., & Tate, W. (1995). Toward a critical race theory of education. *Teachers College Record, 97*(1), 47–68.

May, S., & Sleeter, C. (Eds.). (2010). *Critical multiculturalism: Theory and Praxis.* New York: Routledge.

McLaren, P. (2009). Critical pedagogy: A look at the major concepts. In A. Darder, M. P. Baltodano, & R. D. Torres (Eds.), *The critical pedagogy reader* (2nd ed., pp. 252–260). New York: Routledge.

Milner IV, H. R. (2015). *Rac(e)ing to class: Confronting poverty and race in the schools and classrooms.* Cambridge, MA: Harvard Education Press.

Nieto, S. (2009). Bringing bilingual education out of the basement and other imperatives for teacher education. In A. Darder, M. P. Baltodano, & R. D. Torres (Eds.), *The critical pedagogy reader* (2nd ed., 469–482). New York: Routledge.

Pierce, C. (1969). Is bigotry the basis of the medical problems of the ghetto? In J. C. Norman (Ed.), *Medicine in the Ghetto* (pp. 301–312). New York: Meredith.

Pierce, C. (1970). Offensive mechanisms. In F. B. Barbour (Ed.), *The Black '70's* (pp. 265–282). Boston, MA: Floyd B. Barbour.

Smith, W. A., Allen, W. R., & Danley, L. L. (2007). "Assume the position . . . you fit the description": Psychosocial experiences and racial battle fatigue among African American college students. *American Behavioral Scientist, 51*(4), 551–578.

Solórzano, D. (1997). Images and words that wound: Critical race theory, racial stereotyping, and teacher education. *Teacher Education Quarterly, 24*(3), 5–19.

Solórzano, D., & Yosso, T. (2001). From racial stereotyping and deficit discourse toward a critical race theory in teacher education. *Multicultural Education, 9*(1), 2–8.

Solórzano, D., & Yosso, T. (2002). Critical race methodology: Counter storytelling as an analytical framework for education research. *Qualitative Inquiry, 8*(1), 23–44.

Sue, D. W., Capodilupo, C. M., Torino, G. C., Bucceri, J. M., Holder, A. M. B., Nadal, K. L., & Esquilin, M. (2007). Racial microaggressions in everyday life: Implications for clinical practice. *American Psychologist, 62*(4), 271–286.

11 Learning to Teach for Equity, Access, and Inclusion

Directions for Program Design and Research in Early Childhood Teacher Education

Deborah Wells Rowe

This volume represents the sustained and creative efforts of a team of teacher educators who have concretely taken up the challenge of finding better ways to prepare future early childhood teachers to work effectively with a rapidly diversifying U.S. student population. While it is common for teacher education programs to include issues of language and cultural diversity in university coursework, many programs do little more—even if students are completing their practice teaching assignments in communities with large numbers of students who are emergent bilinguals, heritage speakers of alternate English dialects, or who come from refugee and immigrant backgrounds. Many teacher education programs "talk the talk" but many fewer "walk the walk." The research reported in this volume is remarkable because the faculty of the Community as Resources in Early Childhood Teacher Education (CREATE) program have allowed us to look over their shoulders as they identified a shared set of theoretical premises about conditions supporting the learning of young culturally and linguistically diverse students. We then follow their progress as they worked to iteratively redesign their teacher education program to better support teachers in building the dispositions and skills to enact these premises with young emergent bilingual children and their families.

My goal in this chapter is to consider what I and other researchers and teacher educators might learn from the example provided by the CREATE research program, and also to identify some productive directions for future research aimed at the goal of preparing prospective teachers to teach for equity, access, and inclusion. The terms *equity, access*, and *inclusion* have been interpreted differently over time in relation to decisions about schooling for U.S. children (Lee, 2009). As used in this chapter, these terms are framed by a cultural-ecological framework for learning (Lee, 2009) positing that all children, their families, and communities have resources that facilitate learning and can be used to support children in reaching their full potential. Working from this perspective, Lee (2009) has argued that children's learning is supported "by recognizing salient aspects of their identities, their perceptions of themselves and the tasks that we want them to master, the ways in which their emotional states influence their efforts, and the kinds of guided supports they need to feel competent" (p. 77). From this perspective, teaching for *equity* does not mean that every student is treated in exactly same way in the classroom. Instead, equity requires teachers to recognize and meet the particular needs of individual students (Milner, 2010). Equitable schooling provides all students with *access* to participation in high-level learning opportunities that value and use students' cultural and linguistic resources to bridge their construction of new ideas. Access also involves the provision of material, technological, and environmental supports for such participation. Equitable schooling is *inclusive;* that is, children see positive reflections of their individual abilities, languages, and cultural experiences in the curriculum, and schools productively seek two-way relations with families and community members who can partner with teachers to incorporate family funds of knowledge and language resources into the school curriculum.

Learning to Teach for Equity, Access, and Inclusion

Learning to teach is an amazingly complex process, and even more so for teachers who are learning to interact with students and families whose cultural backgrounds and home languages differ from their own. Prospective early childhood teachers' need foundational understandings of children's linguistic, cognitive, social-emotional, and physical-motor development, as well as specific knowledge of disciplinary learning trajectories in literacy, science, math, and social studies. Teachers apply this knowledge as they design instruction and as they observe and assess students' social interactions, academic skills, and emerging communication abilities. Teaching for equity, access, and inclusion requires an understanding of the ways families' cultural practices may shape children's learning (Lee, 2009) and of pedagogical strategies for culturally responsive assessment (Banks, Cookson, Gay, Hawleym, Irvine, Nieto, & Stephan, 2001).

While teacher education naturally focuses attention on young learners, prospective teachers also need to do considerable identity work of their own. Participating in learning-to-teach events requires that university students take up, critique, and/or remake the teacher "identity kits" (i.e., values, beliefs, ways of talking, acting, and interacting) (Gee, 2003) that are familiar from their own experiences as students or that are introduced in teacher education programs. Teachers need to consider how their own cultural identities intersect with those of their students to impact the classroom learning environment (Milner, 2010).

But learning to teach involves more than developing pedagogical knowledge about learning and assessment, or even interrogating one's own values and beliefs about what it means to be a teacher. Teaching is an applied activity—a social practice. It involves learning about and practicing ways of being in relationship with others—in this case, the groups of children enrolled in the teacher's class, as well as their families and communities. Effective teachers know their students well (Milner, 2010). Teachers need to learn strategies for getting to know their students' out-of-school interests and their cultural experiences at home and in their communities. Teaching for equity, access, and inclusion requires that prospective teachers develop an understanding and appreciation for the positive role family funds of knowledge (González, Moll, & Amanti, 2009), language(s), and literacy practices can play in children's school learning. Prospective teachers need help building strategies for engaging with families and communities to support their students' learning (Edwards, 2016).

Since children necessarily approach school learning tasks using the conceptual frames and linguistic skills provided by familiar experiences and ways of communicating, an important part of learning to teach is developing skill in designing activities that legitimate students' cultures and languages. Teaching for equity, access, and inclusion requires strategies for locating or creating instructional materials that serve as mirrors of students' cultural experiences (Bishop, 1990) and using them as frame of reference for exploring new content, including the perspectives of others (Ladson-Billings, 1992).

Finally, though prospective teachers may largely enter the profession because they want to be engaged in face-to-face teaching relations with children and their families, from the first days observing or participating in classrooms, teachers begin to interact with institutional policies that shape educational practice. Teachers need to learn ways of working within existing systems to provide powerful learning opportunities for all children, and also strategies for challenging unjust institutional ideologies that are embedded in policies and funding decisions affecting classroom teaching and learning (Milner, 2010; Nieto, 2002).

Summary

Overall, learning to teach for equity, access, and inclusion of children from culturally and linguistically diverse backgrounds requires teachers to develop pedagogical knowledge and practices related to the following domains:

1   **Student Learning Trajectories and Assessment:** Teachers need to develop professional understandings of the trajectories for young children's learning, how they may be shaped by cultural and personal experience, and culturally sensitive strategies for observing and assessing what children *can do* as learners.

2   **Teachers' Cultural Identities:** Teachers need to critically reflect on their own cultural identities, values, and beliefs and how they affect the learning context for all students with whom they work.

3   **Student Interests and Family Funds of Knowledge:** Teachers need to develop positive dispositions and strategies for getting to know children

and their families, including children's personal interests, family funds of knowledge, and language resources.

4 **Culturally Responsive Instructional Practices:** Teachers need to develop ways of designing culturally responsive instructional practices and activities that legitimate children's cultures and languages as valuable learning resources.

5 **Critical Consciousness:** Teachers need to develop a critical consciousness concerning the ways systems of power and privilege are embedded in school policy, practices, and materials.

Designing Teacher Education Programs

If we accept the premise that the pedagogical domains described above are crucial to teaching for equity, access, and inclusion, the question for teacher educators is how to design educational experiences that will support prospective teachers in forming the necessary dispositions, pedagogical knowledge, and skills. To further consider how teacher educators and researchers might facilitate this learning, I take up each pedagogical knowledge/practice domain introduced above, asking the following questions:

- What existing research is relevant to the design of teacher education programs that focus on teaching for equity, access, and inclusion?
- What are important questions requiring further study by teacher education designers and researchers?

Student Learning Trajectories

In order to teach young children effectively, prospective teachers need to build pedagogical knowledge related to children's learning processes and expected learning trajectories in key domains including language, socio-emotional development, physical motor development, and content areas such as literacy and mathematics. Lee (2009) points out that existing research on student learning has often been designed from a monologic perspective, studying children sampled from the dominant group and then taking their learning performances to be the norm for all children. Research conducted with children from diverse backgrounds can also perpetuate these normative views of learning by either failing to consider how children's languages and cultural practices shape and impact their performances, or alternately by comparing their performances to dominant group norms. Monologic approaches to research fail to fully recognize children's strengths as learners and often lead to deficit perspectives of culturally diverse children and families.

However, researchers working from asset-based cultural perspectives provide descriptive information on the ways culture and language practices lead to strengths that support school learning. For example, asset-based research shows that emergent bilinguals build the valuable literacy skills of metalinguistic awareness (Bialystok, 2007) and audience awareness (Durán, 2016) as they move between their two languages and use them to speak and write to others. Culturally shaped child-rearing patterns may also lead to skills that support school learning. For example, patterns of adult-child play as well as parental scaffolding of attention to small details in Chinese characters have been posited as contributors to the finding that Chinese-speaking children are more likely than English-speaking peers in the U.S. to learn strategies for attending to and analyzing small details in visual arrays (Pine, 2005)—skills that are especially helpful in learning to read and write.

Studies framed in this way present positive views of learners from diverse backgrounds by specifically recognizing culture and language as positive forces shaping children's learning trajectories and by describing what children can do as learners, rather than comparing them to norms derived from observations of dominant groups. Especially important for teachers of young children, strengths-based research recognizes and values *emergent* performances that are not conventionally correct, but result in learning through creative application of current understandings and hypotheses (e.g., emergent writing, Rowe & Wilson, 2015) or in *hybrid* performances that creatively combine cultural and linguistic resources across languages or cultural settings (e.g., translingual products, Miller & Rowe, 2014).

Teachers of young children from diverse backgrounds need to be introduced to research and broad theories of learning that are assumed to generalize across cultures, but also to theory and research that frame emergence, hybridity, and cultural variation in learning in positive ways. This research can support positive teacher attitudes toward students' learning capabilities, serve as the starting point for culturally sensitive assessment, and provide the foundation for teachers' design of activities that recognize and build on children's existing cultural and linguistic resources.

Directions for Program Design and Research

In the preceding paragraphs, I have argued that existing research provides an important pedagogical knowledge base for prospective teachers' observation and valuing of their students as learners. In designing and studying teacher education programs, we need to consider the extent to which prospective teachers have access to this knowledge base. Questions for teacher educators and researchers include:

- What research and theories do teacher education students have access to in teacher education programs? To what extent does this work positively describe cultural variation and culturally specific learning trajectories?
- What cultural and linguistic groups are represented in the research and theory presented in teacher education programs? On what basis are these decisions made?

Teacher education programs are designed to help prospective teachers transform basic research on children's learning into pedagogical knowledge, in part by applying these understandings to observation and assessment practices. Though my informal analysis suggests that many teacher education programs engage prospective teachers in experiences explicitly designed to teach strategies for observing and assessing student learning, there is little formal research to guide the design of these experiences. While prospective teachers have traditionally been asked to conduct case studies of learners at their school sites using an array of existing assessment tools, it is possible for such observations to be unreflectively rooted in normative practices. Future research and program design needs to theorize and then analyze the conditions supporting prospective teachers' observations of children's cultural resources for learning. Questions for future research include:

- What teacher education experiences can provide prospective teachers with opportunities that are open enough to observe young children's use of cultural and linguistic resources inside and outside of school? What spaces and activities are richest for these observations?
- What teacher education experiences support the development of ethnographic observation skills that produce culturally and developmentally sensitive accounts of young children's emergent and hybrid learning performances?
- How can teacher education programs support critical awareness of the cultural and linguistic frames implicit in the assessment tools currently used in schools?

Teachers' Cultural Identities

Seminal and more recent research on culturally responsive teaching suggests that effective teachers of children from culturally and linguistically diverse backgrounds need to explicitly examine their own cultural identities, values, and beliefs and consider how they intersect with the linguistic and racial backgrounds of their students (McAllister & Irvine, 2000; Nieto, 2002). Researchers (e.g., Florio-Ruane, 1994; Ladson-Billings, 1992; Willis, 2000) have argued that teachers need to critically engage with issues such as color blindness, meritocracy, deficit mind-sets, the operation of systems of power and privilege in education, and systemic institutional barriers. Milner (Milner, 2010), for example, argues that color blind mind-sets that ignore children's racial backgrounds fail to acknowledge a key aspect of student identity and have a negative impact on learning for students of color. For white teachers who comprise the majority of teacher education students, color blind beliefs can lead to Eurocentric instruction, where teachers use their own experience to frame instruction and where children's racial experiences and heritage languages are seen as marginal issues when designing learning activities. As a result, many students will not see their own experiences reflected in the classroom. Similarly, beliefs in meritocracy make it difficult for prospective teachers to recognize unearned advantages supporting the learning of students from dominant groups as well as systemic barriers that operate in the lives of minority students and their families (McIntosh, 1990). These beliefs effectively prevent prospective teachers from deep understanding of conditions that affect student participation and learning. Deficit mind-sets lead to low expectations, and less rigorous instruction focusing on low-level skills, with few opportunities for critical thinking in meaningful activities (Wood, 2015).

While students of color have often addressed these issues in their own experience or in discussions with others, fewer white students may have had reasons to explicitly consider these issues in their own lives (Willis, 2000). Challenges to students' cultural beliefs can generate guilt and resistance in white students. Nevertheless, research shows that teacher education experiences can also provide the impetus for prospective teachers to consider how their own cultural identities and beliefs about culture, race, language, and power affect their work as teachers.

Directions for Program Design and Research

Teacher education programs can find support for their efforts to teachers' self-reflection on culture and cultural identity in the extensive literature on multicultural education. Most commonly, prospective teachers have been asked to complete self-reflective discussions in the university classroom with peers and the course instructor (Milner, 2003), online chats, or other written exchanges. Many activities have been designed with literary and/or writing components. Examples of activities designed to promote cultural self-reflection included: 1) books clubs or courses where participants read, discuss, and write about published narratives of authors' racialized and cultural experiences in learning literacy or becoming teachers (Clark & Medina, 2000; Florio-Ruane, 1994) and 2) interactive journaling focusing on issues of culture with responses by the course instructor and peers (Milner, 2003; Willis, 2000). Other teacher education activities require prospective teachers to engage with issues of cultural identity in interactions with the P-12 students. In an extension of cultural autobiography writing assignments, Xu (2000) engaged prospective teachers in a three-phase activity involving writing their own autobiographies, writing a biography of a student with whom they were currently working, and then discussing and comparing them. Xu comments that prospective teachers found it difficult to learn about students' lives outside of school through interviews and recommended using classroom teachers as additional sources of information. A response to the difficulty of learning about young children's cultural experiences from school interactions is provided by the CREATE program's design of opportunities for prospective teachers to engage and form relations with children and their families in their homes over an extended period of time. (See Chapter 7.)

Questions for teacher education program design and research include:

- What opportunities do prospective teachers have to learn about the cultural experiences and perspectives of children, their families, and communities?
- How are literary, multimedia, and first-hand experiences in schools and homes used most effectively as touchstones for cultural self-reflection?
- How does the intersection of the racial/linguistic background of teacher education instructors and their university students impact the design of experiences intended to promote cultural self-reflection?
- What skills and cultural insights do teacher educators currently have and/or need to support prospective teachers' engagement in cultural identity work?

Student Interests and Family Funds of Knowledge

In order to teach for equity, access, and inclusion, teachers need to know their students well. Ladson-Billings (1992) argues that culturally responsive teaching legitimizes and values students' cultures and languages by putting them at the center of learning activities, thereby making children's experiences a frame of reference for all other learning. Effective teachers get to know children as members of cultural and family groups but also as individuals with personal interests and affinities. Teachers need to understand family and community funds of knowledge (González et al., 2009)—the cultural, linguistic, occupational resources that families deploy to accomplish daily activities and to thrive. It is only through understanding children's interests and the cultural and linguistic resources of their families and communities that teachers can design instruction that uses these resources to support learning in school.

Directions for Teacher Education Program Design and Research

Research conducted within a funds of knowledge framework provides directions for the design of teacher education that supports the development of strengths-based perspectives on family resources and their validation as supports for school learning (González et al., 2009). Seminal work by Moll, González, and their colleagues (Moll, Amanti, Neff, & González, 2005) involved teachers in ethnographic interviews of families with the goal of forming relationships and gleaning information that could be used in classroom teaching. The CREATE program described in this volume has extended this work, breaking new ground by purposefully foregrounding family funds of knowledge throughout the teacher education program. By engaging prospective teachers in a series of experiences with families in their homes, by inviting families to share stories orally around family artifacts returned to school sites in canastas (story baskets), and by authoring books with family photos, the CREATE program has been designed to provide multiple opportunities for prospective teachers to learn about young children's out of school experiences. (See Chapter 11.) Further, prospective teachers had supported opportunities to design school interactions honoring family funds of knowledge and to use them as integral parts of classroom instruction. These activities represent a bold redesign of teacher education to make boundaries between school and home more permeable.

Because teaching for equity, access, and inclusion requires that teachers get to know students and their families well, in and out of school, teacher education program design must be built around answers to the following kinds of questions:

- What teacher education experiences support prospective teachers in adopting a learner stance when interacting with children and their families?
- What teacher education experiences help prospective teachers get to know young children as individuals and as members of families and cultural groups?
- How can teacher educators help prospective teachers work through the tensions that arise when they are required to interact in situations where they are cultural and linguistic novices?

Culturally Responsive Instruction

Culturally responsive instruction cannot be reduced to a set of recommended activities. Instead, teaching for equity, access, and inclusion is a design. Prospective teachers need pedagogical knowledge of key design features that support the participation and learning of students from diverse backgrounds. My initial analysis of a sample of reports describing culturally responsive teaching has identified the following design features. First, culturally responsive teaching is often tailored to children's changing needs through *flexible assembly of materials from a variety of sources*. Instructional materials purchased for schools often fail to represent the experiences of all children in the class. Teachers often have to search for culturally relevant books and materials that can serve as mirrors of students' heritage languages and cultural experiences (Bishop, 1990)—a process that is still challenging, despite increased attention to diversity in children's literature. To address this problem, culturally responsive instruction often combines school content with child/family-composed materials. Examples come from book-composing activities where children and families take photos at home, then collaborate with teachers at school to create and share multilingual books that reflect the children's identities, languages, and experiences (e.g., Bernhard, Cummins, Campoy, Ada, Winsler, & Bleiker, 2006; Bernhard, Winsler, Bleiker, Ginieniewicz, & Madigan, 2008; Rowe & Miller, 2015). Flexible assembly of school and home resources increases cultural connections and allows teachers to use home content as a bridge to new content at school.

Second, culturally responsive teaching involves *collaborative learning relationships* with children and families. Teachers in a rapidly globalizing world, where transnational travel is a common occurrence, must realize that they can't accomplish culturally responsive teaching by themselves. In my local area, many teachers work with children immigrating from as many as 10 nations and speaking 5 to 6 different heritage languages each school year. In addition, the cultural composition of the class shifts from year to year in response to global crises, patterns of refugee resettlement, and changing employment opportunities. Few teachers could be expected to arrive at class with personal knowledge of so many nations, cultures, and languages. Rather than requiring teachers to be experts in all situations, culturally responsive teaching requires teachers to live as learners. Teachers need to find ways of collaborating with families that fit their availability and expertise. New and not-so-new technologies can sometimes be used to advantage. For example, in our own work designing eBook composing activities with emergent bilingual pre-kindergartners (Nieto, 2002), inexpensive digital cameras provided opportunities for families to document and share their interests and cultural practices with teachers and peers. Touchscreen tablets afforded opportunities for parents to quickly record heritage language oral translations at arrival or dismissal times. Both technologies made it possible for children to make family images and voices present in the classroom through a tap of the screen at times when parents were not available to visit the classroom. Effective teachers learn from and with children and their families and use technology and sensitive scheduling to make it possible for parents to participate in their child's schooling.

Third, culturally responsive teaching typically involves designing for *shared sponsorship* (Rowe & Miller, 2015) of instructional content. When family photos or stories are used as the anchors for school activities as in the digital eBook composing activity just described or in the CREATE program's invitations to families to share stories through the artifacts they include in canastas (story baskets), the interests and cultural experiences of children and their families are valued and recognized as part of the official curriculum. Teachers purposefully plan experiences where children, families, and community members take up expert roles, sharing their linguistic and cultural resources to benefit the learning of both the teacher and students.

Fourth, activities are often designed to invite *two-way travel* of materials, information, and people between home and school. As a design strategy, teachers specifically examine what and who travels between home, school, and community spaces and whose expertise gets to shape experiences and materials available in different spaces. Culturally responsive teaching requires a rethinking of traditional one-way, school-to-home communications designed to provide parents with information or tasks to do to support their child's learning. When prospective teachers in the CREATE program travel to children's homes, they have holistic opportunities to learn about family funds of knowledge in contexts where parents and children control the flow of interactions. When family photos or artifacts travel from home to school to be used by children in storytelling or writing activities, children take up expert roles, and their cultural experiences shape and expand school learning activities. (See Chapters 6 and 11.) The goal is more permeable boundaries between home and school, explicit sharing and valuing of family resources and experiences, and the creation "third spaces" (Brandt, 1998) where hybrid practices rooted in both home and school are encouraged.

Fifth, culturally responsive activities are typically designed for *openness*. Teachers design learning events with many different entry points and many acceptable learning products. This allows children to shape their participation in relation to their current cultural understandings and linguistic practices, while also being challenged to make new conceptual connections and learn new ways of communicating. Open-ended activities are often accomplished by inviting children and families to compose their own content. Rather than trying to teach families to use school-based ways of reading, telling stories, or creating graphic/written products, at home families are encouraged to use heritage languages and familiar ways of representing their ideas and experiences (Rowe & Fain, 2013). At school, invitations for children to compose their own content provide opportunities for teachers to become researchers of their students, and for students to learn about one another (Gutiérrez, Bien, Selland, & Pierce, 2011). When teachers use culturally sensitive lenses for observing students' participation, they can recognize the creative genius involved in constructing emergent and hybrid responses that recontextualize (Nieto, 2002) cultural content to meet school learning purposes.

Directions for Teacher Education Design and Research

Teacher education programs need to provide prospective teachers with opportunities to engage in culturally responsive instruction of this kind, but also to learn to design lessons of their own. While my analysis of design features that characterize culturally responsive activities provides a starting place for constructing conjectures about instructional design, more research is needed to develop these ideas. Important questions for the design of teacher education programs and for future research include:

- What are important design features of culturally responsive instruction in early childhood classrooms?
- What teacher education experiences support prospective teachers in learning to design instruction around these key features (e.g., flexible

assembly of resources; collaborative learning relationships; shared sponsorship; two-way travel of materials, information, and people; openness; and so on)?

Critical Consciousness

Learning to teach for equity, access, and inclusion requires development of critical awareness of systems of power and privilege implicit in polices and school practices (Dyson, 2002). Teaching is embedded in and sponsored by (Ladson-Billings, 1992) social and political institutions (public or independent schools, school districts, counties, states, nations,) that use instructional mandates (e.g., educational standards documents, high-stakes assessments, mandated curricular materials), and funding decisions to implicitly or explicitly enact their ideologies about teaching, learning, teachers, students, and families. Nieto (Brandt & Clinton, 2002) contends that when teachers learn with and from students and their families, and when they build on the talents and strengths students bring to the classroom, "they cannot avoid locking horns with some very unpleasant realities inherent in schooling practices, realities such as racism, sexism, heterosexism, classism, and other biases" (p. 219).

Directions for Teacher Education Design and Research

Teacher education programs aimed at preparing teachers to better serve children from culturally and linguistically diverse backgrounds need to consider how to support critical awareness of implicit biases in school practices. Further, they need to help beginning teachers envision ways they can take action individually and with others. Nieto (2002) notes that teachers often have more power to design instruction in their own classrooms than is immediately evident. Even in the face of highly structured curricula, teachers find ways to provide more equitable learning environments by reframing mandated activities in ways that value and build from children's cultural and linguistic strengths. Further, teachers become adept at finding time and space for these activities by "teaching in the cracks." Moving beyond their own classrooms, teachers need to learn effective ways of joining with other educators to discuss and challenge unjust practices that do not serve their students well. Changing school-wide practices is difficult and cannot be accomplished alone. Teacher education programs need to consider how they can help prospective teachers learn strategies for connecting with existing groups of critical educators and for engaging their peers in respectful but critically conscious discussions of school practices.

Questions that require further consideration in designing and studying teacher education programs include:

- What teacher education experiences support awareness and recognition of biases in school practices?

- How can prospective teachers learn to work within their classrooms to reframe and redesign classroom activities to be more equitable, accessible, and inclusive?
- What strategies do prospective teachers learn for making change at the school level and beyond?

Coda: The Potentials of Design-Based Research in Teacher Education

In her 2004 volume, *Walking the Road. Race, Diversity, and Social Justice in Teacher Education*, Cochran-Smith noted that teacher education programs aimed at issues of social justice have received relatively little research attention in part because they are caught between the desires of policymakers for broadly generalizable studies identifying variables impacting teaching outcomes and the incommensurable press by multicultural education researchers for designs that directly study the social and cultural context of teaching and teacher education. I argue, here, that design-based research methods (Nieto, 2002) like those used by the CREATE research team and described in this volume, may be particularly appropriate for supporting theory-based design of programs and for answering questions about the effects of those designs. Design-based research involves engineering the development of particular forms of professional practice, and then studying the development of those practices *in the contexts in which they emerge* (Cobb, Confrey, diSessa, Lehrer, & Schauble, 2003; Cobb, Jackson, Smith, Sorum, & Henrick, 2013).

Design-based studies of teacher education require researchers to make explicit theory-based conjectures about experiences that are likely to support prospective teachers' development of dispositions and skills needed to teach for equity, access, and inclusion. This requires teacher educators to reframe the practical work of course and program design as an opportunity to learn about underlying design features that may be transferable across courses and other teacher education contexts. Design-based research then requires researchers to iteratively test and revise these conjectures using systematically collected data on participants' learning, interactions, and attitudes. Overall, design-based research holds considerable promise for developing context-specific answers to the practical questions raised in this chapter.

Bibliography

Banks, J. A., Cookson, P., Gay, G., Hawley, W. D., Irvine, J. J., Nieto, S., & Stephan, W. G. (2001). Diversity within unity: Essential principles for teaching and learning in a multicultural society. *Phi Delta Kappan*, 83(3), 196–203.

Bernhard, J. K., Cummins, J., Campoy, F. I., Ada, A. F., Winsler, A., & Bleiker, C. (2006). Identity texts and literacy development among preschool English language learners: Enhancing learning opportunities for children at risk for learning disabilities. *Teachers College Record*, 108(11), 2280–2405.

Bernhard, J. K., Winsler, A., Bleiker, C., Ginieniewicz, J., & Madigan, A. L. (2008). "Read my story!" Using the Early Authors Program to promote early literacy among diverse, urban preschool children in poverty. *Journal of Education for Students Placed at Risk*, 13(1), 76–105.

Bialystok, E. (2007). Cognitive effects of bilingualism: How linguistic experience leads to cognitive change. *International Journal of Bilingual Education and Bilingualism*, 10(3), 210–223.

Bishop, R. S. (1990). Mirrors, windows, and sliding glass doors. *Perspectives: Choosing and Using Books for the Classroom*, 6(3), ix–xi.

Brandt, D. (1998). Sponsors of literacy. *College Composition and Communication*, 49(2), 165–185.

Brandt, D., & Clinton, K. (2002). Limits of the local: Expanding perspectives on literacy as social practice. *Journal of Literacy Research*, 34(3), 337–356.

Clark, C., & Medina, C. (2000). How reading and writing literacy narrtives affect preservice teachers' understandings of literacy, pedagogy, and multiculturalism. *Journal of Teacher Education*, 51(1), 63–76.

Cobb, P., Confrey, J., diSessa, A., Lehrer, R., & Schauble, L. (2003). Design experiments in educational research. *Educational Researcher*, 32(1), 9–13.

Cobb, P., Jackson, K., Smith, T., Sorum, M., & Henrick, E. (2013). Design research with educational systems: Investigating and supporting improvements in the quality of mathematics teaching and learning at scale. In W. Penuel, B. J. Fishman, & B. Haugan (Eds.), *Design-based implementation research: One hundred and twelfth yearbook of the National Society for the Study of Education* (Vol. 112, Issue 2, pp. 320–349). Chicago, IL: National Society for the Study of Education.

Durán, L. (2016). Revisiting family message journals. *Language Arts*, 93(5), 354–365.

Dyson, A. (2002). The drinking god factor: A writing development remix for "all" children. *Written Communication*, 19(4), 545–577.

Edwards, P. A. (2016). *New ways to engage parents: Strategies and tools for teachers and leaders, K-12.* New York: Teachers College Press.

Florio-Ruane, S. (1994). The future teachers' autobiography club: Preparing educators to support literacy learning in culturally diverse classrooms. *English Education*, 26(1), 52–66.

Gee, J. P. (2003). A sociocultural perspective on early literacy development. In S. B. Neuman & D. Dickinson (Eds.), *Handbook of early literacy research* (pp. 30–42). New York: Guilford Press.

González, N., Moll, L. C., & Amanti, C. (Eds.). (2009). *Funds of knowledge: Theorizing practice in households, communities, and classrooms.* New York: Routledge.

Gutiérrez, K. D., Bien, A. C., Selland, M. K., & Pierce, D. M. (2011). Polylingual and polycultural learning ecologies: Mediating emergent academic literacies for dual language learners. *Journal of Early Childhood Literacy*, 11(2), 232–261. DOI: 10.1177/1468798411399273

Ladson-Billings, G. (1992). Reading between the lines and beyond the pages: A culturally relevant approach to literacy teaching. *Theory into Practice*, 31(4), 312–320.

Lee, C. D. (2009). Historical evollution of risk and equity: Interdisciplinary issues and critiques. *Review of Educational Research*, 33, 63–100.

McAllister, G., & Irvine, J. I. (2000). Cross cultural competency and multicultural teacher education. *Review of Educational Research*, 70(1), 3–24.

McIntosh, P. (1990). White privilege: Unpacking the invisible knapsack. *Independent School*, 49, 31.

Miller, M. E., & Rowe, D. W. (2014). "Two Voces ": Pre-Kindergarteners' translanguaging practices in dual language eBook composing events. In P. J. Dunston, S. K. Fullerton, M. W. Cole, D. Herro, J. A. Malloy, P. M. Wilder, & K. N. Headley (Eds.), *63rd yearbook of the Literacy Research Association* (pp. 243–258). Altamonte Springs, FL: Literacy Research Association.

Milner, H. R., IV. (2003). Reflection, racial competence, and critical pedagogy: How do we prepare preservice teachers to pose tough questions? *Race Ethnicity and Education*, 6(2), 193–208.

Milner, H. R., IV. (2010). *Start where you are, but don't stay there: Understanding diverstiy, opportunity gaps, and teaching in today's classrooms.* Cambridge, MA: Harvard University Press.

Moll, L. C., Amanti, C., Neff, D., & González, N. (2005). Funds of knowledge for teaching: Using a qualitative approach to connect homes and classrooms. In N. González, L. C. Moll, & C. Amanti (Eds.), *Funds of knowledge: Theorizing practices in households, communities, and classrooms* (pp. 71–87). New York: Routledge.

Nieto, S. (2002). *Language, culture, and teaching: Critical perspectives for a new century.* Mahwah, NJ: Lawrence Erlbaum Associates.

Pine, N. (2005). Visual information-seeking behavior of Chinese- and English-speaking children. In A. Makkai, W. J. Sullivan, & A. R. Lommel (Eds.), *LACUS forum XXXI: Interconnections* (pp. 289–300). Houston, TX: LACUS.

Rowe, D. W., & Fain, J. G. (2013). The family backpack project: Responding to dual-language texts through family journals. *Language Arts*, 90(6), 402–416.

Rowe, D. W., & Miller, M. E. (2015). Designing for diverse classrooms: Using iPads and digital cameras to compose eBooks with emergent bilingual/biliterate four year olds. *Journal of Early Childhood Literacy*. DOI: 10.1177/1468798415593622

Rowe, D. W., & Wilson, S. (2015). The development of a descriptive measure of early childhood writing: Results from the write start! Writing assessment. *Journal of Literacy Research*, 47(2), 245–292. DOI: 10.1177/1086296X15619723

Willis, A. I. (2000). Keeping it real: Teaching and learning about culture, literacy, and respect. *English Education*, 32, 267–277.

Wood, S. D. (2015). *What is critical? An analysis of small group critical conversations with African American second grade males* (Ph.D.), Vanderbilt University, Nashville, TN. (ETD etd-07142015–103303)

Xu, H. (2000). Preservice teachers integrate understandings of diversity into literacy instruction: An adaptation of the ABC's model. *Journal of Teacher Education*, 51(2), 135–142.

Afterword

H. Richard Milner IV

University of Pittsburgh

We are living in tenuous times in education and teacher education: teachers are being blamed for underserving students in pre-Kindergarten–12 environments; parents in urban communities, in particular, are perceived as uncaring and those who do not value education; school administrators are pressured and thus pressure teachers to focus instructional practices mostly on tests and testing in the name of accountability; policymakers are often underprepared to develop policies that address a range of nuances embedded in particular sociopolitical contexts; and too many students in public schools are being grossly underserved—especially Black and Brown students, those whose first language is not English, those who live below the poverty line, and those who need special education services. This is an essential volume—a profoundly constructed must read for any of us determined to improve educational processes and outcomes for our most underserved students in communities. Authors in this volume audaciously tackle the complex, the taboo, the under-examined, and perhaps most importantly *the tenuous* dimensions of our work in education and teacher education in order to advance theory, research, practice, and praxis.

Indeed, outside-of-school realities play an important role in what happens inside of school. Poverty rates, for instance, are highest for African American, Latino American, and American Indian children—39 percent of African American children live in poverty; 32 percent of Latino American children live in poverty; and 36 percent of American Indian children live in poverty. While we should be concerned about all students living in poverty, it is essential not to overlook this reality: proportionally, more people of color live in poverty than white people. Thus, addressing the tenuous in education and teacher education means that we must examine the ways in which outside-of-school issues shape what occurs inside of school. Moreover, addressing the tenuous in education and teacher education means that we must address race, poverty, socioeconomic status, geography, language diversity, sexual orientation, religion, and gender (and not necessarily in this prioritized order and certainly not as independent variables). However, social scientists and educators alike still under-examine race as a tenuous dimension of our work—even in the midst of all the knowledge we have about how people (should) learn and how people (should) teach.

Other tenuous outside-of-school factors that shape inside of school areas include the following:

- Students and family members have suffered physical, psychological, and/or emotional abuse.
- Students and family members and sometimes suffer from harmful addictions such as drug abuse, gambling, or alcoholism.
- Students experience health and nutrition problems. Health problems include high rates of "asthma, ear infections, stomach problems, and speech problems" (Duffield, 2001, p. 326), and their eating patterns may be sporadic, not eating well-balanced meals, or missing meals altogether.
- Students living in poverty attend school fewer days than other children, are transient, arrive at school late, and have difficulty concentrating on learning and interacting with classmates.
- Students and their family members are homeless.

Although the challenges we face in education and teacher education are plentiful, this book provides solutions to some of our most enduring challenges. Explicitly grounded in theory, what this book shows us through empirical evidence, story, statistics, and anecdote is a complex picture of what we are facing in education and teacher education in particular. What can we do to better support students, teachers, parents, and policymakers in designing learning environments that propel all students to reach their capacity? Although the authors do not camouflage the perplexities ahead of us in addressing inequity in education, they also provide insight into the ways in which education and teacher education should be reformed to maximize students' opportunities to learn. And perhaps most importantly, this book is a welcome addition to the literature base as it advances the field and provides insights into what we know and what we *should know* about preparing educators to meet the needs of all students.

Bibliography

Duffield, B. (2001). The educational rights of homeless children: Policies and practices. *Educational Studies*, 32, 323–336.

Contributors

María V. Acevedo is assistant professor of early childhood in the Department of Curriculum and Instruction at the University of Massachusetts, Boston. Her research explores the use of global literature and cultural artifacts to support young children's intercultural understanding and the portrayal of Latino/as, especially Puerto Ricans, in multicultural literature. Her work in classrooms with early childhood educators and preservice teachers focuses on story as a meaning-making process, education as inquiry, and play as transformative experiences for young children. She has published in *Bookbird* and *Young Children*.

Jesus Acosta-Iriqui is originally from Sonora, Mexico. He obtained doctoral degree in Language, Reading, and Culture at the University of Arizona. His research focuses on the impact of language policies on teachers of students of Mexican background. He was a fellow at the Center for the Mathematics Education of Latinos (CEMELA), where he worked with teachers, families, students, and community members on issues related to mathematics education. He has also taught several courses addressing minority language education (K-12) for in- and preservice teachers.

Eliza Desiree Butler is a doctoral candidate in the Language, Reading, and Culture program at the University of Arizona. Her research interests emphasize multimodal literacies, critical literacies, the study of transnational identities, as well as family and community, early childhood education, immigration, and equity in education, In 2016/2017, Eliza will be completing her dissertation, in which she will be researching the transnational and multimodal literacy practices of artists from the Cuban diaspora.

Renée Tipton Clift is associate dean of the College of Education and professor of teaching, learning, and sociocultural studies at the University of Arizona. She received her PhD in curriculum and teacher education from Stanford University. Her research investigates factors that affect the process of learning to teach, which includes preservice teachers' learning, educators' continuing professional development, and educational leadership. She was the 2015 recipient of the Hans Olsen Distinguished Teacher Educator Award, given by the Association of Teacher Educators, and was also named a distinguished alumna by the University of Florida, College of Education.

Nayalin Pinho Feller is a professor of early childhood multicultural education at the University of New Mexico. Her research interests are the bilingual and biliterate development of young Indigenous/diverse children, second language learning, community and culture-based curriculum development, and the development of early childhood and elementary teachers who work with English learners (ELs).

Ana V. Fierro is a doctoral candidate in the Language, Reading, and Culture program at the University of Arizona. Her research interests are related to Emergent Bilingualism and Biculturalism in the Context of Community.

Yi-ping Fu is a doctoral student in language, reading, and culture at the College of Education, University of Arizona. Her research focuses on early biliteracy development and literacy practices in bilingual Asian students and families.

Kelli Gray holds a PhD in language, reading, and culture from the University of Arizona. She currently lives in Chile, where she works in teacher preparation at a large public university in the Valparaíso Region. Her research interests sit at the nexus of critical race theory in education, bilingual and multicultural early childhood education, and social justice in teacher education.

Ana Christina daSilva Iddings is a professor of language, literacy, and culture in the Department of Teaching, Learning, and Sociocultural Studies, College of Education at the University of Arizona. Her research interests are Early Childhood Education, language learning, family and community, biliteracy and bilingualism in early childhood education, immigration and equity in education, and the education and professional development of teachers to work with English learners and their families.

Norma González is professor emerita in the Department of Teaching, Learning and Sociocultural Studies at the University of Arizona. She is an anthropologist of education whose work has focused on language practices and ideologies, language socialization, community-school linkages, bilingual education, and Funds of Knowledge. She is past president of the Council of Anthropology and Education and author of *I am my language: Discourses of women and children in the borderlands* and co-editor, with Luis Moll and Cathy Amanti of *Funds of knowledge: Theorizing practices in households, communities and classrooms*.

Dorea Kleker is an early childhood educator and an instructor for the University of Arizona's early childhood teacher education program (CREATE), where she teaches children's literature and early literacy courses. Working in Latino immigrant communities, her research has focused on cross-border teacher exchanges, cross-border narratives, intercultural understanding, and teacher inquiry groups. She is currently exploring the use of art and literature in classrooms and homes to build family-school relationships, promote learning from and with families, and support students' biliteracy development.

H. Richard Milner IV is Helen Faison Professor of Urban Education and director of the Center for Urban Education at the University of Pittsburgh. His research, teaching, and policy interests are urban teacher education, African American literature, and the social context of education.

Luis C. Moll is professor emeritus in the Language, Reading, and Culture Program of the Department of Teaching, Learning and Sociocultural Studies, College of Education, University of Arizona. His main research interest is the connection among culture, psychology, and education, especially as it relates to the education of Latino children in the U.S. His most recent book, L. S. Vygotsky and education, was published by Routledge Press in 2014. Among his honors, he was elected to membership in the National Academy of Education (1998), and named Fellow (2009) of the American Educational Research Association.

Lauren H. Pangle is an early childhood educator, currently teaching at The Museum School in Decatur, Georgia. She is Nationally Board Certified and has graduate degrees from Western Oregon University and the University of Arizona in Language, Reading, and Culture. Her interests include using children's literature to engage young children in reader response and inquiry-based learning. Her classroom is featured in *Literature for Young Children: Supporting Emergent Literacy, Ages 0–8* (7th Edition).

Iliana Reyes is an associate professor of language, reading, and culture at the University of Arizona, and associated to CINVESTAV, Mexico City. Her areas of expertise include early literacy, bilingualism and biliteracy, and language socialization in immigrant and indigenous communities. Reyes's current research in México explores issues on multilingual education in an indigenous, náhuatl-Spanish community, where family, children and teachers collaborate to revitalize the indigenous language.

Kathy G. Short is a professor in language, reading, and culture at the University of Arizona with a focus on global children's and adolescent literature, literature circles, intercultural understanding, and critical content analysis. She has co-authored many books, including *Teaching Globally:*

Reading the World through Literature, Essentials of Children's Literature, Creating Classrooms for Authors and Inquirers, and *Stories Matter: The Complexity of Cultural Authenticity in Children's Literature.* She is director of Worlds of Words, an initiative to build bridges across global cultures through children's literature, and is past president of the National Council of Teachers of English.

Mariana Souto-Manning, is associate professor of education and doctoral program director in the Department of Curriculum & Teaching at Teachers College, Columbia University. She is a former preschool and primary grades teacher. As a teacher educator, she teaches courses related to early literacy, multicultural education, and critical pedagogy. From a critical perspective, her research examines the sociocultural and historical foundations of early childhood teacher education, early schooling, language development, and literacy practices in pluralistic settings, and focuses on issues of racial and cultural justice.

Kimberly S. Reinhardt is an assistant professor of teacher education and coordinator of graduate teacher preparation at Texas A&M University–Corpus Christi. Her research focuses on school-university partnerships, mentor preparation and the mentoring of teacher candidates, and the development of critical reflection to explore teaching practices that meet the diverse needs of students.

Sheri Robbins is a doctoral candidate in language, reading, and culture in the College of Education at The University of Arizona. Her doctoral research centers on the use of translation as a lens to examine the meaning-making process as teacher candidates traverse between theory and practice both in their teacher preparation program and as beginning teachers. She is a National Board Certified Teacher who currently serves as a Gifted and Talented Specialist in Grapevine-Colleyville Independent School District in Grapevine, Texas.

Deborah Wells Rowe is a professor of early childhood education at Peabody College, Vanderbilt University. Her research focuses on how young children learn to write in preschool and primary grades classrooms. Recent work includes the development of a descriptive measure of early childhood writing and research exploring how the use of touchscreen tablets and digital cameras can provide young emergent bilinguals with opportunities for multimodal, multilingual composing.

Haeny Yoon is an assistant professor of early childhood in the Department of Curriculum and Teaching at Teachers College, Columbia University. She teaches courses on curriculum, language/literacy, and children's play. Her interest in curriculum, teacher development, and children's play stems from working as a staff developer and primary school teacher. She currently studies the intersection of children's cultural practices (e.g., play, language development, social interactions), teacher practice, and curriculum within classroom contexts

Rebecca Zapien is the *Family and Community Liaison* for the CREATE program at the University of Arizona. Her interests are related to the teaching and learning of young children, the families teachers serve in and out school, educational policy and advocacy in the areas of immigration, equity in public education, language, and access to quality preschools and neighborhood schools.

Index